END OF AN ERA:
New Orleans, 1850 - 1860

View of New Orleans from the River — 1855

End of an Era
New Orleans, 1850-1860

ROBERT C. REINDERS

A FIREBIRD PRESS BOOK

PELICAN PUBLISHING COMPANY
Gretna 1998

Copyright © 1964
By Robert C. Reinders
All rights reserved

First printing, 1964
Second printing, 1989

ISBN: 1-56554-506-0

Manufactured in the United States of America
Published by Pelican Publishing Company, Inc.
1000 Burmaster Street, Gretna, Louisiana 70053

THIS BOOK IS DEDICATED TO MY
MOTHER AND FATHER

PREFACE

New Orleans of the 1850's was in many ways unique. It was predominantly Roman Catholic and foreign born in a nation that was Protestant and native born. It was urban in a region that was almost totally rural, and though located in the deep South many of its commercial and political leaders were Yankees. On the other hand it shared with various American cities the problem of adjusting agrarian institutions and ways of thinking to the realities of a new urban society. And the faith in progress, as measured in commercial expansion, was as ardently held in New Orleans as in the nation at large. An account of New Orleans in this decade is the story of a place and time that was different from anything in the American experience. The fifties was the culmination of the ante-bellum commercial grandeur on which the famed (and often incorrect) romantic image of the city is based. At the same time the social, political, and economic forces engendered in this decade are reflected in the problems, issues, and institutions which unite and divide present day New Orleans. It was, more than any other period in New Orleans history, the end of one era and the beginning of another.

This study was made possible in part by a summer grant from the Tulane University Council on Research.

My special thanks go to those helpful archivists and librarians Mrs. Dorothy Whittemore of the Howard-Tilton Memorial Library, Mrs. Connie G. Griffith of Tulane University, Mr. Virgil Bedsole of Louisiana State University, Dr. Llerena Friend and Miss Winnie Allen of the University of Texas, Miss Margaret Ruckert of the New Orleans Public Library, Father Robert Stahl of Notre Dame Seminary in New Orleans, and Mrs. Rosa Oliver of the Louisiana State Historical Society Library. I would like to thank Professors Gerald M. Capers of Newcomb College and John Duffy of the University of Pittsburgh for their suggestions and encouragement. I owe a special debt to Dr. Barnes Fletcher Lathrop of the University of Texas who gave his time, effort, and patience to aid me in preparing this study. Nor should I forget my proof reader-critic, Dorothy Yates Reinders, without whose indulgence and humor this book might never have been written.

R. C. R.

New Orleans, Louisiana, August, 1964

Table Of Contents

Chapter		Page
I	The Place	1
II	The People	9
III	The Wharf	33
IV	Government and Politics	51
V	Protection of Life, Limb and Property	63
VI	An Unhealthy City	87
VII	Religion	112
VIII	Education	131
IX	The Good Times	150
X	The Public Arts	174
XI	Arts and Architecture	197
XII	Literature	213
XIII	The Fourth Estate	226
XIV	The Last Season: 1860-1861	238
	Notes on Sources	246
	Index	251

List Of Illustrations

	Page
New Orleans, 1855 (Frontispiece)	Opposite Title Page
Harbor Scene, 1861	1
Lafayette Square	10
French Quarter Scene	12
German Immigrants	19
Slave Depot	26
Levee Scene	34
River and Levee Scene	38
Levee Scene	49
Firemen In Action	76
Charity Hospital	91
Sick Wards, Charity Hospital	93
Sister Of Charity	94
Yellow Fever Scene	97
Coffin Bearers	99
Burial Vaults	107
Protestant Cemetery	108
Potters Field	109
Street Railroad Car	129
St. Charles Hotel	150
St. Louis Hotel	153
Mardi Gras Parade	156
French Market Scene	162
Lake Pontchartrain Lighthouse	172
Theatre D'Opera	183
Program Of "Le Prophete"	184
Cover Of "The Banjo"	190
Henry Clay Statue	196
United States Custom House	209
Mechanics Institute	210
Charles Gayarre'	212
Title Page Of *The Octoroon*	222
J. D. B. DeBow	225
Louis Moreau Gottschalk	238
Jackson Square, 1860	Opposite Page 48
New Orleans port scene, 1858	" " 49
Canal Street, New Orleans — 1858	" " 80
French Market, 1860	" " 81
Samuel Horton Kennedy	" " 112
Gerald Stith	" " 112
William Mure	" " 112
John T. Monroe	" " 112
A. D. Crossman	" " 112
John Slidell	" " 113
Ben De Bar	" " 113
Rt. Rev. Bishop Polk	" " 113
Pierre Adolphe Rost	" " 113
Paul Morphy	" " 113
James H. Caldwell	" " 144
John McDonogh	" " 144
Glendy Burke	" " 144
Rev. Theodore Clapp	" " 144
Abbé Adrienne Rouquette	" " 145
Abbé Rouquette's Chapel	" " 145
Odd Fellows Home, 1858	" " 192
City Hall, 1858	" " 192
United States Mint, 1858	" " 192
Touro Building, 1858	" " 193
Steele Chapel (Methodist), 1855	" " 193
Christ Church erected in 1847	" " 224
Saint Charles Theatre	" " 225

Foreword

Ask any traveler to name the three most unique cities in the United States and the chances are that New York, New Orleans, and San Francisco will be mentioned — New York for its immensity and diversity, San Francisco for its magnificent setting as the Gateway to the Orient, and New Orleans for its romantic Southern tradition. Embodying the myths of the Old South and having created a mythology of its own, New Orleans has long appealed to the romantically minded.

Robert Reinders brings to his writings a penchant for examining sources and an acutely perceptive mind. Withal he has a healthy skepticism and has no compunction about shattering illusions or discarding traditional beliefs. The period about which he writes, the 1850's, was the heyday of New Orleans, a decade of booming prosperity, of cultural development, and of buoyant optimism. No other writer has attempted to give us so complete a cross section of New Orleans; virtually nothing escapes Professor Reinders' observant eye. He has literally ransacked the archives and unearthed a vast amount of information. In addition, he has familiarized himself with the many articles, monographs and histories of the city.

Interestingly enough, despite the way in which he dismisses legends and slashes away at the thickets of myth, the New Orleans which emerges is even more fascinating than the one of storied fame. His Creole aristocracy are no decadent, genteel dilettantes; they are an energetic bustling crew with no reluctance to engage in trade and commerce, nor with any objections to their sons and daughters marrying into the families of wealthy American merchants. They maintained cultural ties with France, ties which were reinforced by a constant influx of French intellectuals. Their way of life, however, was rapidly changing, and by the 1850's a new Americanized Creole was emerging.

The renown of New Orleans for its theaters and its architecture is well justified, as Professor Reinders points out, but, legend to the contrary, the City was no literary center. Literature was held in such low esteem, that, although New Orleans developed a first rate school system in these years, no significant libraries were established. Social life was gay in New Orleans, and despite removing some of the glamour from the Quadroon Balls, Dr. Reinders demonstrates that the phrase, "the City that care forgot," has a long tradition behind it.

Lurking behind the bright façade of New Orleans was the omnipresent threat of sickness and disease. No nineteenth century city was exempt from epidemics, but yellow fever, a deadly pestilence, struck repeatedly at New Orleans, its attacks reaching a crescendo in the 1850's. It was not without reason that the city became the leading medical center for the South, nor that the State of Louisiana, under the impact of this terrible scourge, established the first state board of health in the United States.

The nature of Dr. Reinders study provided him with a fascinating topic. To it he has brought a discerning eye and the judgment of an historian. The devotees of New Orleans, an enormous group which seems to include the entire citizenry, will find new reasons to appreciate their city; the uninitiated will have to be content with enjoyable reading.

> John Duffy
> *Graduate School of Public Health,*
> *University of Pittsburgh*

END OF AN ERA:
NEW ORLEANS IN THE 1850's

The Crescent City — Harper's Weekly, March 30, 1861

Chapter I

THE PLACE

New Orleans has been [built] upon a site that only the madness of commercial lust could ever have tempted men to occupy. . . .[1]

A brief picture of the physical setting of New Orleans is necessary for an understanding of much of its history and economic and social institutions. The city's geology and topography are products of the Mississippi River. The river created the site of the city, for the land upon which New Orleans rests consists of alluvial deposits accumulated over an estimated 25,000 years. So recent are the deposits, geologically speaking, that they are still water-soaked; New Orleans quite literally floats on a thousand feet of muck.

The city is at all inhabitable because the river deposits built up a natural levee along the bank; later European settlers and their descendants widened and strengthened the levees though not always successfully as crevasses occurred and the river often broke through to flood vast areas of the surrounding land. In front of the levee, especially on the inside of a "U" shaped meander of the Mississippi River where New Orleans was located, silt deposits were formed. This new land, called a batture, eventually solidified sufficiently to sustain wharves, buildings, streets, and new protec-

—1—

tion levees. From the founding of the city to 1850 over three city blocks were added in some places by this process.

From the levee the land sloped downward gradually to a vast swamp which in the 1850's began about a mile and a half back from the river and extended for five miles to the shores of Lake Pontchartrain. The lake, which lies, roughly speaking, north of the city, was on nearly the same level as the swamp — indeed parts of the swamp are below sea level and thus lower than Lake Pontchartrain itself — and when its waters were driven by high winds or enlarged by heavy rains it overflowed into the swamp. Not until the present century were adequate protection levees or sea walls erected on the lake shore. Rising above the level of the swamp were two ridges which were in reality levees left when the Mississippi flowed to the Gulf of Mexico by way of Lakes Pontchartrain and Borgne. Metairie Ridge crossed the swamp from the river to the lake in the area above Canal Street; Esplanade Ridge parallelled the Bayou St. John, a narrow stream which ran from the "high" land near the levee to Lake Pontchartrain. Though only four to six feet above the level of the swamp, the ridges were vital to New Orleans because they offered the only feasible land connection between the river and the lake and indicated the line of habitation if the city expanded beyond the restricted area of the levee.

The swamp was dismal and unhealthy, and, until the twentieth century, largely unpopulated. To inhabitants of ante-bellum New Orleans the swamp was a mosquito-ridden, "oozy" marsh, "reeking with filth, and sheltered by cypress forest, matted with shrubs, vines, and aquatic plants. . . ."[2] To a traveller, whose short stay allowed him to be romantic about the swamp, it appeared as a "luxuriant forest growth, festooned with graceful ribbons of the wild vine, the funeral streamers of the tillandsia, or Spanish moss . . . the long thick grass, the palm and palmetto."[3] A man in the swamp might hear now and then the heavy cough of an alligator, the flutter of a covey of brant or ducks, the splash of frogs, the ring of the ever-present mosquito, the high-pitched whistle of the two railroads that crossed the swamp, the crunch of a horse and carriage on the single shell road to the lake, or the distant barked commands to the crew of a barge or pirogue passing along one of the two commercial canals. But by and large the illusion of a primordial swamp remained; unless the individual looked towards the direction of the river and saw the spires of the city's churches and the white dome of the St. Charles Hotel, there was no indication that he was only a few miles from a city of over one hundred thousand persons.

In spite of the unprepossessing character of the topography the area of New Orleans had certain advantages which prompted its original settlement by the French. The levee was relatively high and dry and was only ninety miles by way of the river from the Gulf of Mexico. Equally important it provided the shortest portage route from the river to Lake Pontchartrain and thence to the French settlement at Biloxi. Bienville, commander of the French forces on the Gulf coast, aware of these advantages and realizing the necessity of establishing a major French post on the Mississippi River, in April or May, 1718, sent twenty-five convicts and about an equal number of skilled workers to the task of clearing land and constructing a few huts. Bienville named the village Nouvelle Orléans after the somewhat disruptable regent of France, the Duc d'Orléans.

Four years later, when New Orleans became the headquarters of French government in the lower Mississippi, it boasted one hundred houses and five hundred inhabitants. The plan of the town, prepared by the engineer De Pauger, was roughly a parallelogram 4,000 feet along the river by 1,800 feet in depth divided into regular squares of three hundred feet on each side. Though the entire parallelogram was not occupied for many years, it became the boundary for the Vieux Carré or French Quarter of New Orleans. For a century the principal settlement was in this district and along the Bayou St. John.

New Orleans grew rapidly under the sponsorship of John Law's Mississippi Company, but with the failure of the Company in 1725 the colony of Louisiana came under royal control. The French government brought over settlers — including the famous "casket girls" — encouraged religious communities, and provided soldiers for protection against Indians. In general however the French policy toward the colony was that of systematic neglect.

Life in the city was enlivened early in the eighteenth century by occasional Indian attacks, while internal dissension between Capuchins and Jesuits or between the Governor and his enemies provided sources of interest and excitement in the comparatively simple life of colonial Louisiana. Much of the labor in the city and on nearby plantations was performed by Negro slaves introduced in the early years of the colony. The area was nearly self-sufficient; goods needed from Europe were purchased by sale of myrtle wax, indigo, and furs to the mother country or illegally to English traders. The presence of the Governor in New Orleans offered a crude approximation of court life and led plantation owners into the habit of spending part of the winter season in the city.

This slatternly utopia was rudely interrupted in 1763 by the transfer of the Louisiana territory to the Spanish after the Seven Years War. Some settlers in Louisiana opposed the change of governments and in October, 1768, they forced the Spanish governor, Don Antonio de Ulloa, to flee New Orleans. But the revolt was short-lived; the issue was decided on August 18, 1769, when a Spanish fleet with 3,600 soldiers under Alejandro O'Reilly arrived in New Orleans. O'Reilly, Spanish commandante, combined affability with force to squelch the revolt. Leaders of the abortive insurrection were executed or imprisoned. O'Reilly instituted Spanish laws and governmental systems — except for the Inquisition. He incorporated local French practices, and by cleverly giving local Frenchmen positions of importance he was able to secure the transfer with amazing ease. Under the able rule of O'Reilly's successors, Unzaga, Galvez, Miro, Carondelet, de Lemos, and Casa Calvo, hostility between Spanish and French largely disappeared.

Shortly after O'Reilly entered New Orleans he restricted the English merchants, of whom there were a considerable number in the city, from trading in the area. However trade with the English continued, and under O'Reilly's successors it was tacitly, then openly, allowed. New Orleans prospered and by the 1780's attracted English and Americans in increasing numbers. The population was further augmented by French settlers, their slaves, and a number of free Negroes from Santo Domingo following slave revolts there in 1791.

Galvez favored the Americans during their Revolution, but United States independence was in the long run unfavorable to the continuance of Spanish rule in Louisiana. As settlers poured into Kentucky, Tennessee, and Ohio, the Mississippi and its tributaries offered the only avenue for their commerce; but the Spanish hesitated to open the Mississippi to them, realizing that settlers might follow the stream and simply engulf the Spanish by numbers. The most enlightened policy the Spanish could evolve in face of this danger was periodically to close the river to traffic and then employ the promise of free navigation as a means of separating Kentucky and Tennessee from the United States.

Meanwhile the rise of Napoleon brought the Louisiana colony

into the maelstrom of European affairs. The First Consul obtained Louisiana from the Spanish, but being unable to exploit its resources, he chose in 1803 to sell the colony to the United States. A French colonial prefect formerly recovered the Louisiana territory from Spain on November 30, 1803, and on December 20 he transferred it to W. C. C. Claiborne and General James Wilkinson, the American commissioners.

Claiborne was made first Governor and established his headquarters in New Orleans. At that time most of the city's 7,000 were quartered within the bounds of the original Vieux Carré. The population was predominately French, but the economy was largely in the hands of Americans and other foreigners who had arrived in the city during Spanish rule. Claiborne appointed Étienne Boré as first mayor of the city, a position roughly equivalent to the one Boré held under the Spanish. After the United States Congress established the Territory of Orleans, the territorial council in 1805 granted a charter to the city. "With its adoption," a historian has stated, "the real history of New Orleans, as distinguished from the remainder of the Province or Territory, may be said to begin."[4] The charter provided for an elective common council, but the mayor continued to be appointed until 1812 in which year the Constitution of the new State of Louisiana provided for an elected mayor.

With American occupation the city's population had grown rapidly. By 1806 there were 12,000 people (7,500 whites) in New Orleans and within four more years the population doubled. Americans swarmed into the city as did a wave of Santo Domingans who had fled to Cuba in the 1790's, and came to Louisiana when war broke out between France and Spain in 1809. The city was disturbed in these early years by factional disputes between West Indian immigrants and the older population, by the Burr conspiracy, and by a bitter conflict over ownership of the batture. The city was subject to periodic riots, to arsonry, and to bloody fights between American and European mariners. Pirates, who operated out of the nearby coastal swamps, brazenly walked the city's streets. Claiborne had a difficult time keeping a semblance of order in New Orleans.

The War of 1812 and the presence of British troops below the city had the effect of providing some unity among local factions. The military force with which Andrew Jackson met the British comprised his own Tennessee and Kentucky frontiersmen, local Creoles, pirates, Santo Domingans, an assortment of Americans and foreigners from the city, a group of Choctaw Indians, and slave and free Negroes. The victory won by this polyglot army established an important tradition and symbol of unity in New Orleans during the following generation.

With peace the Mississippi Valley was opened to settlement. The result was another period of rapid growth and commercial prosperity for New Orleans; by 1820 the city had 41,000 people. This was the era of the flatboats; thousands came down the river yearly with products of the West. The crude frontiersmen who manned them horrified and terrorized the older Creole population and undoubtedly embarrassed cultured Americans. To entertain flatboatmen the already large bistro and brothel business was expanded. From the East came speculators, lawyers, gamblers, and merchants on the make, eager to attain a fortune in the growing city. The coming of the steamboat reduced the flatboat trade and the flow of frontier visitors, but had no appreciable effect on population growth. According to the census of 1830 there were 46,310 residents of New Orleans.

The expanding population overflowed the original city and moved upriver into a former truck garden area that James H. Caldwell and Samuel J. Peters purchased from Jean Gravier. Here, with the support of other American entrepreneurs, they opened a commercial and residential center. By 1835 this new quarter rivalled in population and exceeded in wealth the Vieux Carré. Below the old city Bernard Marigny, who had foolishly declined to sell land to Peters and Caldwell, developed his own Faubourg Marigny.

The residents of the area above Canal Street, Americans and some Creoles, found their economic prosperity not reflected in political recognition. With the aid of the state legislature, a degree of political independence was obtained through the formation of a tri-parte municipal government in 1836. Under a new municipal charter New Orleans was divided into three corporations or, as they were called, municipalities. The First Municipality included the area between Canal Street and Esplanade Street-Bayou St. John and the river to the lake; the Second Municipality included all of the city above Canal Street and the Third Municipality all of the city below the Esplanade-Bayou St. John line. There was an over-all city government but its powers were negligible and for all practical purposes each municipality was a separate city. The system worked badly and in 1852 the three municipalities were re consolidated and the suburb of Lafayette added to the city.

The Panic of 1837 temporarily halted New Orleans' booming commercial prosperity. Recovery was slow and characterized by caution and a business conservatism not seen in the inflationary period of the 1830's. It was not until 1845 that the city had recovered from the crash of 1837. Population however continued to grow stimulated by waves of German and Irish immigrants in the 1840's. They were to provide the cheap labor force so essential to the business boom of the 1850's.

New Orleans in 1850 had 116,375 people; it was the fifth largest city in the United States and, excluding Baltimore, it was vastly larger than any southern city. Like any urban center it also boasted of a metropolitan area of satellite towns and suburbs, or, to use the local term, faubourgs. Directly across from New Orleans on the "right" or "west" bank of the river were the small communities of Algiers, Belleville, McDonogh, and Gretna. Though only a short ferry trip from New Orleans, the West Bank maintained a small town, semi-rural atmosphere throughout the fifties. A traveller who wandered over to Algiers reported that it was "a kind of suburb . . . where everything bears the marks of decay; muddy roads, broken wharfs, nothing neat or cared for; some warehouses at the river side, where a few ships . . . unload or load occasionally."[5] The area below the city was too swampy for settlement, but above the city several suburbs were formed or were forming by 1850. The largest of these, Lafayette with 14,000 people, was, as noted above, annexed to New Orleans in 1852. The upper boundary of the city and the Parish of Orleans was then placed at Toledano Street. In 1848 a number of faubourgs were incorporated to make Jefferson City, which extended about a mile and a half along the river from Toledano Street to the present-day Joseph Street. Though it was to grow rapidly in the 1850's, Jefferson City had little community identification, being merely a hodge-podge of real estate developments. Farther up the river four potential communities, Hurstville, Bloomingdale, Burtheville, and Greenville had been carved out of the Boré plantation. As towns they had little to recommend them other than their owners' optimism. The last and the largest of the up-river suburbs was Carrollton. Platted as a town in 1833 and incorporated in 1845, it had 1,470 people by 1850. It was the upper terminus of the New Orleans and Carrollton Railroad and chiefly functioned as a resort and truck farming center. On Lake Pontchartrain, at the juncture of the Bayou St. John and the lake, was the small community of Milneburg. Like Carrollton and Bucktown (another lake shore community) it served as a railroad terminal and resort center.

On New Years Day, 1850, an editor of the New Orleans *Picayune* remarked that "A fresh era of time has come upon us, with all its unknown events of weal and woe." It is hoped in the chapters that follow to describe New Orleans of the 1850's with all its "weal and woe." And to depict the city in this last, and perhaps most significant, ante-bellum decade as it moved from its promised "fresh era of time" to its climax in the tragic American Civil War.

NOTES

[1]"Yellow Fever in New Orleans and Mortalty in New York," *Illustrated London News*, XXIII (September 10, 1853), 203.

[2]Bennet Dowler, "Researches into the Natural History of the Mosquito," *New Orleans Medical and Surgical Journal*, XII (September, 1855), 191.

[3]Charles Mackay, *Life and Liberty in America: or, Sketches of a Tour in the United States and Canada in 1857-8* (New York, 1859), 174.

[4]John Smith Kendall, *History of New Orleans* (3 vols.; Chicago, 1922), I, 70.

[5]J. W. Hengiston, "More of the Ohio — the Mississippi and New Orleans," *The New Monthly Magazine*, XCVIII (June, 1853), 251.

Chapter II

THE PEOPLE

... one here meets with various races of people, hears many different languages spoken, and sees the production of various zones. Here are English, Irish, Germans, French, Spaniards, Mexicans. Here are negroes and Indians.[1]

THE UPPER CLASS.

Traditionally historians of New Orleans have presented what may be called the "romantic" version of ante-bellum class and social relations in the Crescent City. They divided the city between two camps, the "Creoles" and the "Americans." According to the romantic approach, the Creoles were "uniformly genteel and cultured aristocrats" of Spanish and French colonial descent who created the social and artistic temper of the city.[2] As disdainful of money lust as of physical labor, they stood above the vulgarity of business and politics. Creole men were handsome, well educated, and extremely conscious of individual and family honor; their women folk were attractive and virtuous. Theirs was a society of "grâce," "elégance," "simplicité," "éxquise politese," "amabilité."[3] Anglo-Americans, on the other hand, were a herd of money-grubbing, semi-literates embodying the worse features of the Kaintuck and the Yankee. The Creoles, cried Grace King, "were as children before the keen-witted Americans," who fleeced them of all save honor.[4] Resentment by the older Creole population against the American intrusion brought about a division of the city into three municipalities in 1836. The Americans, occupying the Second Municipality, prospered in their avaricious way, while the Creoles in the French Quarter waned economically but waxed rich culturally. Canal Street divided the Creoles from the Americans in politics, economics, and social life.

The romantic view is false in two respects. First it does not present an accurate view of the character and behavior of either the Creoles or the Americans and completely ignores the larger immigrant and Negro population; second, the Creoles and wealthy Americans were not "two class systems which differed in every way,"[5] but rather merged to form the main economic and social components of what was the upper class in the 1850's.

The Creole was not necessarily blessed with all of the above mentioned favorable traits. Indeed, he might not even be of

Lafayette Square, New Orleans—Ballou's Pictorial XVI, April 30, 1859
(Ballou's Pictorial Drawing Room Companion-1855)

Spanish-French ancestry, for the word Creole in ante-bellum usage simply meant someone native born and there were American, English, and German as well as French and Spanish Creoles.[6] The best description of a Creole for the fifties was an individual who belonged to one of the old families dating from the Colonial and early national period or who had, like John Slidell, married into and identified with the old families. Nor was the Creole, as such, especially genteel and aristocratic — or even very literate. He was not averse to taking an active part in the city's commercial life; for every Bernard Marigny who frittered away his fortune, dozens of Creoles could be found prospering as bankers, brokers, commission merchants, and so on. The Creole could, a visitor reported, "teach a Yankee tin peddler lessons in economy."[7] Creole women were probably not the ravishing beauties that the romantic writers have portrayed and they were more than likely, in view of their limited education, to be crashing bores. Furthermore, Creole politicians seemed as adept at political skullduggery as any American.

The actual picture of the American was not nearly so black as the romantic viewpoint holds. The American generally was less provincial and better educated and even more artistically inclined than his Creole brother. Indeed, the Americans and foreigners who migrated to Louisiana were often select, aggressive, and able men. Nor can it be proved that Canal Street was a rigid social curtain drawn between Creole and American. A striking example to the contrary is the fact that Samuel J. Peters, the individual most responsible for the development of the uptown business area, married into a prominent Creole family as did his children. Land holdings above Canal Street were in the hands of the older French settlers who were to profit most by an uptown movement and just as some of these "Creoles" lived above Canal Street so many "Americans" lived downtown — the census returns prove what romance denies.

The traditional view of New Orleans society implied that the Creoles and Americans were members of separate castes with no social or economic contact between them. However a closer study of New Orleans reveals that whatever the ethnic cleavage might have been in the earlier history of the city, differences between Creole and American had nearly disappeared by 1850 — if not before. Creoles, Americans, and some immigrants of wealth and power had, by 1850, formed a distinct upper class that was neither Creole, nor American, not immigrant, but a composite of all. Proof of this class unity might be illustrated in intermarriage between Creoles, Americans, and a few immigrants, in economic cooperation, and in a common political policy.

Where intermarriage between groups exists, anthropologists inform us, caste barriers no longer have meaning. It is one thing to accept an uneasy peace between heterogeneous groups at a dinner party, it is quite another to share a bedroom and accept caste differences.[8] Even in the early history of the territory and state, Americans readily intermarried with Creoles. Such prominent Americans as John L. Lewis, George Eustis, Evan Jones, Samuel J. Peters, John Slidell, James Wilkinson, W. C. C. Claiborne, Richard Proctor, Albert Blanchard, and Edward Livingston, and natives of France such as Pierre Soulé, Étienne Mazareau, and Pierre Rost had taken Creole wives. Marriage of an American or immigrant into a Creole family brought him a great deal of prestige

View in French Quarter — Harper's Weekly, March 30, 1861

and occasionally an improved economic position. In the early period American males usually married Creole women, but by mid-century marriages of Creole men and American women were also common. The Creoles, stated a traveller in the 1850's, "are now ... very sensibly seeking alliances with the go-ahead blood of the Anglo-Saxon."[9] The result of this intermarriage, noted J. J. Ampére while attending a soiree at the Slidell home, was a "melange du sang français et du anglo-saxon."[10]

Any real measurement of intermarriage in the fifties would be difficult to ascertain, but the following list of marriages among prominent families will indicate something of its extent:

Husband	Wife	Husband	Wife
Adams	Deslonde	Heerman	Didier
Balfour	Musson	Hite	Rousseau
Ballejo	Whitewell	Howard	Boulemet
Bartlett	Gagnet	Hymans	Trudeau
Bell	Musson	Hubbard	LeBreton
Blanc	Palfrey	LeBlanc	Clark
Bouligny	Montgomery	Lesassier	Pritchard
Bradbury	Chabert	Logan	Soniat
Breaux	Locke	Miller	Belleveau
Brothers	Bredou	Mitchell	Freret
Burke	de Bolle	Neville	Gasquet
Capella	Roselius	North	Le Mercier du Saucy
Carleton	Dupuy	Poullalier	McClosky
Chapman	Fortier	Power	Dupré
De La Cruz	Hall	Pritchard	LeBlanc
Denegre	Morgan	Quentell	Baquié
Dennett	Dufilho	Rodewald	Fortier
Elliot	Giraud	Rogers	Macarty
Foute	Campbell	Rousseau	Jones
Fowler	La Croix	San Roman	Robb
Freret	McCall	Seguin	Norcom
Friedericks	Gaiennie	Stille	Bienvenue
Gaiennie	Neelis	Taylor	Mouton
Gardner	Mouton	Thomas	Landry
Gayarré	Buchanan	Treppanier	Humphreys
Gottschalk	Prieur	Williams	Bienvenue
Hart	Gayoso	Williams	Legendre
		Young	Lasassier

Of course marriage into an old family was not always necessary by the 1850's to attain upper class status. Class lines were not rigidly drawn and upward mobility was possible for the enterprising wealthy individual. Self-made men were admitted to the inner social circle with little hesitation, provided they were residents of the city and not mere winter-time entrepreneurs. Upward mobility is aptly illustrated in the career of James Robb.

Born without benefit of lineage or wealth in Fayette County,

Pennsylvania, Robb came to New Orleans in 1837 with a few hundred dollars. He formed a partnership and opened a broker's office on Camp Street. Where others went bankrupt during the depression, Robb succeeded. In 1840 he helped found the firm of Robb and Hoge, private bankers, and later founded the Bank of James Robb with branches in Liverpool, London, San Francisco, St. Louis, and New York. He purchased nearly worthless stock of the New Orleans Gas Light and Banking Company, becoming its leading stockholder and president in 1852. By efficient management the company showed profits and the value of its stock rose. In the early 1850's Robb was the principal instigator of the New Orleans, Jackson, and Great Northern Railroad, serving on its board of directors and as its president. In 1845 he was elected to the council of the Second Municipality and in 1852 to the state senate with Judah P. Benjamin where he led the movement to consolidate the municipalities of New Orleans.

Even though Robb could be considered nouveaux riche, he was accepted socially. His home was one of the show places of the city, his art collection far and away the finest in the community. One of his daughters married into Spanish nobility (with a blood line sufficient to satisfy the most discriminating Creole), one into the Creole Miltenberger family (St. Louis branch), and one into a prominent Philadelphia family.

Proof of upper class economic ties transcending ethnic lines are not difficult to discover. Creole, American, and immigrant names were found on the directorships of the city's railroads and most of the city's banks, insurance companies, and other commercial enterprises. Booster organizations, such as the Chamber of Commerce, the railroad conventions, and the Mechanics and Agriculture Fair Association included Creole, American, and immigrant names. The directory of 1858 lists over forty Anglo-Creole partnerships and considerable number of Anglo-immigrant and Creole-immigrant partnerships. There were, of course, many economic ventures conducted entirely by Americans, and a few by Creoles alone, but the repetition of names in joint organizations illustrates a tendency toward a shared economic life.

The leaders of the major political parties in New Orleans came from an American-Creole upper class and evinced nearly identical political philosophies. Not ideological differences, which were few, but tradition (somewhat wilted) and personal ambition served to separate the parties. The leaders of the city's Whigs and Democrats favored the constitutional changes and the consolidation bills of 1852 which set the tone for an accelerated capitalistic development in the city. The "independent" movements during the decade made an appeal to the commercial classes and cut across party lines, though it is true that the Whigs and later the Americans took a more active role in these movements than Democrats. As the historian Roger Shugg has stated of this period in Louisiana, it was "Government by Gentlemen" regardless of which political party was in power.[12]

In 1860 there were still Creoles who undoubtedly felt resentful at the American intrusion and who did not consider Anglo-Saxons as their social equals, but active conflict had ended by then. As one writer has concluded:

> The fruits of six decades of conflict and intercourse between Creole and Anglo-American in Louisiana was a society [that] ... though often disagreeing [was] ... usually contented and neighborly ... something of a common standard had been cultivated.[13]

There was no doubt among many Creoles a nostalgic longing for the "olden days" when they had been dominant. This nostalgia, nurtured ironically by French immigrant intellectuals, was reflected in a rather artifical attempt near the end of the decade to preserve Creole customs, history, and language. But it awaited a post-war generation to create the "romantic Creole" and the misleading picture of New Orleans' class structure.

THE BOURGEOISIE.

Historians of the New Orleans scene have described in detail the wealthy Creoles and Americans, that is, the upper class; and there are available sources on the lower class, both immigrant and native American. But the middle class does not seem to have existed for many students of New Orleans ante-bellum history. Even Roger Shugg in his study on the class structure of Louisiana has largely neglected the middle class in New Orleans. However a close glance at New Orleans society in the 1850's reveals a well established middle class, although it is often difficult to obtain any exact picture of its number, character, and influence.

What might be called upper middle class was composed of wealthier Creole, American, and immigrant shopkeepers, managers of large business ventures, and members of leading professions. It was less homogeneous than the upper class as there was a tendency to form associates along ethnic lines. Thus an American upper middle class family lived within a social circle of fellow Anglo-Americans with the same economic status. Unlike the upper class, marriage between Americans, Creoles, or immigrants in this group was rare. They did however emulate the upper class in political views and to an extent in social behavior.

Perhaps typical of the upper middle class was Thomas K. Wharton, an English emigrant who had entered the United States at the age of seventeen. After a program of self-education and two failures in attempts to establish colleges, Wharton found himself in 1850 a draftsman and architect employed on construction of the United States Custom House in New Orleans. His social circle was composed almost entirely of middle class Anglo-Americans who lived a life similar to his own. He ate regularly at home with his loving wife and child. After his day's work he preferred, as he states, to "sit down at home and rest for awhile [sic] in my rocking chair" and spend his leisure time "in the bosom of my family." He read eastern newspapers, took long walks stopping only long enough for "ices," and occasionally invited friends to his home for supper. He worshipped sporadically in the Presbyterian or Baptist churches, but formed few other associational attachments, though he had a fairly strong sense of social responsibility, favoring the political figure whom he felt would be "a man of family and status in the community." He himself was appointed to the board of school directors of the First District, where he worked diligently to improve the standards of the public schools. Significantly perhaps his superior at the Custom House, P.G.T. Beauregard (upper class), several times visited Wharton's home, but only once (after Beauregard's second marriage) was Wharton invited to the Beauregard home; he was awestruck by the mansion, its furnishings, and the graciousness of Beauregard's wife. It is quite obvious from his diary that he felt out of his class. On the other hand he certainly felt superior to the immigrants who lived in squalor near his home; towards Negroes he seemed to have almost no contact and no opinions. In general Wharton led a dull bourgeois kind of life which hardly differed from that of a man of the same class in the Northeast and was probably far more common in New Orleans than many writers have imagined.[14]

The largest element in the lower middle class were the clerks who worked in the many mercantile establishments in the city.

They were often from the Northeast or the upper South, though as the decade progressed an increasing number were recruited from the foreign-born and from young men who were natives of New Orleans. Clerks frequently resided in boarding houses, isolated from any social or familial life, and their chance of surviving the periodical yellow fever epidemics was about as low as their salaries. They were motivated by thoughts of promotion or partnership which was common enough in the city to balance out fever and boredom. In addition to the clerks, the lower middle class contained proprietors of oyster houses, groceries, dairies, tobacco stores, market stands, butcher shops, and other small retail stores. Many of these small businessmen were foreigners who worked in the city as laborers and after accumulating a nest egg opened a shop. Typical perhaps was the case of Louis François Hezeau who arrived penniless from France in 1840. He began selling artifical flowers on the streets, saved money, and opened a profitable flower shop and invested in real estate and cemetery lots. Unfortuntaely Louis' commercial ventures were somewhat disturbed by the financial demands of his wife whom he had abandoned in France and the revelation that his help-mate he had brought with him from the old country was not his legal spouse. To the above lower middle class might be added salaried officials of the national, state, parish, and city governments. They more often than not were native born and, given the spoils system, were probably poorer relations of upper class families.

THE PROLETARIAT.

The working class in New Orleans was mainly of foreign origin, and a discussion of it must therefore be largely concerned with immigrants and lives of immigrants. Between 1850 and 1860 the foreign-born population in New Orleans increased by 13,000, although the number which passed through the city for points north and west was many times more. The immigrants who left the European ports of Liverpool, Havre, Bremen, and Hamburg were packed into steerage—German ships were especially notorious for overcrowding—where they faced an uncomfortable voyage of up to six weeks. On landing in New Orleans they were ignored by the state and municipal governments (except for a fee of $2.50) and were, if they had no organization of fellow countrymen, literally dumped in the city, where they became fair prey for baggage thieves and dishonest employment agencies. In the words of a sympathetic observer, the immigrants

> plunged into this chaos, raw and ignorant, speak no language but an unknown one, know not where to go, have no friends . . . and are quite certain, in their own minds of being woefully cheated. . . . [15]

The largest immigrant group in New Orleans was the Irish. The famines of the 1840's had sent thousands to the United States, many by the inexpensive route from Liverpool to New Orleans—it was either bricks or Irishmen for ballast. Throughout the 1850's the Irish continued to arrive, though the numbers declined on account of the improvement of conditions in Ireland, adverse publicity depicting New Orleans as a "wet grave," and the rise of the bitterly anti-immigrant Know-Nothing party. In 1850 the city had 20,200 natives of Ireland; by 1860 the figure had increased only to 24,398.

The Irish who landed in New Orleans were generally impoverished. They did not, as the Germans did, find awaiting them at the docks an agency of fellow nations to arrange for board and employment. After landing, the Irish immigrants generally moved into the Third District or into the "Irish Channel" between Camp Street and the river in the First and Fourth Districts, where they resided in overcrowded tenement houses or in dilapidated shanties. From these ethnic bastions they poured out to fill the demand in the city for unskilled labor.

German immigrants, most of whom were from Bavaria, Baden, Wittenberg, and the Rhenish provinces of Prussia, generally passed through the city on their way to Texas or upriver to the northwestern states, though undoubtedly a good many worked in the Crescent City before leaving for other destinations. Because of epidemics and the institution of slavery few Germans with money or zeal stayed in New Orleans and therefore the city's German population was not composed of the pick of the Teutonic immigration. For example, some German-speaking Swiss communes and the state of Baden rid themselves of paupers by sending them to New Orleans where they more than likely died in the first epidemic. One effect of the poor selection of immigrants was the lack of militant and able leadership which characterized other German communities. The 48'ers simply did not reside in New Orleans. But in spite of the city's drawbacks, and because of the immirgants' poverty or the attractions of the city, the German-

German Immigrants in New Orleans
(Eremson's Magazine and Putnam's Monthly — October, 1857)

born population of New Orleans increased from 11,220 in 1850 to 19,675 ten years later.

On arriving in the city the needs of the German immigrants were met by the German Society (Deutschen Geselschaft.) This organization, founded in 1847, did much to make economic and social adjustments easier for the immigrant; it provided immediate housing, facilitated transportation for those travelling beyond New Orleans, and it operated an employment agency. The Germans that remained in the city tended to settle in the Third and Fourth Districts among the Irish and French nationals, and on truck farms at the edge of the city and in the suburb of Carrollton. Like the Irish, they handled jobs requiring physical strength.

The French-born, numbering 10,564 in 1860, were the third largest immigrant group in New Orleans and the largest French colony in the United States. Some of the city's French had fled their homeland for political reasons after the failure of the revolution of 1848, but most were voluntary immigrants who took advantage of the cheap passage from Havre. This latter group—many of whom were Gascons—settled in the Third District or operated dairy and truck farms on the outskirts of the city.

The table following shows the number of foreign-born in New Orleans in 1860 from countries other than Ireland, Germany, and France:

Nation	Immigrants
England (including Scotland and Wales)	3849
Spain	1390
Italy (including Sardinia)	1019
West Indies	796
Switzerland	600
British American	562
Mexico	261
Denmark	227
Belgium	168
Holland	167
Sweden	140
Poland	119
Portugal	109
Asia	51
Russia	38
Norway	38
Atlantic Islands	31
Central America	22
South America	18
Greece	13
China	10
Africa	3

Many of the English immigrants were probably men of means, but larger numbers were impecunious upon landing. The patient list at Charity Hospital — a good index to relative national poverty — showed a heavy influx of English-born. Italians and Spaniards frequently came as single men and operated fruit stands, market stalls, cigar stores, and coffee shops. In the eyes of the Americans they were seldom differentiated; the term "dago" was used to cover them and even an occasional Cuban or Mexican. West Indians, chiefly from Santo Domingo and Cuba, were attracted to New Orleans because of climate, ethnic associations in the case of the French-speaking, and the position of New Orleans as a center for filibustering expeditions to Cuba.

Besides immigrants, the working class of New Orleans consisted of many native Americans born principally in the upper South and the Northeast. Little information about this group is available, but census data indicates that they provided at least one-half of the skilled labor in he city. And there were other

Americans in search of employment who simply worked with the immigrants on the wharves. There must have been many like Joseph Cooper, a seventeen year old from Pittsburgh, who drifted into the city and slept among the cotton bales until arrested as a vagrant. Poor Cooper contracted yellow fever and died eight days after his arrival in New Orleans.

How well the working class fared economically in the city is often difficult to ascertain. Wages were high, around two dollars a day for unskilled dock workers to three and four dollars for skilled labor. However because New Orleans depended on seasonal crops, unemployment was common during the summer months, though mitigated somewhat by construction work and city street paving projects. Some surplus labor was drained off by demands for workers on railroad gangs and as canal diggers and plantation ditchers in Louisiana and Mississippi.

There certainly is evidence that the workers had organizations which, though under the title and form of benevolent and burial societies, functioned as labor unions. One group called the Associated Pilots of Louisiana insisted upon standard wages for trips up-river. "Who ever goes for less is regarded as an 'outsider'," a local paper announced. The object of the Fireman's Low Pressure Steamship Association was "to compel the owners of all seagoing vessels to take only such men as belong to that society." The Association employed runners "who go on board every steamer arriving here and if there be members on board who are not of their organization they are required to leave, and unless they leave, none of the association will remain on board."[16] On the docks violence flared as stevedores struck for higher wages in October, 1850, the strikers assaulting scabs and setting up picket lines which were eventually broken by the police. In 1852 and again in 1854 deck hands walked off steamboats demanding sixty dollars a month, but employers used Negro scabs and after some violence the strikes were broken. Men armed with slung shots and brass knuckles often boarded incoming ships and prevented them from landing until certain wages were paid. More frequently they boarded a steamboat shortly before its departure and forced the crew to strike for higher wages. How far these "levee bullies" who also prevented dock workers from working "for fair rates of wages" and excluded Negroes entirely from the wharves were labor racketeers, which is the way the newspapers viewed them, and how far they were legitimate trade unionists it is impossible to say. Efforts to keep unions—or racketeers—off the docks was made by the State which passed a law in 1858 against picketing and made it illegal to prevent any worker from laboring on the wharves or on board river and ocean craft.

The evidence of militant trade union action—only a few of the strikes are discussed above—does not denote any well formulated class struggle. The working class was simply not articulate; it lacked leadership and all of the instruments of information were controlled by an upper class elite. "Class struggle was not to be expected in a society where only one class was articulate and conscious of its interests."[17] Most important the ominous shadow of the Negro—slave and free—made unity of all classes a necessity to maintain white supremacy.

MEN OF COLOR.

The Negro in New Orleans was part of a separate caste; he was excluded from marriage outside his group and his life pattern was narrowly restricted by the mores of the society in which he found himself. In the words of a contemporary: "Neither wealth, virtue, talent, beauty, nor accomplishment can elevate them above their caste."[18] The Negro accepted this scheme, albeit with certain mental and a few physical reservations, and constructed an institutional and class framework within the circle of caste limitations.

The caste system was made complex by the existence of both a free and a slave Negro population. Because there were important and essential legal distinctions between them, even if, in the eyes of the white population, there was little social distinction, the Negroes were divided in a sense into two separate castes. Of these only the free Negro was able to develop a class system vaguely approximating that of the dominant white class. The free Negroes had, Charles Gayarré wrote, "among themselves different classes, social distinctions, and objected to association with slaves."[19]

Free Negroes were usually called free men of color, "f.m.c.," or "f.w.c.," free women of color. In French they were designated by the initials "p.c.l." — personnes de couleur libres, "h.c.l." — hommes de couleur libres, or "f.c.l.—femmes de couleur libres. In their own circles the native born, French-speaking, free Negroes usually referred to themselves as "Creoles de couleur." Since the free Negroes were often racial hybrids, a terminology was developed to denote the degree of admixture. The most common terms were "quadroon" (one-fourth Negro), "octoroon" (one-eighth Negro), "mulatto" (one-half Negro), and "griffe" (three-fourths Negro). These appellations were commonly interchangeable with the term "free Negro."

There were 9,961 free people of color in New Orleans in 1850 and 10,689 ten years later. Census returns indicate that four-fifths of the free Negroes were racial admixtures, that three-fifths were women, that most were born in Louisiana with a few hundred originally from Virginia and the West Indies, and that most lived in the two districts below Canal Street. Other sources reveal that most of the free Negroes spoke French and were members of the Roman Catholic Church.

The economic position of free Negroes was often quite favorable. They owned an estimated $15,000,000 worth of real estate; a few free men of color owned entire city blocks. *Cordons bleus*, as wealthy free Negroes were called, served as jewelers, brokers, tailors, and money lenders. In the eyes of the white community they were "respectable and useful men," who emulated upper class whites wherever possible.[20] However most free Negroes were engaged in crafts or small businesses as barbers, cabinet makers, carpenters (355 in 1850), cigar makers, clerks, coopers, masons (325 in 1850), mechanics, painters, and shoemakers. Free women of color were employed as domestic servants, dressmakers, hairdressers and the like. An unknown number operated or worked in the booming prostitution business while others doubled as flower sellers and street walkers or offered themselves as mistresses for a remuneration greater than love. There was also a transient free Negro population that worked on ocean ships and steamboats or spent the winter season working on the wharves — only to fly North as the weather proved unhealthy and the work scarce. Some of these transients were skilled workers who came from the northern and western states to work in the city during the busy winter season. As the decade progressed laws made it increasingly difficult for free Negroes to cross state lines, but many northern free Negroes met the problem with forged passes.

During the 1850's unskilled free Negroes were replaced by cheaper Irish and German labor. Immigrants took over former free Negro jobs as domestics, hotel employees, dray drivers, and cab men. On the other hand free Negroes held their own in the skilled trades and travellers noted Irish waiters serving Negro artisans and Irish hod carriers employed by free Negro masons. It is possible that this economic relationship created antagonism between the free Negro and white laborers which in turn entrenched caste differences and made impossible an united working class.

Though the free Negro was able to maintain much of his economic position, his legal status, already severely restricted, declined during the decade. The state legislature in 1855 prevented the incorporation of any new religious, charitable, scientific, or literary society composed of free people of color. Out-of-state free Negroes were excluded from Louisiana, and free Negroes on board ships docking in New Orleans had to be registered; in 1859 the law was changed to require all free colored sailors to be lodged in the parish jail until twenty-four hours before sailing time. The 1859 legislature made it illegal for a free Negro to keep a coffee house, billiard table, or retail store where liquor was sold. The same legislature in a stroke of magnanimity allowed free Negroes the boon of choosing their own masters and becoming slaves for life. The city re-enforced the state law on illegal entry by allowing recorders (police judges) to commit all free Negroes who entered the state illegally to the work house and an 1856 ordinance supplemented a state law by preventing free people of color from obtaining liquor licenses. In addition the city had its own proscriptions; they ranged from minor limitations on shooting off fire crackers by free Negroes, playing cards and dominoes and having balls with slaves, to a general ordinance preventing any assembly of colored people, free or slave.

Of course no law is stronger than the degree of its enforcement and in New Orleans, with its inadequate and inefficient police force, the laws against free Negroes were frequently ignored. However there is some evidence to indicate that the police, especially in the later 1850's, enforced city ordinances dealing with free Negro assembly, illegal passes, vagrancy, suspicion, and contacts with slaves than had hiterto been practiced.

The free Negro faced not only the tightening bonds of legal restrictions but also an almost overwhelming hostility from the press. As North-South tension increased the newspapers viewed the free Negro as a questionable element in southern society; they "are not a desirable population and they may be a dangerous one" the *Picayune* reported. In more modern terms the free Negro was a fifth column agent who would lead the placid slaves astray and serve as local agents for the abolitionists; in brief, they were un-Southern. The result was a daily outpouring of invective from the city's journals which may have depressed, where it did not disgust, the local free Negroes and forced many of them to consider leaving.

Some Negroes apparently did leave. France had always been a refuge for wealthy free Negroes and a handful moved to Liberia through the cooperation of the American Colonization Society, but a larger group fled to Haiti. After the restrictive laws of 1855, Lolo Mansion, a wealthy free man of color, provided funds for his associates wishing to emigrate to Haiti or Mexico and in 1858 the Haitian Emperor, Faustian Soulouque, sent an agent to New Orleans to encourage emigration. In the following year a "literate and respectable" group of two hundred free people of color left New Orleans for Haiti, and in January, 1860, another ship with eighty-one more free Negroes sailed for the island. It is the opinion of one student that "many more" free Negroes emigrated to Haiti.[21] Except to note a few dissatisfied free Negroes who returned, the press offered little information about the movement to Haiti.

The Negroes who migrated were probably among the most sensitive and capable, the ones who might have offered a focus of protest. Such prominent artists, musicians, and writers as Edmund Dedé, Victor Sejour, Eugene Warberg, Richard Lambert, Nelson Debroses, Joseph C. Rousseau, Pierre Dalcour, and Camile Thierry found New Orleans life too restraining and they fled to France where their talents might develop and be appreciated. There were free Negro leaders and intellectuals who remaind however and though they hibernated — "survived" as Abbé Sieyès would say — the arrival of the Union army brought them forth again complete with a program of emancipation and with cogent criticisms of the old regime.

There were two groups of slaves in New Orleans; slaves who were brought into the city and sold in slave auctions and slaves who were owned by New Orleans residents.

As a slave trading center New Orleans was the greatest in the South. The bull market in slaves, which lasted throughout the 1850's for the Southwest, made this one of the major "products from the interior" sold in the city. Slaves were sold by auctioneers or by slave dealers; the former received a commission on the sale, while the latter generally purchased slaves in the upper South, transported them by sea, steamboat, or in overland coffles to the city. If the slaves were from Louisiana and spoke French they would be designated "Creole Negro"; if from the upper South they

Slaves for sale: A scene in New Orleans.
(Illustrated London News, XXXVIII — April 6, 1861)

would be advertised as "Virginia Negro" or "American Negro." There were also a small number of slaves brought directly from Africa, smuggled into the Delta area and sold in New Orleans.

Slaves for sale were kept in "jails" or "yards," that is, compounds open to view for prospective buyers and containing quarters for slaves. There were at least twenty-five of these slave depots within a half mile of the St. Charles Hotel, mostly on Gravier, Baronne, Magazine, and Esplanade Streets. Sales were made at the depot or by bi-lingual auctioneers in the rotundas of the St. Charles and St. Louis Hotels. In New Orleans at least there was no disapprobation connected with being a slave auctioneer; indeed, some, as Joseph A. Beard, Julian Neville, C. F. Hatcher, Thomas Foster, and N. Vignie were community leaders.

In the interest of the slave dealers, their charges were well fed and well dressed. When up for sale they were attired in their "Sunday best." Men wore good quality blue cloth suits with vests, ties, white shirts, well shined shoes, and high beaver hats; women were adorned in multi-colored calico dresses with bright silk bandanas. When not on an auction black slave dealers had their charges stand outside the depots for inspection which, according to a local newspaper editor, presented a not entirely edifying sight.

> Scarcely anyone desires to pass such places; while to the ladies it is like running the gauntlet, to be exposed to the prying, peering gaze of lengthened lines of grinning negroes of both sexes ranked in Indian file; and who have nothing to occupy their attention stare 'out of countenance' with their very large and saucer eyes. . . . They hardly await the passing of persons before they extended lines, ere they commence making their comments and those eke out lengthened and amusing conversation for each other.[22]

Aware of these nuisances the city council passed an ordinance in December, 1856, to control slave marts. No future slave depot was allowed in the city without common council approval and if the majority of people in a four block area of a slave yard protested its presence the mayor could force the removal of the depot. The slave quarters had to meet standards of health, cleanliness, and privacy and Negroes were not be displayed on the streets or sidewalks in front of the slave pens.

Since the number of slaves for sale in the city during June was small, the bulk of the slaves listed in the censuses of 1850 and 1860 were locally owned. What is perhaps surprising is that Orleans parish was the third largest slave holding parish in the state with 18,068 slaves in 1850 and 13,385 in 1860. As in the free Negro population, women outnumbered men at a ratio of approximately eight to five; in contrast however to the free Negroes, the number of blacks was significantly higher than the number of mulattoes.

There were very few large slaveholders in New Orleans.

In 1860 there were in New Orleans 1435 individuals who owned one slave each; 821 who owned two slaves each; 609 who owned three slaves each; 369 who owned four slaves each; 203 who owned five slaves each; and 128 who owned six slaves each. After that the numbers in one column diminished sharply while they increased in the other. Thus there were but forty persons in the city who owned fifteen slaves each; three who owned forty each, and but two who counted one hundred slaves among their possessions. There was nobody who owned as much as two hundred slaves. The total of 14,484 slaves in New Orleans was distributed among 4,169 owners.[23]

As can be observed from the above, holdings were small, with one-third of the slave holders possessiong only one slave, and one-half owning two or fewer.

The majority of slave holders in New Orleans were whites. The exact figure of slaves owned by free people of color is unknown, but by 1860 it was probably somewhat lower than 1830 when 749 free Negroes owned slaves. Free Negroes customarily purchased relatives or close friends; because the conditions of manumission were often difficult to meet, and after 1857 impossible, the purchase of a slave would at least overcome the spirit of slavery if not the exact letter. There were however free Negroes who purchased slaves as investments or as servants and their relations toward these slaves probably did not differ vitally from those of whites toward their slaves.

The major employment for slaves in the city was as house servants in the form of cooks, washwomen, maids, valets, butlers, carriage drivers, hair dressers, gardeners, and general handymen. Slaves were also used by merchants as porters, laborers and unskilled laborers. German and Irish immigrants occasionally invested in slaves to operate drays or hacks. There were several industries in New Orleans which were large employers of slaves, among which were the Leeds and the Armstrong foundries, the gas works, the Canal Banking Company, and several cotton presses. The gas works had a Negro compound with all facilities for the slaves' room and board—even the overseer was slave. It should be noted however that an extensive use of slave labor in New Orleans industry never developed. More commonly large slave holders rented bondsmen to private individuals as servants or to various companies as laborers. One example of the slave rentier was Isaac Pipkin who brought his slaves from Virginia to New Orleans and hired them out chiefly as dock workers, employing his nephew as an overseer. After the elder Pipkin's death the nephew employed thirty-nine slaves and by hiring an assistant overseer, collecting slave wages daily, and efficient management he made a profit of $16,538 in two years.

Like the free Negro in this decade, the slave saw his position become subject to more stringent legal bounds. The state government declared that slaves accused of a capital crime in Orleans Parish were to be tried by a jury of six slaveholders. The penalties for slave offenses were made stricter in 1855 and then even more elaborate in 1857. In addition various restrictions on the slaves' mobility were enacted in the 1850's. By state law slaves were not allowed out after 9 P.M., before dawn, or on Sunday and loitering in front of a tavern or warehouse was a punishable crime. City ordinances were more binding than even state laws. Along with free Negroes, slaves were not allowed either to congregate in numbers or shoot fireworks; slaves had to have the approval of the mayor for Sunday dances; they could not carry sticks or guns, could not ride in public vehicles without their master's approval, and could not play cards with whites or free men of color; and they might not purchase any article over five dollars without written permission from their master. In case they had forgotten anything the city fathers proclaimed: "All slaves are forbidden to quarrel, yell, curse or sing obscene songs, or in anyways disturb the public peace, or to gamble in the streets, roads or other public places, or on the levee."[24]

The slave who wished to escape his servitude had several recourses. The first and most obvious was by manumission. Since a slave in New Orleans could often earn money, the wherewithal for buying his freedom was not always lacking. Slaves often were freed in their masters' wills or by personal act of a white or free Negro benefactor or relative. Manumission was obtained also through a direct legislative enactment and through the instrumentality of a local branch of the American Colonization Society. During the ante-bellum period two hundred and ninety slaves were sent to Liberia from Louisiana under the auspices of this Society. Of these, one hundred and twenty-one had belonged to the famous miser-philanthropist John McDonogh.

As community prejudice against free Negroes increased it became more difficult for slaves to be emancipated. By an act of 1852 manumission was to be allowed only if the slave were to leave the country. This act was repealed in 1855 and emancipation was allowed by a suit for freedom in the state courts. The appellate had to be of good character and have an unblemished past. If the court permitted the individual to remain in the state after manumission, he had to post a thousand dollar bond that he would not become a public charge. Finally in 1857, in the shortest law on the statute books for the decade, the state closed the legal door to emancipation; it simply stated: "That from and after the passage of this act no slave shall be emancipated in this state."[25] In an almost equally terse manner the state Supreme Court upheld this law.

A few New Orleans slaves attempted to escape their bondage by running away. The average runaway of course was uninterested in a thousand mile trip to free territory. He probably intended merely to escape from some immediate task; or he preferred to live by his wits in the anonymity of the city. But for a few Negroes at least freedom via the underground railroad beckoned. Cases of Northerners or free Negroes being arrested for enticing, secreting, or transporting slaves were common enough to indicate that New Orleans was a way-station for slaves seeking freedom. The *Picayune*, noting a case of free Negro sailors who attempted to hide two slaves on board a ship, advised local police and slave holders "to keep a bright look out for these colored cooks, stewards and crews of foreign vessels, who are but too often the instruments which abolition fanatics use to carry out their nefarious designs."

In practice the New Orleans slave was not always as restricted as the nature of slavery was thought to be. Negroes were often free to seek their own hire and even their own room and board; in turn the master asked only a certain remuneration. Slaves worked as street and market vendors and flower girls with little or no regulation over their conduct. Occasionally slaves served as prostitutes with the tacit knowledge or even the overt direction of their masters. Furthermore laws to regulate slaves were often unenforced. There were constant complaints of slaves congregating with free Negroes and whites. One newspaper deplored the fact that the corner of Perdido and Baronne was "continuously blocked up with a great number of impertinent negroes, mingled with the lowest class of white people male and female. . . ."[26] Slaves gambled, drank, and went hunting directly contrary to municipal and state laws. And, according to newspaper accounts, there were male slaves who were known to share time and bed with some elements of white southern womanhood.

Though there is no source for the personal view of any slaves in New Orleans concerning their position, it can probably be concluded from their actions that they were, on the whole, contented; certainly the urban slave had more freedom and adventure than the plantation Negro. It might well be however that the comparative tolerance the slave found in New Orleans only whetted his desire for freedom. The fact that in 1857 all possibility of freedom was legally terminated by the state leigslature must have produced an added resentment in the slave community toward white society and made them, as all contemporary accounts indicate, more than unusually pleased to see the "Bluecoats" in 1862.

NOTES

[1] Frederica Bremer, *The Homes of the New World: Impressions of America* (2 vols.; New York, 1854), II, 213.
[2] Joseph G. Tregle, "Early New Orleans Society: A Reappraisal," *Journal of Southern History*, XVIII (February, 1952), 22.
[3] [Madame Frédéric Allain] *Souvenirs d'Amerique et de France par une Créole* (Paris, n.d.), 190.
[4] Grace King, *Creole Families of New Orleans* (New York, 1921), 43.
[5] Selma Louise Klein, "Social Interaction of the Creoles and Anglo-Americans in New Orleans, 1803-1860," (unpublished M.A. thesis, New Orleans, Tulane University, 1940), 27.
[6] Several contemporary sources contend that the word Creole meant native born and as late as 1873 Creole was defined as "all who are born here . . . without reference to the birth place of their parents." Edwin L. Jewell, ed., *Jewell's Crescent City Illustrated: The Commercial, Social, Political and General History of New Orleans Including Biographical Sketches of Its Distinguished Citizens* (New Orleans, 1874), 15. This book was prepared in part by Charles Gayarré and Albert Fabre, descendants of old Spanish and French families, and one may perhaps infer that the definition met with their approval. Not until thirty years after the Civil War is it possible to discover a definition of the Creoles as "white descendants of the French and Spanish settlers." Alceé Fortier, "The French Language in Louisiana and the Negro-French Dialect," Modern Language Association of America, *Transactions*, I (1884-1885), 98.
[7] James Creecy, *Scenes in the South and Other Miscellaneous Pieces* (Washington, 1860), 13.
[8] Intermarriage of course also involved a shared social life and an accepted upper class set of customs and leisure values. In later chapters it will be shown that wealthy Americans adopted and accepted a particular pattern of social life associated with the Creoles.

[9] Henry A. Murray, *Lands of the Slave and Free; or Cuba, the United States, and Canada* (London, 1857), 144.
[10] J. J. Ampére, *Promenade en Amerique* (2 vols.; Paris, 1855), II, 153.
[12] Roger Shugg, *Origins of Class Struggle In Louiisana: A Social History of White Farmers and Laborers during Slavery and After, 1840-1875* (Baton Rouge, 1939), 121, 155.
[13] Lewis William Newton, "Creole and Anglo-Americans in Old Louisiana — A Study in Cultural Conflicts," *Southwestern Social Science Quarterly*, XIV (June, 1933), 48.
[14] Thomas K. Wharton, diary, 1852-1862, in Division of Manuscripts, New York Public Library; microfilm copy in the Archives of the Howard-Tilton Memorial Library, Tulane University, New Orleans. Wharton's salary on the Custom House work was $175 a month until 1859 when it was raised to $250. He supplemented his income by other governmental duties and by doing part-time architectural work. For a pattern of daily life similar to Wharton's see the Thomas R. Markham Papers, 1850-1859, Archives of the Louisiana State University, Baton Rouge. Markham was a Presbyterian divine whose diary shows a life spent in beating carpets for his wife, dusting his library, puttering in his garden, preparing his brimstone sermons, and talking to his Anglo-American friends.
[15] "Up the Mississippi," *Emerson's Magazine and Putnam's Monthly*, V (October, 1857), 436.
[16] New Orleans *Weekly Picayune*, August 7, 1854. Unless otherwise stated all newspapers cited in this study were published in New Orleans.
[17] Shugg, *Origins of Class Struggle in Louisiana*, 30-31.
[18] Philo Tower, *Slavery Unmasked: Being a Truthful Narrative of a Three Years' Residence and Journeying in Eleven Southern States. . . .* (Rochester, New York, 1856), 325.
[19] Charles Gayarré, "The Quadroons of Louisiana," unpublished study, quoted in Mary Scott Duchein, "Research on Charles Étienne Arthur Gayarré" (unpublished M.A. thesis, Baton Rouge, Louisiana State University, 1934), 137.
[20] Louisiana Attorney General, *Report*, 1857 (Baton Rouge, 1857), II.
[21] Donald Edward Everett, "Free Persons of Color in New Orleans, 1803-1865," (unpublished Ph.D. dissertation, Tulane University, New Orleans, 1952), 128-130.
[22] *Daily Orleanian*, January 20, 1852.
[23] John Smith Kendall, "New Orleans' 'Peculiar Institution,'" *Louisiana Historical Quarterly*, XXIII (July, 1940), 871. The census returns listed slaves held in depots as locally owned, so it is reasonable to assume that some of the large holdings were not actually owned by permanent residents of New Orleans.
[24] Resolution 500, December 18, 1852, in Common Council Ordinances and Resolutions, 1852-1856; Ordinance 3203, January 7, 1857, in *ibid.*, 1856-1866, City Hall Archives, New Orleans Public Library; Henry J. Leovy, comp., *The Laws and General Ordinances of the City of New Orleans. . . .* (New Orleans, 1857), 257-262.
[25] *Louisiana Acts*, 1857, 55 (No. 69).
[26] *Louisiana State Republican*, March 31, 1855.

Chapter III

THE WHARF

> This levee is the grandest quay in the world. Tyre, nor Carthage, Alexandria nor Genoa, those afore time metropoles of merchant princes boasted no quay like the levee of New Orleans.[1]

The heart of New Orleans economic life in the ante-bellum period rested on the waterfront; almost the entire economy directly or indirectly was related to activity on the thin line of wharves and levees which rimmed the Mississippi. Here the traveller viewed a port

> crowded with vessels of all sizes and of every nation, together with hundreds of large and elegant steamers, and a multiplicity of river craft. Nothing can present a more busy scene than the *levee* at this time: the loading and unloading of drays transporting the varied products of the Great West, is truly exhilarating, and impresses the beholder with an idea of the vastness of the commerce that requires all this commotion in its prosecution.[2]

To an emotional traveller from France, the levee

> offered a bizarre and curious contrast. Here was a strange concert of oaths, questions, cries, and savage noises. While several steamboats heated up for their departure and several draymen passed at a fast pace, shaking the pavement under the weight of their iron carts, the Negroes and Irish proceeded to unload other recently arrived boats and rolled to earth bales of cotton or hogsheads of sugar, under the eye of the commissioners.... The mixture of voices spoke every language. There was the *by God* of the Yankee, the *per la madona* of the Italian, the *caramba* of the Spaniard, the *Diou bibant* of the Gascon, the gutteral *God dam* [sic] of the Irishman.... In all a living Babel....[3]

Perhaps the most succinct remark on beholding the forest of ship masts, the smoke and noise of a hundred steamboats, and the levees piled high with western and southern produce, was made by an amazed American who on arriving in New Orleans burst out, "Well, what an almighty fine country is ours."[4]

On the other hand, during the summer months, when weather and fever kept the merchants out of the city, and before the year's cotton and sugar crops began to arrive, the wharves were almost abandoned. "The levee looked like a desert ... all seemed dreary

The Levee at New Orleans
(Illustrated London News XXXII — June 5, 1858)

and desolate," wrote one summer visitor.[5] Only the occasional sail of a skiff or a schooner bringing produce to the market dotted the muddy river.

In the center of the port, along the levee between Toulouse and Julia Streets, was the steamboat dock where during the 1850's, 30,567 steamboats tied up. In the busy winter season arrivals were so frequent that the port wardens and harbor masters, who regulated the flow of river traffic, were often forced to request steamboat pilots to anchor their vessels out in the stream until room was available.

The average steamboat was a single-deck, six hundred-ton, side-wheeler about 250 feet long and twenty to thirty feet wide. It had simple lines and functioned primarily as a carrier of freight. In contrast, the larger river craft were veritable floating palaces of the most advanced type of steamboat gothic architecture. These boats were, in one writer's view, "built in the most fantastic manner and painted in the most gaudy colors."[6] While another considered his boat a "Huge, tall white pasteboard castle of a steamer. . . ."[7] Luxury steamboats might be three hundred feet long, thirty-five feet wide, with a side-wheel thirty-eight feet in diameter and buckets twelve feet wide. For the passenger's comfort there were bathing rooms, a fancy saloon, a children's nursery, ten or more state rooms, and berths for as many as 160 cabin passengers. The large steamboats took pride in a host of safety devices, e.g., steam gauges in each room and floating doors, which undoubtedly eased nerves easily frayed at the thought of sleeping above the boat's five boilers.

Steamboats were divided according to the service they rendered into three classifications: the transients, the packets, and the lines. The transients, by far the largest number, were the free lancers of the business; they announced their desination by advertisements in local papers and by handbills distributed at hotels, and if these measures failed to obtain sufficient freight and passengers, the owners or captains employed "runners" to scare up customers by promise of cheap freight and low cost fares. Packet boats offered service between two points at scheduled intervals; they usually operated on tributaries of the Mississippi or between New Orleans and communities in Louisiana and Mississippi. A line consisted of two or more boats providing regular service between distant points; thus a line offering daily departures on the New Orleans-St. Louis run requried twelve steamboats.

There were as many as two hundred ocean vessels in the harbor at once during the winter season. These ships, which docked at wharves extending at right angles from the levee out into the stream, were mostly sailing vessels, varying from large packets to small schooners, brigs, and barks. Competing with sailing vessels were the larger, though less picturesque, steamships. Because they were able to carry a greater cargo, an especially important consideration when handling cotton, they were preferred to sailing ships and as a result by 1860 the number of ocean ships docking in New Orleans was fewer than in 1850, but the total tonnage carried from the port had increased.

The bulk of the ships were American, mostly coastal packet lines running to and from New York. There were also scheduled lines operating between New Orleans and Gulf Coast ports and California. There were no regular lines connecting New Orleans and Europe — a source of much irritation to the local citizens — so a traveller wishing to sail to Europe had to watch the newspapers for announcements of non-scheduled ship departures.

The Mississippi provided a highway for the lowly flatboat, but the trade was only a fraction of what it had been in previous decades. The number of flatboats, which had declined from 2,763 in 1845-6 to 541 in 1856-7, were of so little importance after 1857 that harbor officials ceased to keep statistics on their arrival. Instead of the earlier troublesome Kaintucks floating down the river with whiskey and lard, the flatboat traffic by the 1850's was composed almost entirely of more prosaic hay from Indiana and coal from Pennsylvania. The flatboats were unloaded at specific sections of the port set aside for them and then either towed back upstream or broken up and used in street and home construction.

In addition to steamboats, ocean ships, and flatboats, there were a host of smaller ships plying the river: small schooners, sloops, skiffs, pirogues, and barges brought sugar and garden truck to the city from nearby plantations and farms; public ferry boats loaded with humans, cattle, horses, and goats crossed the river between New Orleans and the west bank communities; private skiffs and pirogues darted about the harbor like water beetles, carrying sailors, merchants, and thieves from ship to ship; stubby steam towboats maneuvered about the harbor bringing up ships from the Gulf and taking on new tows in turn; and finally the city nuisance boat which made a daily voyage with the city's garbage and refuse to the middle of the stream where it dumped its contents, its crew hoping, but not always successfully, that the "cargo" would float "unvexed to the sea."

The most important product handled on the wharves of New Orleans was cotton. In the season of 1850-1851,[8] New Orleans cotton receipts from the interior amounted to 995,036 bales valued at $48,756,764. With the exception of 1853-1854 and 1856-1857, when crops were small, the decade saw a steady increase, the volume reaching 2,255,448 bales in 1859-1860 with a value of $109,389,288. The city was the leading cotton port in the nation, handling an average of forty-eight percent of the total United States crop for the 1850's. The great and growing importance of cotton to the commercial life of New Orleans is demonstrated by the fact that in 1850 it accounted for forty-five percent of the value of all products received from the interior, and that by 1860 the value had risen to fifty-nine percent of the total.

Sixty percent of all the cotton received in New Orleans was raised in Louisiana and Mississippi, most of it brought to the city on steamboats. But smaller amounts came by coastal ships from Texas, Alabama, Florida, and Mississippi, by small ships from across Lake Pontchartrain, and, after 1856, by rail from parts of Louisiana and Mississippi. After processing, most of the cotton from New Orleans was consigned to English firms. During the 1850's the amount of cotton sent annually to England rose from 582,723 bales to 1,426,966 bales, well over one-half of the total New Orleans exports. Such statistics prompted one English writer to declare that "Manchester is no less needful to New Orleans than is New Orleans to Manchester,"[9] and later undoubtedly led the Southern Confederacy into its unsuccessful King Cotton diplomacy during the Civil War. French consumption of cotton in the same period increased from 125,067 bales to 303,157 bales. There was also a significant growth of cotton shipments to the new textile industries of northern Italy, the German states, and New England. The chief European ports for New Orleans cotton were Liverpool, Havre, Bremen, Genoa, and Trieste, while the principal American ports were Boston and New York, though much of the New York bound cotton was later trans-shipped to Europe.

The first bales of the annual cotton crop arrived in mid-August, but it was late in September or early in October before news items such as the following appeared in the local press: the "dull monotony which for several months has pervaded the Levee ... was broken by the arrival of five river steamers with 6,059

River and Levee at New Orleans from the Northeast angle of the new Customhouse. Drawn by T. K. Wharton, October, 1855. (Reproduced by permission of the New York Public Library)

bales."[10] Gradually cotton receipts would increase and by December the river was thick with steamboats and the levee covered with cotton bales. The flow of cotton into the port would continue until March; the supply would then slowly diminish and by May only a trickle reached the city.

The cotton that landed on the wharf was labeled by a steamboat clerk with the mark of the planter from whom it came and the mark of the commission merchant to whom it was consigned. Because of the usual illiteracy of the Negro and immigrant stevedores, a flag designating the consignee — a "black cross," "blue cross," or "red ball" — was stuck into the bales and they were rolled to a section of the dock set off for the consignee and marked by the same flag. With forty to fifty thousand bales often on the levee at the same time, this routing system led to occasional confusion but in general was satisfactory.

The commission merchant had previously arranged to have one of the twenty cotton presses handle the bales and at the docks draymen loaded between five and fifteen bales of cotton, depending on the state of the streets, on wagons and with an African, Hibernian, or Teutonic curse started their unwilling mules toward the press. At the press the cotton was unloaded by a three-man yard gang, one of a number of such gangs each in charge of a "store" of eighty to one hundred bales. As soon as possible the bales were placed in a gigantic steam press and reduced further in size. The planter's bagging and rope was used again unless the planter was using one of the new-fangled iron hoops, which were removed and standard rope and bagging substituted.

Meanwhile a six-ounce sample from each bale was taken by the commission merchant's clerk and inspected in his office and classified according to quality (*inferior, ordinary, good ordinary, low middling, middling, good middling, middling fair, fair, good fair, good,* and *fine.*) Jurisdiction over the cotton soon passed from a factor or commission merchant to a cotton broker. He had it classified, re-weighed, and ship-marked; that is, marks were placed on the bagging which made it possible to trace the cotton back to the ship, the broker, the cotton press, the commission merchant, and to the planter. This was a necessary precaution because one of these agents, usually the planter, occasionally substituted, advertently or not, rocks, brush, gin dirt, and other foreign matter for cotton.

After pressing, cotton bales were hauled by dray to storage or to a ship wharf. At the wharf the drayman's receipt was signed by a ship's clerk, and stevedores began the task of loading the cotton aboard ship. Since in ships carrying cotton, space was more important than weight, "screw men," working in five-man gangs, were employed to force the cotton by means of "jack screws" into a limited space. When the loading was completed, the ship's crew collected from the groggeries on Gallatin Street and a towboat attachment made, the ship was ready to head down river to the sea and distant ports.

Behind the physical movement of cotton from plantation to mill lay a complex financial and mercantile organization. The banker, exchange merchant, insurance underwriter, and ship broker played essential roles, but the two most important functionaries were the commission merchant or factor[11] and the cotton broker. The commission merchant was the planter's agent in the port of New Orleans and served as intermediary between the planter and the mercantile world. It was the duty of the commission merchant to receive the planter's cotton, protect it, and sell it at the most advantageous price. In return the merchant charged a commission of two and one-half percent. He might also serve as a "broker" in purchasing goods for the planter, a "banker" in loaning the planter money or giving him credit against future crops, a financial and legal advisor, and, judging from contemporary letters, a general confidant. The brokers were engaged in filling orders for buyers usually in the North Atlantic states or abroad. Some brokers were independent operators, others were representatives of private investment houses, and yet others were direct agents of cotton importing houses or even of manufacturers.

The second most valuable crop handled in New Orleans was sugar. Almost all of the sugar and molasses was grown and processed on Louisiana plantations and transported to New Orleans by steamboat, river schooner, or, after 1854, railroad. The 1850's saw marked ups and downs in sugar crops and for that reason sugar and molasses varied greatly from year to year. Thus in the low year of 1856-1857 only 62,463 hogsheads of sugar and 84,169 hogsheads of molasses were marketed; the high year was 1858-1859 when 257,225 hogsheads of sugar and 353,715 hogsheads of molasses reached the New Orleans market. The yearly average for the decade was about 177,000 hogsheads of sugar and 260,000 hogsheads of molasses. Sugar was sent to commission merchants in New Orleans under a system similar to that for cotton. The commission merchant in turn sold to a broker, or, as happened increasingly in the fifties, directly to a representative of a sugar refinery or a distributor. Unlike cotton, sugar marketed through New Orleans was largely shipped upstream or to eastern ports; few shipments went abroad. Very small amounts of sugar were even imported from Cuba (or smuggled in and relabeled "Louisiana") and distributed throughout Mid-America.

New Orleans was a major center for the handling of tobacco. In 1850-1851, 64,030 hogsheads arrived in the city, and in 1859-1860 the total was 80,995; the high year was 1857-1858 with 87,141 hogsheads. Upon arrival in New Orleans, tobacco was stored in state-approved warehouses for a year, after which it was inspected by state officials who classified it according to quality and condition. Following inspection the tobacco was subject to the order of its owner, who would then have it pressed and recasked. The greater part was shipped on consignment to Europe (chiefly Bremen) and eastern United States ports. Later the tobacco might return to New Orleans as "Havana" cigars and be trans-shipped for sale in the New Orleans trading area. A few New Orleans companies imported finished tobacco from Virginia, Cuba, and Germany for chewing or smoking — including cigarettes for the "senoritas of Mexico" — which they packaged under such alluring titles as "Star of the South," "The Gold Leaf," "Virginia's Boast," "Kookinoor," and "The Pancake."[12]

There were several other products from the interior which were worth a million dollars or more yearly. Pork and pork products brought to New Orleans in 1850-1851 were valued at $13,-145,148. During the decade that followed the quantity of pork and pork products shipped to the city declined, a decline obscured however by a rise in pork prices over the ten year span so that the total value of pork in this period dropped only about a half million dollars. Dressed pork (and beef) received in New Orleans was inspected by state officials and given a grade of "mess," "prime," or "cargo." Most of this meat was then reshipped to southern coastal cities and to areas in the Mississippi valley dependent upon New Orleans for retail and wholesale supplies. Flour shipped to New Orleans in 1859-1860 was valued at $6,036,625, an increase in value of nearly two million dollars in a ten year period; like pork, the increase was the result of a price rise and not an increase in quantity. Flour brought to New Orleans was classified by state inspectors as "super," "Fine," or "middling." About a third of the flour was shipped to coastal ports from Galveston to Boston; less than a tenth was sent to Europe and Latin America with the remainder consumed locally or distributed in the city's trading area. The only other products worth a million dollars or more in 1859-1860 were corn ($3,051,274), whiskey ($1,665,378), coal ($1,160,000), and bale rope ($1,126,861).

Excluding cotton and sugar, the value of products from the interior increased from $32,615,573 in 1849-1850 to $57,631,146 in 1859-1860. It should be pointed out again that much of this increase was due to a general price rise in the 1850's and that, with the exception of a few products like hay, oats, porter and ale, shingles, and coal which made spectacular advances, the tonnage of most products remained nearly constant and in a few cases, like furs and lead, declined precipitously.

Though the bulk of New Orleans trade was composed of foodstuffs and raw materials carried to the city from the valley of the Mississippi, the city also served as a center for receipt and distribution of manufactured goods. The many ships which plied between European ports and New Orleans provided cheap transportation for European imports. But the import-export values were not balanced; generally imports came to only one-fourth or one-third of the value of exports and incoming ships often carried only immigrants, or sand and bricks for ballast. Ships from New York and other eastern ports brought in finished northern manufacturing products and from California came gold and silver from the newly opened mines.

The 'fifties in New Orleans was an era of "flush times, high wages, high profits, and high prices."[13] As a result the commercial community often overlooked, or underplayed, the evident shortcomings of New Orleans' economic structure. In spite of the statistics in the *Price Current* which revealed an annual growth of export and import receipts, New Orleans was becoming a financial satrapy of New York and to a lesser degree of Liverpool, and trade was only relatively increasing as iron rails took the commerce of the upper Mississippi valley eastward rather than south via the river system.

The bulk of New Orleans trade was channeled through New York City by means of coastal packets which brought cotton to New York where it was trans-shipped to vessels bound for Europe. The same coastal packets returned to New Orleans with European goods. By this system, Robert Greenhalgh Albion declares, the "New York command of Southern commerce was remarkably complete."[14] It was estimated that New York merchants made forty cents on every dollar paid for southern cotton. It was felt in the city that direct shipping lines to Europe would free the community from the economic stranglehold placed upon it by New York. If New Orleans had such steamship lines, one newspaper announced, "the sinking of New York, Boston, and Philadelphia would affect us no more than a gentle zephyr affects the monarch of the forest." With direct lines, the paper predicted, "New Orleans . . . commercial and financial grandeur would baffle calculation."[15] But nothing was accomplished despite agitation. After Louisiana entered the Confederacy the project was given the incentive of patriotism; before anything concrete was accomplished, the city was captured by Federal troops.

The practice of securing foreign and eastern products by way of New York also tended to limit New Orleans as a trading center. To make a profit New Orleans wholesalers had to charge higher prices than their New York suppliers. Country merchants could therefore save by purchasing directly from New York and preferred to do so. "New York," wrote William T. Sherman from Alexandria, Louisiana, in 1859, "is the great commercial center of America, and it would be in my judgment extreme squeamishness to pay more for a worse article elsewhere."[16]

In banking as in the import and export trade, New Orleans was in great measure dependent upon New York and Europe. Not that New Orleans banks were poorly operated; on the contrary they were highly profitable and much more stable than eastern banks as revealed in the banking crisis of 1854 and 1857 when New Orleans banks survived money panics that drove many other banks to insolvency. The city had simply too few banks with a small total capitalization. Attempts to increase banking facilities by the establishment of "free banks"[17] during the 1850's gave New Orleans a stronger financial position, but the increased capitalization was not sufficient for the volume of trade. Therefore many of the exchange, discount, loaning, and credit functions that might have been managed by New Orleans banks were handled by New York firms or their branch houses in the Crescent City. A British banking journal reported: "The Southern trade may be said to have been always the mainstay of the New York bankers. Everything that the South has produced and purchased has been represented in bills of exchange which have passed through New York bankers' hands." "The weak point," stated the same publication, "of western trade by way of New Orleans is thus the absence of banking facilities."[18]

If shipping and banking costs were largely determined in New York, prices of cotton were determined by middlemen in Liverpool. This had great disadvantages; the purchasing of cotton was rendered highly speculative and American planters and merchants were limited by a price setting mechanism over which they had little control. In 1855 a commercial convention in New Orleans urged direct sales from the shipping port (New Orleans and other southern ports) to manufacturing concerns, thus destroying the "Liverpool monopoly." The movement for direct sales was supported by the planter class, but the New Orleans commercial community took little interest (the commission merchant and broker was always assured of a profit barring a complete collapse of the market) and nothing was accomplished. It is true that speculation in Liverpool might have been limited if cotton buyers had been aware of crop prospects, but lack of rapid communication between North America and England prevented prompt adjustments of price. There was hope that the trans-atlantic cable would improve communication, but it broke and was not relaid until after the Civil War. Speculation was also abated by the absence of a crop reporting service in the South. English buyers had to rely upon such unofficial sources as southern newspapers and personal correspondence. The greatest of all marketing improvements needed was a local cotton exchange, but this was not even broached in the ante-bellum period.

The influence of New York and Liverpool on the city's economy led local citizens to fear that New Orleans might become "scarcely more than a . . . point for trans-shipment to the Northern Cities,"[19] and fostered as a result a movement for economic diversification to include the development of local industry. Certainly no form of industry appeared to be so eminently practicable for the city as cotton mills. Only public apathy prevented New Orleans from becoming another Lowell according to an anonymous writer in *De Bow's Review*;[20] the city had easy access to southern cotton, established river and ocean connections for shipping finished cloth throughout the Southland, and a growing supply of cheap immigrant labor to say nothing of the fact that, as one editor insisted, "our suburbs swarm with poor children, growing up in idleness," who might be put to work in factories.[21] In 1850 a cotton mill was "projected," but it failed to materialize. Five years later the Louisiana Manufacturing Company opened in the Fourth District; though engaged mainly in processing hemp for northern rope-walks, it did manufacture some cotton rope and in 1856 the company began to spin cotton, producing only six hundred pounds daily. By the end of the decade two new cordage plants and a cotton factory were in operation, but they were minor concerns. New Orleans in 1860 was hardly closer to Lowell's position than it had been in 1850.

The unusual situation of New Orleans as a major port of both river and ocean traffic called for the development of a ship building industry in Algiers. The West Bank was already a center for ship repairs with several dry docks, the largest of which could handle vessels up to four hundred feet. With this background and encouraged by a small state subsidy, the West Bank boat building industry expanded during the decade. From 1850 to 1861 seventeen steam vessels of small tonnage were launched in Algiers and Gretna, whereas only five had been completed in the previous decade. By 1860 there were ten ship and boat building firms in Orleans Parish; they were capitalized at over a half million dollars and employed nearly three hundred men.

The city's foundries and machine shops, which did a two million dollar business yearly, offered the most promising future to New Orleans industry. Originally the foundries were merely expanded blacksmith shops and were engaged in repair functions almost exclusively. But the needs, especially of steamboats and cotton presses, for heavy equipment and the cost of transporting such equipment led foundries and machine shops into the field of manufacturing. Among their products were boilers for ocean ships, steamboats, and sugar houses, cotton gins, draining machines, cotton presses, saw mills, iron posts and grills, and incidental brass and iron work. Foundries like Leeds & Co. and the Belleville works in Algiers were among the leading employers of labor in New Orleans.

There were other assorted industries and crafts in the city, but they were of minor importance. Indeed New Orleans was simply not a manufacturing center; though the number of people employed in local factories and shops increased from 3,134 in 1850 to 5,060 in 1860, the increase was only about proportionate to the population growth during the decade. New Orleans in 1860 was the sixth ranked city in the nation in population, but it ranked only seventeenth in value of its manufactures. The average New Orleans industry employed only a few workers and operated with limited capital; production was primarily designed to fill local needs. New Orleans on the eve of the Civil War was as far removed from Pittsburgh as it was from Lowell.

Far more catastrophic to the city's commerce was the gradual loss of western trade. The *Price Current* in 1850 noted with alarm "the increased facilities for reaching the Atlantic markets through the canals and railroads which Northern enterprise is constantly multiplying and extending" that led to the diversion of goods to the East which had formerly been sent to New Orleans. Only by rail lines emanating from the Crescent City could the once rich traffic of the upper Mississippi be recovered and new areas inaccessible to river boats be exploited. There were of course those in the city who scoffed at the idea that rails would seriously injure local commerce — surely nothing could replace the mid-continent's great liquid highway! — but the relative decline of the city's trade was obvious to all who would read the signs.

There were in 1850 already three short railroad lines operating out of the city. The oldest of these railroads was the six-mile New Orleans and Pontchartrain Railroad which carried passengers and freight from a dilapidated depot in the Third District down Elysian Fields Street and through the swamp to the lakefront at Milneburg. In 1852 the *Orleanian* reported that the line had not paid dividends in years, but track repairs and improvements in facilities at the lakefront breathed new life into the company and its stock doubled in the five years after 1855. The New Orleans and Carrollton Railroad, constructed a few years after the Pontchartrain line, transported passengers and mail from Tivoli Circle (now Lee Circle) down Nyades (now St. Charles) Street through the woods along the river to the resort town of Carrollton. In 1853 the Carrollton line made contact with the Jefferson and Lake Pontchartrain Railroad which ran between Carrollton and a point on the lake shore called Buck Town. This line, after several unsuccessful years, was purchased by the Carrollton Railroad. The longest of the pre-1850 railroads was the Mexican Gulf Railroad which began in New Orleans and ran for twenty-seven miles to Proctorville (reached in 1846) on Lake Borgne. The original intent had been to extend the line to a suitable point on the Gulf of Mexico and thereby tap much of the coastal trade, but limited finances had prevented any advance beyond the hamlet of Proctorville and the road served chiefly as a milk line for local planters.

In 1851 and 1852 railroad conventions were held in New Orleans "to deliberate upon and concert such measures as will be likely to influence the construction of a system of railroads connecting the Gulf States with those of the West and North West."[22] Out of these conventions evolved the New Orleans, Jackson and Great Northern Railroad and the New Orleans, Opelousas and Great Western Railroad. The Jackson Railroad was intended to extend to Canton, Mississippi, and eventually to the Ohio river; by so doing it would be able to regain and increase New Orleans trade in the upper Mississippi valley and also frustrate the pretensions of Mobile which hoped to capture the same trade by means of the Mobile and Ohio Railroad. In the words of its promoters, the Jackson Railroad

> will form the stem on which all the railroads east of the Mississippi leading to New Orleans will be engrafted. Its branches will amount to many thousands of miles; and as a grand trunk, its relations to other railroads will be the same as the Mississippi to its numerous tributaries.[23]

The Opelousas line was planned to run from New Orleans to Opelousas; from that point extensions or connections were envisaged into Texas and inevitably on to California to form America's first transcontinental railroad.

Both railroads were granted abundant state and local financial support and additional funds were obtained from private individuals in this country and abroad. The city of New Orleans subscribed to bonds worth $4,000,000 for the Jackson line and $3,000,000 for the Opelousas road; it also provided the railroads with rights-of-way and with wharf and ferry privileges. But in spite of this governmental generosity the railroads, especially the Jackson line, had shaky financial careers. The *True Delta* reported in 1855 that the officials of the Jackson road had squandered six million dollars and had played on public credulity in its appeal for money. By 1857 the road was nearly bankrupt, but after a change in directors stability was restored and two years later the railroad's total earnings exceeded one million dollars.

Starting construction from New Orleans, the Jackson Railroad had by August, 1854, reached Osyka, eighty-eight miles from New Orleans, and on March 31, 1858, it reached Jackson, Mississippi.

The line had earlier incorporated a railroad which had already been constructed from Jackson to Canton, Mississippi, a distance of 206 miles from New Orleans. By 1861 the road was transporting 180,000 bales of cotton and 165,000 passengers yearly and by connections with other lines tied New Orleans to most of the major soutern and northern urban centers.

The eastern terminus of the Opelousas Railroad was in Algiers with ferry service to New Orleans. The road progressed slowly, reaching Brashear City on Berwick Bay in 1857 — a distance of eighty miles — when construction ended for the decade except for an isolated section of the line from New Iberia to Opelousas. At Brashear City a line of steamers connected the railroad with the port of Galveston in Texas.

Several other railroads extending from New Orleans were proposed in the 1850's but nothing was accomplished beyond legislative incorporations and the publications of extremely optimistic prospectuses. So after a decade of agitation New Orleans was still not a railroad center; a road running two hundred miles northeast and one eighty miles west were not much in comparison with the railroads operating out of Chicago — even the Chicago of 1860. Perhaps, as one student has suggested, New Orleans had "started too late and moved too slowly."[24] Another scholar contends that New Orleans' failure to develop as a railroad hub was inevitable, for

> regardless of how railroads might have radiated out of New Orleans, the general direction of railroad construction for the United States was to be East-West, it is doubtful whether New Orleans could have maintained the pre-eminence it attained during the steamboat period. Railroads supplied the missing link between the industrial and mercantile East and the agricultural Mid-West.[25]

In spite of the problems in the New Orleans economy, the city in the 1850's had something of the character of a boom town, though the boom was far removed from the brash inflationary exuberance of the 1830's. The commercial houses that had survived the panic of 1837 and the slow pace of the early forties were not interested in a boom-to-bust economy; they preferred a situation under which the city's business was "chiefly confined to comparatively old or well established firms."[26] Furthermore, the growth of trade associations in the 1850's tended to produce — in a few cases by means of force or bribery — a more stable, if less

Jackson Square showing the Cathedral and surrounding buildings, 1860.

New Orleans port scene, 1858 (From a painting by Sabron in possession of Tulane University)

flexible, economy. But by and large if there was any underlying theme in the thought of the commercial community of New Orleans in the decade, 1850-1860, it was the fervent and optimistic belief that commerce was king and New Orleans was his prized domain. Only a few railroads, a few more banks, and direct ship lines to Europe were needed and New Orleans would become the economic capital of the New World. It was a heady romantic belief.

Levee scene at New Orleans
(Emerson's Magazine and Putnam's Monthly — October 1857)

NOTES

[1] J. H. Ingraham, *The Sunny South; or, the Southerner at Home, Embracing Five Years' Experience of a Northern Governess in the Land of Sugar and Cotton* (Philadelphia, 1860), 338.

[2] *Colton's Traveller and Tourist Guide Book Through the United States of America and the Canadas* (New York, 1854), 132-133.

[3] Marie Fontenay, *L'Autre Monde* (Paris, 1855), 74.

[4] A. T. Cunynghame, *A Glimpse at the Great Western Republic* (London, 1852), 98.

[5] William Henry Allen, "The Last Trip by a Steam-Boat Clerk," *Knickerbocker, or the New-York Monthly Magazine*, XLVI (December, 1855), 597.

[6] Alexander Mackay, *The Western World; or, Travels in the United States in 1846-1847*. . . . (5th ed., 3 vols.; London, 1851), II, 291.

[7] "Roundabout Papers — No. XVII — A Mississippi Bubble," *Cornhill Magazine*, IV (December, 1861), 756. The rococco character of the steamboat was heightened by adding steam calliopes to the boat whistles. *Weekly Picayune*, November 24, December 22, 1856.

[8] A season extended from September 1, to August 31.

[9] James Stirling, *Letters from the Slave States* (London, 1857), 172.

[10] *Commercial Bulletin*, September 30, 1853.

[11] The terms "factor" and "commission merchant" are here used interchangeably. In as far as there was a difference between them, the factor usually served only as a functional middleman between planter and broker. The commission merchant served the planter in several capacities.

[12] *Semi-Weekly Creole*, April 21, 1855.

[13] T. L. Nichols, *Forty Years of American Life* (2nd ed.; London, 1874), 134.

[14] Robert Greenhalgh Albion, *The Rise of New York Port, 1815-1860* (New York, 1939), 95-96.

[15] *Daily Crescent*, October 20, November 30, 1857.

[16] Sherman to D. F. Boyd, December 15, 1859, in Walter L. Fleming, ed., *General William T. Sherman as College President: A Collection of Letters, Documents, and Other Material . . . 1859-1861* (Cleveland, 1912), 92.

[17] Free banks are allowed to issue notes based not only on specie, but also upon securities in the form of national, state, and local bonds, and on stock of certain corporations such as railroads and canals.

[18] "American and Canadian Banking: The New York Banks," *Bankers' Magazine*, XXI (July, 1861), 470; "New York and New Orleans," *ibid.*, 615.

[19] *Price Current*, September 1, 1851.

[20] "Establishment of Manufactures at New Orleans: Remarks on the Practicality of the Establishments, and Profitable Prosecution, of the Manufacture of Cotton in the Immediate Vicinity of New Orleans," *De Bow's Review*, VIII (January, 1850), 5.

[21] *Daily Crescent*, May 27, 1858.

[22] *Price Current*, August 2, 1851.

[23] New Orleans, Jackson and Great Northern Railroad, *Fifth Annual Report*, 1857 (New Orleans, 1857), 14.

[24] Erastus Paul Puckett, "The Attempt of New Orleans to Meet the Crisis in Her Trade with the West," *Mississippi Valley Historical Association, Proceedings*, X (1920-1921), 495.

[25] Harry A. Mitchell, "The Development of New Orleans as a Wholesale Trading Center," *Louisiana Historical Quarterly*, XXVII (October, 1944), 945.

[26] "Commercial Prosperity of New Orleans," *De Bow's Review*, XXI (December, 1856), 621.

Chapter IV

GOVERNMENT AND POLITICS

I am a believer in the sacred and inalienable rights of property . . . [and I believe] that the practical character of every government is the result of a state of property.[1]

Electioneering is the order of the day, treating the order of the night, and shaking hands with 'greasy mechanics' and sun embrowned and toiling laborers common on every side by the kid glove gentry. . . .[2]

Conflict between conservative Creole real estate owners and politicians and the expanding American population above Canal Street, joined by land developers above and below the Vieux Carré, led in 1836 to a division of the city into three separate municipalities. The municipalities possessed separate corporate rights, could sue and be sued, and hold property; they were, by law, separate cities. Each municipality had an elected aldermanic council and recorder (police court judge) who governed the municipality, appointed officials, made and enforced laws, and carried out public works. The municipal councils sat together as a General Council for the whole city and were presided over by a mayor who was elected by the city at large. The General Council had power (1) to fix uniform wharfage and drayage rates; (2) to tax carriages and ferries and to issue licenses for peddlers, hawkers, and taverns; (3) to set the salaries of the mayor and secretary of the General Council; (4) to enact all police regulations of a general nature; (5) to represent the city in corporations in which the city owned stocks or bonds. The individual municipal councils retained control of their own finances, except that they could not alienate any real estate valued at $2,000 or over without permission of the General Council. Unquestionably, this was the most curious, and the clumsiest municipal organization in the varied history of American cities.

The first formal attempt to change the tri-municipality system occurred in 1850 when a special election was held to determine if the municipalities should be reconsolidated or whether the status quo was to be maintained. A majority of the voters favored retaining the system of separate municipalities. However the advocates of consolidation continued to press for reunification. In the fall elections of 1851 the city's Whigs campaigned on a program of municipal consolidation and constitutional changes to allow governmental aid to internal improvements, a better public school system, and a program for free banking. On this platform the Whigs swept the city and joined a Whig majority in the state legislature.

The change in attitude toward consolidation grew out of several social and economic forces. By 1850 Creole-American animosity had diminished as an upper class composed of both elements had formed over the years. An expanding middle and working class had become convinced that consolidation was essential to their economic well-being. Then too lack of cooperation between municipalities allowed criminal elements to escape from one municipality to another, and, after a levee burst in 1849, the failure of the municipalities to act in a concerted fashion led to excessive flooding. Probably the most important reason for change was a clear recognition by business men and property owners that the city government was on the brink of bankruptcy and that their "stationary or perhaps retrograding fortunes" could be related to the tri-municipality system.[4] In 1850 a report on the sinking fund of the city revealed that the fund

> seems from year to year to be growing less and less, and if there be no change in its management, will ere long be entirely exhausted, without having liquidated any portion of the debt for the payment of which it was created.[5]

In the following year a Board of Liquidation, designed to settle the financial problems of the city, was declared unconstitutional. "And after two years of tedious and expensive litigation," Mayor A. D. Crossman complained, "we find ourselves thrown back to the point whence we started and actually in a worse position than before."[6]

Unless the city could obtain a suitable credit status, it would be unable to engage in programs of internal improvements, the editor of the *Commercial Bulletin* insisted. "Our domestic credit at home and abroad is impaired—yes destroyed," but a re-united city would mean "brighter and better times" with a "steady, rapid and permanent revival in the commerce of the city, in all trades and professions, and in every description of industrial pursuits." The *Bulletin* also argued that the tri-municipal government should be ended because it "alienated from each other American citizens who should be one in name as in feeling and interest." The *Bee*, official journal of the First Municipality council, argued strongly for consolidation on the grounds it would simplify municipal administration, reduce expenditures, extinguish sectional prejudices, and give the city commercial "homogeneity and strength." The paper doubted the idea that one part of the city would be sacrified for the betterment of another: "Such fear we regard as groundless, for sectional hostility and rivalry are rapidly dying out of themselves...." A Democratic paper hoped that with consolidation the city would be "blended into one harmonious whole acting together and sharing together all blessings and benefits." The paper also favored a proposition to annex the suburb of Lafayette to the consolidated city. The annexation of Lafayette, the editor predicted, would bring "a new epoch in the history of New Orleans."[7] The *Delta,* an uptown paper, favored annexation of Lafayette and consolidation of the municipalities because it would break down sectional prejudice and give every citizen "all the protection and advantages of a rich and powerful corporation." The *Picayune* reasoned that consolidation and annexation would give New Orleans a "larger area, an improved system of finance, which secures the dimunition of debt, the increase of credit, and the growth of resources, and all the material and opportunities for lifting this city to a high degree of prosperity."

The council of the Second Municipality and the city council of Lafayette strongly favored consolidation and annexation. The council of the First Municipality backed any consolidation measure, but a minority of its members opposed the introduction of Lafayette into the city. Party differences were not important. The first two municipalities were Whig bailiwicks while Lafayette was a Democratic center. The main opposition to the movement came from the polyglot Third Municipality. Its principal newspaper, its council, and mass meetings of its citizens all voiced an antogonism toward annexation of Lafayette and to a lesser degree toward consolidation. It was felt that the addition of Lafayette would shift the political and economic balance in the city above Canal Street and jeopardize the already shaky economy of the Third Municipality. As alternatives to a reorganized city there was talk in the Third Municipality of separate incorporation, of secession, and of annexing Algiers to balance Lafayette. The common council of the municipality sent W.C.C. Claiborne to Baton Rouge to lobby against the annexation measure. Supporting the Third Municipality against annexation was the *Courrier de la Louisiane* (its English-language side favored annexation) and the Lafayette journal, the *Spectator*.

While editorial differences raged in New Orleans, James Robb and Henry Lathrop in January and February, 1852, engineered through the legislature the consolidation of the three municipalities and the annexation of Lafayette. Both Whigs and rural Democrats were solid in their support of the measures; the only concerted opposition came from assemblymen representing the Third Municipality. According to the new charter, the First Municipality became the Second District, the Second Municipality became the First District, the Third Municipality became the Third District, and Lafayette became the Fourth District. Each of the first three districts was divided into three wards and Lafayette into two.

The lawmaking body of the newly consolidated city was a bicameral council, composed of a board of twelve aldermen to serve two-year terms, and a board of twenty-seven assistant aldermen elected each year.[8] The boards met separately and each had the power to originate or reject any ordinance or resolution; like the national Congress the lower body had the power to impeach, the upper to try all cases of impeachment. The council had the power to appoint non-elective officials which after 1856 included all but the mayor, four recorders, comptroller, and street commissioner.

The mayor possessed the traditional prerogatives of vetoing bills of the common council, demanding reports from subordinate city officials, and convening the council. He controlled the granting of licenses and, for part of the decade, had direct jurisdiction over the police. Circumscribed by independently elected executive officials, by common council appointees, and by the control of city finances through common council committees, the mayor had very little effective control over the government.

The passage of the consolidation and annexation measures corresponded to an upturn in the economy and the antagonism toward re-unification nearly disappeared. In less than a month the *Orleanian* had discovered that Lafayette was only an "imagined rival" and that prosperity was assured for the Third District. The Common Council by early 1853 congratulated themselves on the fact that notwithstanding the brief period of its existence, and the difficulties inseparable from the entire alteration in the complete machinery of our city government, the Consolidated system has worked well, and bids fair to accomplish all that its most ardent friends desired.[9]

The only carping notes came from the Fourth District where with Calhoun-like reasoning the *Louisiana State Republican* stated that the district should secede since its compact had been violated. During the decade there were public meetings in the Fourth District to protest high taxes, removal of a recorder court (soon restored), and a movement to consolidate the school systems which might lead to removing Bible readings from the schools. Some of these protests were bogus; none was taken seriously by the city government.

In the first election following consolidation, the interests of class overcame the interests of party. On March 16, 1852, a group of merchants met at the American Theatre and organized the Independent Party to insure a common council favorable to commercial interests. They chose "non-partisan" candidates from both the Democratic and Whig slates, and nominated a few of their own candidates as well. They made no choice for mayor, probably because it might arouse factional feelings and because both Lewis (Democrat) and Crossman (Whig) could be regarded as "safe" candidates. For recorders, aldermen, assistant aldermen, and administrative officials Whigs were heavily favored by the Independents. Though some elements in the local press opposed circumventing party lines, most of the newspapers backed the Independent movement.

In the election—a peaceful one by New Orleans standards—A. D. Crossman was reelected to his fourth two-year term as mayor and a majority of the aldermanic candidates backed by the Independent Party were chosen. A Whig treasurer, a Whig-Independent comptroller, and a Whig-Independent street commissioner were elected. Secure in its belief that the city government was controlled by a conservative bloc of merchants, the *Commercial Bulletin* on the day after the election predicted

> the dawn of a new era in New Orleans, when with restored credit, unfettered resources, and sagacious and wise municipal legislation, our city will be able to take her proper position among the proudest and greatest in the union.

— 55 —

The city council responded to their trust by reforming the city's finances through consolidation bonds, by issuing revenue bonds for two railroads, and removing the city from the realm of business by farming out services formerly handled by the municipalities.

From 1854 to the Civil War, the New Orleans political scene was subject to periodic influences of outside issues: local elections sometimes hinged on events in Baton Rouge, Washington, Kansas, Cuba, and elsewhere. But if these outside issues are eliminated in order to ascertain purely local currents, it seems obvious that politics in New Orleans revolved, in great degree, around efforts of the commercial classes to retain control of the city and to prevent the rise of political machines based on immigrants and laborers. The symbols of mercantile control in these years were the "reform," "independent," or "citizens," movements, and to a lesser extent the American Party. The Know Nothings of course did not originate in New Orleans, but they came to have a local character not found in other sections of the nation. The Louisiana American Party was founded in February, 1854, and from the beginning deviated from the national party on the religious issue. In its desire to enlist the native-born population it softened the overt anti-Catholicism of the national organization. Catholic Creoles and Protestant Americans as well as Democrats and Whigs were encouraged to join. The essential key to membership was native American birth; the "Creoles of America" as a Know Nothing paper called the native born. Thus the party enlisted old line Whigs like Randall Hunt and Democrats like Bernard Marigny, the "Creole of Creoles" in Grace King's words. On other planks the state party followed the national body; it favored restriction of immigration and it affirmed the party's unionist sentiments, both of which reflected the attitudes of the commercial class. The party's candidates were "mainly men successful in business," and it "received considerable support from the property holders everywhere. . . ."[10] The business elite feared the rising tide of immigrants voting for Democratic candidates (especially loco foco Democrats) and like their hero, Henry Clay, they feared the spirit of disunion. Only the American party would calm their fears:

> The repeal of the naturalization laws, arresting the conversion of thousands of immigrants, soon after they land on our soil, into voters is necessary effectually [sic] to quiet sectional

strife and restore that fraternal feeling between the North and South which marked the early history of the country.[11]

Furthermore the super-patriotism of the Know Nothing movement—"screechings of intense Americanism"[12]—had perhaps an appeal to the native-born businessman who might imagine himself as some flag-enshrouded Horatio defending the bridge of republicanism against foreign hordes.

Certainly the American Party press was vociferous in its denunciations of immigrants. According to the *Semi-Weekly Creole*, both Irish and Germans failed "to comprehend the genius of our republican institutions, and regard with disfavor the restraints of law and the operations of long established usages." The *American Exponent* solidly supported the party's "principle of anti-foreignism" because the "foreign influence is alarmingly increasing and endangering the permanence and purity of our republican institutions. . . ." "Immigration is," pronounced the *Daily Creole*, "the fountain of abolitionism—Europe is prevaded by a hatred of negro slavery." The *Picayune* came off its pedestal of party neutrality to announce its support of the "principle of the new party that Americans should rule America."

The anti-immigrant feeling of the Know Nothings threw into the Democratic Party diverse and at times antithetical groups. The conservative Catholic press and the Whig *Orleanian* from the heavily immigrant Third District joined editorial forces with the middle of the road *Delta*, *True Delta*, and *Deutsche Zeitung*, and with the radical *Louisiana Courier* and *Staats Zeitung*. Unfortunately the Democratic Party lacked internal cohesion and made a poor agency to oppose the Americans. Party control was in the hands of men who were hardly different in outlook from the Whigs — J. L. Lewis, Democratic leader in the city, was, in the view of the *Orleanian*, a Democratic Know Nothing. Immigrants were courted for their votes, but their representatives were not brought into the party's councils. The state Democratic Party was little concerned with municipal elections and asked the local machine to turn out the vote only on state and national elections. In the last half of the decade the Democratic Party was split into two rival factions — the one supporting John Slidell, the other Pierre Soulé — whose animosity toward each other was greater than toward the opposing political party. However in the early years of the decade the party was not yet impotent on the city level; the

Democrats captured a majority of the aldermanic seats in the spring election of 1853.

The following year a Reform Party made its appearance and chose candidates "without reference to party considerations." Composed of a "large number of our most respectable and influential citizens," it was obvious that the party was a front organization for the newly organized American Party. When the votes were counted it was discovered that Lewis, the Democrat, was elected mayor, but the "reformers" had gained a large majority on the common council.

The Reform Party's respectable veneer was belied in this election by the presence in the Seventh Ward of Know Nothing hoodlums who forcibly kept Democratic voters from the polls. Disorder had not been unknown in New Orleans elections, nor had the Democrats been averse to using strong-arm tactics, but the American Party carried violence to a height shocking even in the Crescent City. Hoodlums, evidently recruited from a native-born criminal class who spent their winters in the city, used threats, force, and murder against the immigrant. Even after the election groups of thugs roamed the streets of New Orleans for days beating and stabbing immigrants. In the September, 1854, state elections, parts of the city were turned into battlegrounds between Irish and Know Nothing gangs. The employment of hoodlums spread into the shaded walks of Carrollton, where "Red Bill," "Big Tom," and nearly thirty other cocky thugs patrolled the streets one election day while the outmanned constabulary looked on helplessly.

The spring, 1855, aldermanic elections saw the Americans (no Reform label now) peaceably rout the Democrats, but in the fall election wholesale "intimidation, violence, and bloodshed" was used to keep Democrats and naturalized citizens from the polls.[13] "Ruffianism appears to have reigned triumphant" reported a state legislative committee.[14] The legislature denied senatorial seats to four American candidates who had been elected through fraudulent means and it passed rigid voter registration laws to eliminate floaters and made the city of New Orleans responsible for damages caused by mobs during election campaigns. Their efforts were of little avail.

By the spring election of 1856 respectable individuals in the city began to realize that they had created a monster; therefore on March 17, a group of prominent merchants and lawyers who had figured in the Independent movement of 1852 and the Reform

Party of two years later, met at Banks Arcade to select a "Citizens" ticket without reference to party. It was an abortive movement as American Party hecklers and tough broke up the meeting. The Know Nothings nominated Charles Waterman, a timid merchant, for mayor and the Democrats put up the colorless William A. Elmore. The election was a brutal farce.

> No man's life was safe, drunken crowds of brutes, whose faces were unknown to our citizens paraded our streets, shouting forth the various Know Nothing candidates and indiscriminately insulting and beating all they met.[15]

Thomas K. Wharton wrote in his diary: "Scenes of violence and bloodshed at the Polls — naturalized citizens were the object of enmity and very often not permitted to vote at all." "Who now or hereafter," asked an editor bitterly, "will regard citizenship as worth a straw. . . . [?]"[16] The terrorism continued after election day as the police through fear or collusion did nothing. Election returns showed that the American Party had elected its candidate for mayor and his slate, and that the Democratic vote had declined by over two thousand from November, 1855. The Democrats carried only three of the city's twenty-five precincts.

For the first time in the decade, if not the century, a merchant clique was not in control of city government. Though it is difficult to document, it appears that the American Party leadership had shifted to a group who found the spoils of office superior to reform politics. The party had become, as the *Crescent* accused its one-time associates, a "machine to promote purely selfish ends."[17] Under the leadership of the shrewd and able Gerard Stith, a typographer elected police judge, the American Party recruited support from the working class and by 1858 had so lost its anti-immigrant character that it was making a strong appeal to the German voter. Indeed the transformed American Party was the first of the immigrant-labor machines which, with few exceptions, dominated New Orleans politics until 1946.

The Whig-American candidate, Millard Fillmore, carried the city in the national election of 1856. The loss of two or three lives on election day seems almost bucolic by previous standards. The following spring the Democrats were rendered so impotent by an intra-party squabble between Soulé and Slidell they did not even enter a slate of candidates. Only two thousand votes out of a possible sixteen thousand were cast; the American Party elected a comptroller, a recorder, and twelve aldermen unopposed. The Know Nothing movement may have been on its deathbed nationally and in the country parishes, but it was very much alive in New Orleans.

Business leaders attempted to challenge the political base of the American Party by introducing a bill into the state legislature excluding all but certain property holders and license payers from the franchise in municipal elections; it did not pass. Having failed to obtain the desired suffrage law, businessmen turned to yet another "non-partisan" political organization. In the Spring of 1858 a group calling itself the "Independent Voters of New Orleans" nominated Major P. G. T. Beauregard, who was in charge of constructing a United States Custom House, as its candidate for mayor to oppose Gerard Stith, the American Party choice. Beauregard's "commercial and professional standing" was extolled by the Independent voters. Even Pierre Soulé agreed to back Slidell's brother-in-law as did Isaac Marks, a prominent Jewish merchant who had written the constitution of the original American Party of Louisiana. The six hundred citizens who publicly endorsed Beauregard were certainly the *créme* of New Orleans society.

The election was one of the most fantastic in New Orleans history. An unofficial "Vigilance Committee," which had been formed in 1857 "to free the city of ruffianism," supported Beauregard and stated its intention to patrol the streets during the election in order to insure peaceful voting.[18] When the city fathers refused to grant committee members official status as election watchers, the committee sympathizers under Lieutenant J. K. Duncan, one of Beauregard's army subordinates, seized the state arsenal on St. Peter Street, barricaded the streets entering Jackson Square, and established an armed camp. Meanwhile an opposing "army" gathered in Lafayette Square. Fortunately for the welfare of the city, the rival forces confined their animosity to verbal taunts and refrained from rifle or artillery shots, though the Vigilance Committee "troops" did manage to kill four of their own scouts by firing grape at them down a narrow alley. Mayor Waterman became completely befuddled by the turn of events; he was deposed by the Common Council and alderman H. M. Summer was appointed mayor pro-tem. Under his orders extra policemen were sworn in.

On election day the Vigilance forces were confined within their self-imposed fortress, helpless to carry on their task of securing peaceful voting and a fair count. The election was quiet; only seven thousand votes were cast and Stith and most of his ticket were elected. The next morning Jackson Square was empty, since during the night Vigilance Committee leaders escaped to the steamboat *Princess* and steamed upriver until safer days, while the "troops" fled to the lower limits of the city and hid in the swamps. Eventually the police rounded up a few members and after several were tried and fined as an example to the rest, the incident was forgotten. Beauregard shrugged off his defeat and returned to less exciting duties at the Custom House.

Stith, contrary to all signs, was probably the best mayor of the decade. He kept tight reins on his party through an assiduous employment of the spoils system and at the same time secured sizable support from the commercial interests. The city was prosperous, extensive street improvements were carried on, the municipal government was reasonably efficient, and even the crime rate was lowered. Political opposition all but vanished; the American Party elected most of their aldermanic candidates in 1859, and in 1860, over token opposition from a group of disgruntled Know Nothings, they elected John T. Monroe, a one-time stevedore. There was no violence and few voters took the trouble to cast their ballots. Two years later Monroe was elected again only to spend most of his term in a federal prison.

A. D. Crossman, the first mayor of the decade, was a Whig, a unionist, a merchant, and a native of Maine; John T. Monroe, the last mayor of the era, was an American, a secessionist, a laborer, and a Virginian. The differences between the two men symbolize the far-reaching political transformation, fostered by violence, which took place in New Orleans in the 1850's.

NOTES

[1] James Robb, a New Orleans banker, as quoted in Shugg, *Origins of Class Struggle in Louisiana*, 138.

[2] *Daily Orleanian*, March 18, 1852.

[3] The 1836 split is usually cited as the most blatant example of Creole-American hostility. In fact, the division is not that simple. Bernard Marigny who was developing a faubourg below Esplanade Street had as much reason to be irritated with the failure to extend docks out of the French Quarter and the conservative business principles of his fellow Creoles as any American. Samuel J. Peters, the man most intimately associated with the formation of the American section, moved uptown only after he was refused certain advantages in the Faubourg Marigny. Peters was married to a Creole and so were his sons; there is no evidence that Peters was hostile to Creoles on the basis of language, religion, or ethnic derivation. The land above Canal Street was owned almost entirely by old Creole families who gained by a move out of the Vieux Carré.

[4] "New Orleans — Consolidation of Municipalities, Banks, Rail-road Enterprises, etc.," *De Bow's Review*, X (May, 1851), 586.

[5] Commissioners of the General Sinking Fund, *Report*, 1850 (New Orleans, 1850), 4.

[6] A. D. Crossman to Common Council, November 10, 1851, Mayor's office, Messages, 1850-1851 (MS), Archives of the New Orleans Public Library.

[7] *Louisiana Courier*, February 5, 14, 1852.

[8] In 1856 the aldermen were reduced to nine and assistant aldermen to fifteen.

[9] Resolution 662, March 5, 1853, in Common Council Ordinances and Resolutions, 1852-1856.

[10] *Semi-Weekly Creole*, March 28, 1855; *Bee*, June 4, 1856.

[11] *Daily Creole*, July 1, 1856.

[12] *Louisiana Courier*, May 30, 1856. The American Party was preceded by earlier nativist movements in New Orleans. In 1835 a Louisiana Native American Association was established to oppose immigration. Fifteen years later a local branch of the Order of the Lone Star was established; it was spread-eagle in sentiment but passive in action. In the same year E. Z. C. Judson, "Ned Buntline," already famous for his adventure and anti-Catholic novels, came to New Orleans to propagate nativist doctrines. He was unsuccessful.

[13] Governor of Louisiana (Paul O. Hebert), *Message to the Legislature*, (Baton Rouge, 1856), 4.

[14] Louisiana General Assembly, Senate Committee on Elections, *Majority Report and Resolution on the Petition of Henry M. Hymans, Henry St. Paul and D. D. Withers Contesting the Right of Leonce Burthe, J. J. Michel, and Glendy Burke to their Seats as Senators from the Parish of Orleans* (Baton Rouge, 1856), 16.

[15] *Louisiana Courier*, June 5, 1856. The bloodiest events occurred in the Second District where a mob shot two Sicilians and destroyed market stalls owned by Italians and Spaniards — "dagos."

[16] *Daily Orleanian*, June 5, 1856.

[17] Quoted in the *Daily Delta*, May 31, 1860. The *Crescent* was the last paper to reach this conclusion; four years earlier the *Orleanian* pointed out that the Americans had lost their Whig principles.

[18] Wharton, diary, June 3, 1858.

Chapter V

PROTECTION OF LIFE, LIMB, AND PROPERTY

It behooves the citizens of New Orleans to come to some understanding by which complete protection to life, limb, and property may be secured.[1]

In the middle of the nineteenth century American cities grappled with problems for which our rural past could provide no immediate answer. Following the pattern of farmer-dominated state governments, cities were governed by two-house legislatures and the powers of the mayor were severely limited. The system was grossly inefficient and simply did not fit the realities of an urban community. Then too the nature of cities demanded certain social services for which there were only vague approximations in a rural society. Adequate sanitation, police protection, maintenance of order, and fire protection were essential to urban centers, and in the mid-nineteenth century American cities, New Orleans included, made efforts, often unsuccessful, to deal with them.[2]

POLICE AND CRIME

As the city of New Orleans grew in the ante-bellum years its efforts to control lawless elements demanded a constant expansion of the police force and by the 1850's the city employed between 250 and 300 policemen. Unfortunately the increase in police was not accompanied by an intelligent and regular system of control by municipal officials. Before the consolidation act of 1852 there were in reality separate police forces in each of the municipalities; the mayor's power over the police was only nominal. After the re-unification of the city, the mayor was designated "conservator of the police"; he had power to appoint and discharge policemen with the consent of the board of aldermen. A year later the legislature created a police board composed of the mayor and the four recorders. Political differences (three of the four recorders were Democrats) between members of the board led to bickerings and at times to chaos. In 1854 the recorders, over the mayor's protest, fired the police chief and so disrupted the force that the militia had to patrol the city for several days. The police board was dissolved in 1856 and control over the police was given to the mayor; this centralized administration and may have been a factor in the relative improvement of the police force in the latter 1850's.

There is no question but that appointment of police officers was based on political considerations. Thus after the 1856 law, naturalized citizens appointed to the force when the Democrats controlled the police board were removed and American Party followers were readily accepted. Their "high toned nationality," the *Creole* rationalized, "makes them more sensitive to the honor of the city, for peace and reverence of law." Mayor Gerard Stith said it in a more realistic manner.

> It is not denied that the force is mainly constituted of men favorable to the principles which are professed by the American Party. . . . Under the present organization of this [police] department of the city, it is impossible to ignore the friends of the party in power.[3]

Needless to say the police did their utmost, by force if necessary, to see that the opposition parties found voting a hazard. Much of the success of the American Party after 1856 can be attributed to its control of a pliable police force.

Most police in New Orleans were patrolmen who walked a beat. There was a small staff of detectives and in 1854 a twelve-man river patrol was formed. A few policemen were stationed in the lockups and the workhouse while a lone officer served as an syndic (constable) in the swamp lands of the Third District. In appearance the local gendarmes were somewhat less than prepossessing; in fact, other than wearing caps they had no uniforms until 1855 when a blue coat, brass buttons, and stand-up military collar was prescribed. Patrolmen were equipped with "rattles," clubs, pistols, and handcuffs ("Pittsburgh Bracelets"). Each district had the standard horse-drawn "Black Maria" for carrying criminals to the lockup or, in times of epidemic, transporting the ill to hospitals. During the decade the police were aided by the introduction of the city's first rogues' gallery when the the council appropriated $250 to make daguerreotypes of a number of well-known criminals. Late in the decade police work was improved by a telegraph system connecting the main district stations with central headquarters in the city hall. The messages which have survived reveal the police to be semi-literate and given to pithy descriptions. For example: "J. Bentz Keeper of a beer house on Marigny bet[ween] Moreau and Casacalvo St. blowed out his brains." And another, "Joe Davis was found by two frenchmen name unknown, naked on the left bank of the river about 15 or 16 miles below with two balls in the head."[4]

The average policeman worked long hours and received only forty-five dollars a month. Nor were his superiors richly rewarded; in 1855 captains received a yearly $2,000, Lieutenants $1,000, and Sergeants $700. Furthermore police salaries, like those of other municipal employees, were not always paid regularly and police were often forced to seek other means of remuneration, e.g., unleashing goats or other animals and dragging them to the city pound where their irate owners had to redeem them at the rate of $2.50 of which the police officer received half. Police also brought in "runaway" slaves for the ten dollar reward. More serious, the police were bribed or collaborated with criminals and owners of prostitution houses, gambling dens, and illegally-managed liquor stores. Drunkenness on duty, irresponsibility, brutality, and outright cowardice were other charges thrown at the police force.

In view of the political control of the police force and its ill-paid and ill-staffed employees it is no wonder that New Orleans had one of the highest crime rates in the United States. "The proportion of crime to population is, to an European, perfectly astounding," declared one visitor.[5] There is no record of the number of crimes reported, but the arrest rate offers some indication of the extent of crime in the Crescent City. In the year September 1, 1857 to August 31, 1858, the police made 25,417 arrests: 20,655 men and 4,762 women. The majority of these arrests — sixty percent of the total — were for misdemeanors such as breach of peace, disturbing the peace, intoxication, vagrancy, and violating city ordinances. The arrest rate was highest in the winter months when the population had expanded and when employment meant a full whiskey bottle as well as a full dinner bucket.

One reason for the high crime rate in New Orleans was the influx of a professional criminal class who came to "live by their wits" during the winter months, "following the tide of travellers as the shark does his prey, unerringly and relentlessly."[6] They were usually fugitives from eastern states or foreign countries who preferred the lax law and the balmy clime of a New Orleans winter. The police often met boats and arrested known criminals — remembered from previous years — as "dangerous and suspicious." Cooperative recorders then sentenced these suspicious characters to three months in the workhouse and by the time they were released the winter season would be almost over. If all else failed a charge of vagrancy might be attached to the professional criminal and a six-month sentenced levied.

The criminals who came from other parts of the United States were sustained by a sizable home-grown product as well. While perhaps less adept in the ways of the underworld, the local "Liverpool Irish," as immigrant hoodlums were called, helped fill police blotters. They had a near-monopoly on disturbances of the peace and they were well-represented in such criminal categories as petty larceny, strong-arming, and homicide.

The most expert of the professional criminals in New Orleans were the swindlers. The presence in the winter of wealthy upriver planters, of gawking Hoosiers and rube Texans, of Southern planters and cracker farmers, of Californians long on gold and short on experience, and of mystified immigrants, offered lucrative pickings for the glib-tongued and quick-handed whose offerings were as amorphous as their morals. One of the easiest and most common ways of separating fools from their money was the mock auction. A likely prospect was approached and offered three or four "genuine gold" watches at a very low sum. He was then informed that he could sell the time pieces in a nearby auction shop by putting them up and starting the bidding. He was invariably left with the bid and if he refused to pay on his own watches they were kept by the auctioneer. If he did pay or kept a watch back he found that neither the works nor the "gold" case were valuable. A variation on this swindle was simply to have the "mark" bid on worthless goods. The police frenquently cracked down on these "Peter Funk" places, but conviction was difficult to obtain and the swindlers were highly mobile. The sale of gold bricks was not recorded in this decade, but a far more clever gold dust swindle was employed. Less subtle were immigrants who operated on the wharves as "watch stuffers," selling fake gold watches and glass jewelry to their unsuspecting conutrymen.

First cousin to the swindlers were forgers and counterfeiters. One dapper individual posed as an army officer and was admitted into the most exclusive clubs; once there he cashed forged sight drafts and obtained advances on bogus bills of exchange from his unsuspecting hosts. Counterfeiting was simple where banks issued their own money and it seems to have been a regular problem in the city. Perhaps the biggest haul was made by a group that passed out between $60,000 and $70,000 of bogus Citizen Bank notes in ten-dollar denominations. Less ostentatious was a ring of Irish girls who were caught manufacturing fifty-cent pieces. To these might be added several cases of bank tellers fleeing for points unknown with entrusted funds and the City Treasurer, William Garland, who was captured near the mouth of the Mississippi, only a few miles from freedom, with $25,000 of the city's funds.

The riverfront provided a fertile field for criminal activity. The various cheap boarding houses patronized by sailors employed "runners" who by fair means or foul forced or induced sailors and immigrants to lodge in their places. According to a *Picayune* account:

> As soon as the ships touch the wharves hordes of them [runners] clamber on board, in defiance of all law and order, and, with the fierce ruffianism of their class, they bundle ashore the sailors and their traps and woe to the luckless tar or officer that dares to resist them! Shoulder hitters and 'Hyer'-law bullies are these bravo runners, and by no means sparing with their knock down arguments. Every Captain who pretends to claim authority on board his ship, and every sailor that expresses the slightest inclination to patronize the 'Seaman's Home' rather than the whiskey cribs of Barracks or Gallatin Street, is felled without compunction and pays dearly for his daring.

In these cootie-ridden waterfront boarding houses a sailor could find prostitutes and cheap liquor, but he might also find himself robbed, beaten, drugged, and shanghied. Certainly the port of New Orleans deserved its unenviable reputation for "slung shots, doctored liquor, Shanghai-ing, and warf [sic] ratting. . . ."[7] On the other hand desertion was common among sailors who preferred the jaunty times of Gallatin Street to the lonely life at sea. The deserters probably added to the floating criminal population.

The wharf area was also menaced by intrepid river pirates who during the day resided along the banks of the Third District and Algiers. At night they launched swift-moving skiffs; silently they boarded ships, overpowered watchmen, and looted. The most common victim was a fully loaded steamboat whose deck would almost be at water level, but on one occasion brazen river pirates locked the crew of a sailing ship below deck and leisurely plundered the vessel. Goods stolen on these midnight forays were sold in the city or peddled on nearby plantations. The handful of river police were unable to cope with the menace.

Thievery along the waterfront was aided by the hopelessly inadequate lighting on the wharves and by the practice of dismissing night watchmen one hour before the day police came on duty. This "burglars' witching hour" was understandably popular among thieves. A great deal of ingenuity was utilized in stealing from the wharves. Some individuals stood beneath the docks and slit open coffee bags piled on the wharf; the coffee poured between cracks into convenient containers. Others dumped barrels over the docks to be collected by confederates below. Most simply pilfered — everything from cotton to cases of champagne.

Over and beyond the "professional" criminals the city had its quota of simple toughs. These "lions of the strychnine whiskey district,"[8] loitered in the neutral ground on Canal Street, along Gallatin Street in the Second District, Perdido and Calliope in the First, Elysian Fields in the Third, and the St. Mary's Market in the Fourth, while behind the city they could be found along the Shell Road. They made a living at armed robbery, pimping, boarding house running, and serving as strongarm men during elections. When not wrecking havoc with the law-abiding citizenry they fought among themselves. Notices like the following were common in the daily papers.

> Self-Defense — Frank Powell, in self defense it would appear, struck Dan Shannon with a slung shot, on Annunciation Street, and was arrested — It being proven in evidence that he did so to prevent himself from being killed by a gang of fellows, the recorder discharged him.

At times uptown and downtown gangs fought each other in the Canal Street neutral ground, thus terrorizing innocent folk — and the police.

These hoodlums in broadcloth coats and pants tucked into boots made a colorful appearance. They were armed with brass knuckles, slung shots, pistols, and Bowie or switch blade ("Sicilian") knives. They often showed complete contempt for the police, and if perchance they were menaced they merely transferred their operations to another district. Actually because of the inept police force they were seldom arrested and even less often convicted. In 1856 the Grand Jury, reviewing 471 assault and battery cases on the court docket, contended that at most two hundred of these would ever be found for trial. A murderer had a good chance of being undetected and, if caught, almost no chance of being given the death sentence.

Perhaps it was difficult for the police and the courts to operate in an atmosphere where there was a community sanction for carrying — and using — weapons, and where the public was indifferent to the lives of the lower classes. "Human life is a cheap commodity" in New Orleans, a traveller observed.[9] Symptomatic perhaps of the indifference toward human life was the prevalence of dueling. Few responsible individuals in the community rose to oppose the practice, and city and parish officials rarely made attempts to halt duels. Not a single paper opposed dueling; indeed, the press announced duels with occasional relish, but usually with bored detachment. Duels fought at the "Oaks" in City Park or behind the Halfway House on the Metairie Ridge were often attended by a loud, cheering, and probably gambling crowd. Contrary to romance few people were killed in these duels; if swords were used success was measured in drawing a bit of the opponent's blood and dueling pistols were notoriously inaccurate and at any distance generally were not fatal. During one duel at the "Oaks" two merchants exchanged several shots and succeeded only in killing a horse grazing nearby. There were few men like José Llulla, owner of a fencing academy and, rather appropriately, a cemetery, who sent several men to their doom. Nor as romantic legend would have it were duels confined to hot-blooded Creole aristocrats; free Negroes and lower class whites also settled their animosities on the field of honor. If they did not always have the traditional weapons or the skill to use them, bowie knives, shotguns, and even rough and tumble fights sufficed.

Criminal action in New Orleans was not of course a monopoly of white males; free and slave Negroes, women, and children also made important contributions to the city's criminal reputation. Slaves were usually brought before recorder courts for minor infractions such as not having passes, running away, loitering on street corners and at taverns, and renting rooms. Slaves were seldom inclined toward violence, but were slightly more disposed toward house breaking and petty larceny than whites. Free Negroes were remarkably law-abiding; except for possession of illegal passes and being in the state in contravention of the law, they were rarely arrested. In 1860 there were only three free Negroes from Orleans parish in the state prison — less than two percent of the prison population.

Women generally demonstrated their criminal tendencies in less violent ways than men. The fair sex were most commonly charged with disturbing the peace and intoxication. Slave women were picked up now and then for pilfering, congregating illegally, or wandering the streets after the evening gun. However from brief notices in the local press, it is obvious that a few doxies were as dangerous as male criminals. For example:

> It appears that Bridget [Fury] and some of her female friends were drinking coffee in the market when [Patrick] Croan wantonly insulted the women by applying vile epithets to them, when she ordering him to leave plunged a knife into his abdomen so as to cause his death.

This was not Bridget Fury's first criminal affair; she and her nemesis, "Irish Kate" Winters, provided bloody entertainment for tenderloin habituees and newspaper readers throughout the decade. Then there was Julia Campbell, who in beating up Wilhelm Kornruniff "made use of the most indecent and obscene language, caught hold of his hair, and struck him a severe blow in the face," and Mary Egerton, arrested for "getting drunk, screaming so as to be heard for half mile, biting a piece out of officer Peterson, and attempting to gouge out his eyes." And not to be overlooked were "Rosana" and "Charley" Smith who, to the horror of local belles, smoked cigars, swore strongly and wore male attire.

New Orleans, complained the *Mirror*, had "something more than a fair average share of the depraved members of the rising generation."

> On our streets children from ten to twelve years of age may be met, with cigars in their mouths and deadly weapons in their pockets, who have already become familiar with vice in its most disgusting forms.

The most common types of delinquency were street begging and pilfering cotton from bales on the levee. Juveniles were often encouraged by their parents, who, perhaps, took a certain pride in their nimble offspring; less charitable was Mayor Crossman who insisted that such parental guidance would only lead children into the "brothel and penitentiary."

To a young criminal unlucky enough to be caught, or simply lost, abandoned, or vagrant, the city reserved a place for them in the Boys' or Girls' Houses of Refuge. Though there had been talk of a juvenile detention home since 1847, it was not until 1853 that the Boys' House of Refuge was opened. In that year a *Delta* reporter investigated the home and critically affirmed that it was in a "disgraceful condition" and a "positive stain upon the character of the city." The entire place was enclosed by a high fence and according to the reporter the building was more suitable for cattle than humans. The Superintendent was a "kind hearted fellow" but he had limited funds and the health of the inmates suffered. Whenever possible, boys were indentured to the tender cares of land holders in the nearby parishes Until 1858 the only manual training offered was cobbling, but in Mayor Stith's administration a full scale program of schooling (most of the boys were illiterate) and training in manual skills were begun.

The Girls' House of Refuge, established in 1852, held one hundred inmates aged two to seventeen. The institution had a "sad and sombre look," but it was a "paradise" compared with the Boys' House.[10] The girls were subject to rigid discipline and given some manual training; on Sunday they were treated to moral lectures by Joseph A. Maybin, a crochety Presbyterian elder and prominent businessman. What the "graduates" thought of their experiences in the House of Refuge is not recorded.

The first prison that adult criminals entered was the lockup or police jail located in each district. A contemporary reported that the lockups "are not the cleanest, sweetest-smelling or best ventilated dormitories in the city; on the contrary they abound with villainous smells, filth and fetid atmosphere."[11] Prisoners spent only time enough in the police jails to be arraigned by a recorder court and then freed or transferred to another prison.

Individuals sentenced for misdemeanors were confined in the city work house, an overcrowded structure containing 350 "vagrants, drunkards, thieves, and prostitutes."[12] Until 1857 when the chain gang was abolished, men and women, Negroes and whites, were democratically assigned by the workhouse to cleaning streets, digging canals, policing parks, and doing other tasks. Prisoners worked long hours in carpenter, cabinet, and tin shops, in an oakum pickery and at a blacksmith forge; they made chairs for the city schools, coffins for the poor, and various products sold in the market. In 1856 the city farmed out prisoners' labor to a lessee who had them pack oakum and make clothes, boxes, and cigars. Food in the prison was as simple as the uniforms were coarse — bread, rice, beans, salted meat, vegetables, and molasses — and if an inmate were sick he was treated with liberal doses of opium derivatives and quinine. Actually it wasn't really such a bad prison; it was clean, prisoners were rewarded for extra work in the shops, and discipline was lax.

The parish prison, built to house 400, was the largest jail in New Orleans. It contained prisoners held before trial in district courts, convicts to be transferred to the state penitentiary at Jackson, a number of short term prisoners, and an occasional prisoner awaiting execution. One newspaper stated that "It *looks* like a prison," but it was hardly operated as one. Cells were seldom locked and prisoners walked about the corridors, sunned themselves on the galleries which ran the length of the two main buildings, or conversed with friends through the fence. Prisoners were encouraged to decorate their cells with paintings which prison officials respected in their twice-weekly white washings. Food, medical treatment, and clothing was on a par with the workhouse. The monotony of prison life was broken occasionally by an escape or by the "edifying spectacle" of a public execution attended by gentlemen with cigars and mint juleps and by ladies "gay with ribbons" and "flaunting dresses." All awaited the final act when the prisoner, or prisoners as the case might be, dressed in a white shirt and white pantaloons, ascended the scaffold; they listened while the doomed man said his last words — cursing the crowd, proclaiming his innocence, or, to the joy of the black robed minister, announcing he was in Jesus' care — and watched with horror and delight the trap door spring and the noose tighten.[13]

Attached to the parish prison from 1848 to 1854 was a three-story Temporary Asylum for the Indigent Insane; "temporary" because the inmates were supposedly awaiting transfer to the new state mental hospital in Jackson. Conditions in the asylum were wretched; a *Delta* reporter stated that forty-three men and women were "cribbed, cabined, and confined within the dreary limits of a common paved jailyard." Their clothing was "of the coarsest kind" and they were fed a "miserable and inadequate diet" of the "cheapest and poorest quality." After an investigation of the institution the city fathers re-opened the old Third Municipality workouse to keep the indigent insane. If any of the mentally ill thought their condition would improve by the transfer they were disillusioned. "Call it a lock-up, Calaboose, or mankennel if it pleases you," Dr. Stanford Chaillé bitterly wrote, "for surely no benevolent lexicographer could so outrage humanity and the English language as to justify the city fathers in terming it an *Asylum*."[14] The place was overcrowded and unsanitary; aged, beggars, criminals, and insane of both sexes and races were mixed together. The attendants were workhouse prisoners who reduced their sentences by serving in this cross between Bedlam and Bleak House. One wonders how solicitous "Baltimore Jimmy" or "James George, alias M. Bird" were toward their charges.

The first step to judgment faced by almost every accused person in the city was an appearance before one of the four recorder courts.[15] The recorders, after an initial hearing, transfered felony cases to the jurisdiction of a district court and tried and sentenced prisoners charged with most criminal misdemeanors. The recorder could ordinarily determine the amount of bail and he had power to sentence free and slave Negroes for various offenses. They were important political figures in the city and election to the office was hotly contested. Gerard Stith from his recorder post was able to erect a political machine which eventually catapulted him into the mayor's chair. Every newspaper covered daily events in the recorder courts and the presiding judges were the most publicized in the city. In particular the press recorded the antics and sayings of "Awful John" Suzeneau of the Third District, who administered law in the "old, rickety, worm eaten, rat infested, spider infested, and mildewed" court on the corner of Greatman and Elysian Fields.[16] In these sleazy surroundings he dispensed justice as casually as whiskey in a Moreau Street bar. His attitude toward prostitutes who peddled their wares across the street from the court, and toward drunkards and disturbers of the peace, was one of quiet and amused tolerance. Reformers failed to impeach him, but, alas, in the great American Party sweep of 1856 he was defeated.

By a law of 1846 five district courts were established in New Orleans. The First District Court was responsible for criminal cases not within the jurisdiction of a recorder or the justice of the peace and it served as a final criminal court of appeals for the state of Louisiana. There were complaints that this court was overtaxed with cases, with slovenly handling of juries therein. In one case a jury was allowed to consume during a recess six bottles of claret, a bottle of brandy, a bottle of champagne, and one glass for each juror of anisette and of absinthe. In a masterpiece of understatement, a Supreme Court judge declared "that one or more of the jurors were not in possession of that unclouded intellect which the accused had a right to demand."[17] The remaining district courts had jurisdiction over civil cases. The Second handled succession cases, the Third, justice of the peace appeals, the Fourth, commercial cases, and the Fifth served as a general court; a Sixth District Court was formed to serve the Lafayette area. Each court had an elective clerk who was also the court reporter and handled probate matters. The parish sheriff was the agent for the district court, not, as in common law states, an investigating and enforcing official. Attached to his staff were docket clerks, deputies, and a coroner.

The State Supreme Court held sessions in New Orleans during the months from January to June. This body, elective after passage of the 1852 constitution, heard only civil cases. On the high court bench during this decade sat some of the outstanding figures of the Louisiana bar: Pierre Rost, Thomas Slidell, George Eustis, and Isaac T. Preston. Notable among the men representing the State before the Supreme Court as attorney general were the brilliant, hot-tempered, E. Warren Moise and the able and sarcastic T. J. Semmes.

There were two United States courts in New Orleans, regular United States District Court and a yearly meeting of the Fifth Circuit Court. Through most of the decade Theodore H. McCaleb was District Judge and the Supreme Court Judge on circuit was John A. Campbell. The United States courts handled all matters pertaining to the Federal Government and issues involving interstate suits; in addition the District Court also served as a court of admiralty. To enforce the dictates of federal law in the city there was a United States marshal and a United States commissioner and their deputies.

THE FIRE DEPARTMENT

The spectre of the loss of property by fire was always present in ante-bellum New Orleans. Though nothing comparable to the disastrous fires of 1788 and 1794 occurred in the fifties, there were several extensive and costly fires, of which two at least were on a million-dollar scale. In 1854 whole blocks of stores, warehouses, and homes burned along Tchoupitoulas, Lafayette, Magazine, and Commerce Streets, and in 1859 a large cotton press burst into flame that spread to an area four blocks square. The most death-dealing fire consumed six ships in the harbor and killed forty-two persons. The largest building burned was the first St. Charles Hotel; sixteen adjoining buildings were partially or completely destroyed along with it. Other victims of fire included the

Mechanics Institute, the American Theatre, the Planter's Press, and the Verandah Hotel.

Minor fires, numbering about two hundred a year, were inevitable where open fireplaces and wooden building materials were in use. To remedy severe losses the common council passed ordinances which required new buildings on the riverfront and in the business sections to be constructed of brick or other fireproof material. The city required the assistant chief fire engineer to inspect new homes under construction and gave him power to force contractors to make changes. There were also ordinances regulating stovepipe erection and the construction of bakery ovens.

The main defense against fire rested of course in the fire department. The Volunteer Fire Department No. 1, formed in 1829, was the first effective fire-fighting organization in New Orleans. It was followed by similar groups and the establishment of a city-wide fire department in 1837; by 1850 there were over twenty fire companies in the city. "The early membership of these companies," wrote the historian of the New Orleans fire department, "was . . . composed of the leading men in the city, in various walks of life."[18] However with the growth of the city and an increase of fires the upper class found fire-fighting bothersome and time-consuming and they were gradually replaced by immigrants. For example, the records of the Orleans Company show that within five years a sedate middle class organization was transformed into a rather undisciplined Irish-German aggregation. The first foreman and one of the company founders complained in 1854: "I have done my best for the prosperity and the fame of my beloved Company[;] it is not my fault [they have] . . . disgrace[d] a company . . . [which] used to be the flower of the fire department."[19] By 1857 over one half of the firemen in the city had Teutonic names and the chief engineer, John F. Gruber, was a German immigrant. However a few companies, such as the American Hook and Ladder Company No. 2, continued to enroll wealthy Anglo-French members.

The volunteer companies, operating under such names as "Vigilant," "Perseverance," "Tom Thumb," "Neptune," "Red Rover," "Young America," and "Jackson," were semi-autonomous. They had elective officers, initiations, ceremonies, and benevolence programs; in other words they had most of the features of a lodge. There was a fire commissioner, with limited powers, who was chosen by the foremen of the companies, usually from among

The burning of the ALABAMA Cotton Presses. 20,000 bales valued at $1,000,000 were destroyed. One of "the most fearful conflagrations New Orleans has ever seen." (Illustrated London News March 19, 1853)

themselves. The city government put up the larger part of the funds for equipment and stations and the Board of Insurance Underwriters, obviously interested in lowered fire losses, contributed formally through a city tax and informally with contributions for the purchase of equipment. Other funds were accumulated through company balls, dues, and initiation fees.

The volunteer companies were criticized by the Board of Underwriters who by the mid-fifties became increasingly concerned over a spate of expensive fires. The Board was seconded by elements in the local press and together they were able to bring political pressure on city officials. The common council acted in June, 1855, by disbanding six volunteer companies. In protest over this action and over the penury of city appropriations for equipment, the volunteer companies marched to Lafayette Square and there publicly disbanded. The demonstration was dramatic, but the city fathers were unperturbed. They enlisted a temporary fire-fighting force and requested bids from some organization which would operate a fire department. After turning down two $100,000 bids the city accepted a $70,000 bid by the Fireman's Charitable Association. This organization, founded in 1834, was a typical benevolent society providing sickness and burial benefits and aid to widows and orphans of firemen. It owned the Cypress Grove Cemetery on Metairie Ridge; graves were reserved for members and lots sold for the financial benefit of the association. By assuming the city fire department contract, the Charitable Association made possible an efficient transfer from a volunteer to a paid department. The semi-independent character of the companies was maintained, but the authority of the newly appointed chief engineer and the president of the Fireman's Charitable Association was strengthened. Companies could now be dropped or added to improve efficiency. Funds, no longer available from the underwriters' tax, were replaced after 1857 with appropriations received from the state government.

In 1855, after the paid department was formed, there were thirteen engine companies, four hook-and-ladder companies, a hose company, and a steam engine company plus two bell ringers. Four years later there were nineteen engine companies with 1,056 men, four hook-and-ladder companies with 164 men, a hose company in charge of a steam engine with thirty-four men, and a steam engine crew of nine men, for a total of 1,263 firemen. Engines were usually made in New York or Cincinnati and cost between $1,100 and $2,600 depending upon the degree of ornamentation. Some of the fire trucks must have been simple, but others bordered on the gaudily ostentatious. A hook-and-ladder truck purchased in 1858 carried seven ladders, each having rounds capped with alternate silver stars and buttons. The engine was painted a marine blue "tastefully striped with red, white, and gold." The cradle and the perch were carved, the iron work brightly polished, and the running gear silver mounted. It was "chastely beautiful and rich" a local editor crowed. Steam fire engines were introduced in 1855 with the arrival of "Young America." It was a bulky machine pulled by four horses and requiring an auxiliary hose carriage and fuel wagon. To the joy of the hand-engine men, "Young America" went through a wooden bridge on its first fire. But in spite of this obstacle, and the fact that the engine was too heavy to use on the wharves and there were only sixteen large hydrants available for it, the steam engine overcame criticism and by the Civil War six steam engine companies were in operation.

The police were responsible for discovering fires and for sounding fire alarm bells in the district stations. The bell tower of St. Patrick's Church was used as a lookout for fires and its bells were rung to designate the district in which the fire was located. Smaller bells then picked up the sound and gave the warning. The loud clang of a fire bell amidst services must have detracted somewhat from the piety of the parishioners, but the pastor apparently did not complain. An improved fire warning system which employed alarm boxes sending telegraphic signals was introduced in 1860.

Since there was no standard fireman's uniform each company could design its own. For example, members of the Orleans Company No. 21 wore a black cap with a gilded eagle and the number "21" stitched in white on the top. They had dark blue flannel shirts with white silk trim in the sleeves, black pants, and white gloves. The shirt was adorned with sixteen white buttons, white patent leather stars on the collars, a white patent leather star with "No. 21" inscribed in black, and a ribbon with "Orleans" printed on it. The men wore wide black belts with a red '21" in front and their motto "Trust in Us" on the back. Needless to say the scene of a fire involving several companies must have presented a riot of color.

New Orleans firemen were not plagued with the curse of their New York brothers; they kept out of politics and fighting at fires was rare. On only two occasions in this decade did companies engage in brawls at the scene of a conflagration and even then the groups involved expiated their sins in the daily press. There were of course firemen who were not always intrepid fire fighters. Drinking at the scene of a fire was common—the Orleans Company once simply stayed at the Banks Arcade bar instead of returning to the station—but cases of looting, other than appropriating liquor, were rare.

Firemen provided entertainment for the citizens and for themselves in other ways than by fighting fires. Fire companies were called out to parade in honor of a special occasion or an holidays and on March 4, of each year, the anniversary of the founding of the department, firemen from the city and surrounding communities paraded through the streets. Each company was led by one or two honorary marshals and two boys carrying the company name on a banner. Between the companies were bands keeping firemen in step with tunes like "Oh Suzannah" and "Dan Tucker." In describing the 1852 parade the *Commercial Bulletin* declared: "The firemen never looked better; the engines were covered with floral and ribbon ornature, wrought in the most artistic style, and blended with exquisite taste, and the procession, admirably marshalled, moved with military precision." The parades were followed with lengthy patriotic perorations by an "Orator of the Day," races between companies, water throwing contests, and general celebrating. One rather critical observer remarked that after a parade the firemen "dispersed to take a share in the convivial glass, which was circulated somewhat too freely on that afternoon."[20]

Each winter season some of the companies sponsored balls. The social prestige of the company determined the dignity and the expense of these dances Thus the ball of the Pelican Fire Company of Algiers, held in the Belleville Foundry, was by all advertisements, not to be "one of your stiff necked, cold formal aristocratic affairs, but a social democratic assemblage, where both sexes can intermingle, whisper love sonnets in each other's ears and naturally amuse and delight." The frolicking Algerians danced "voluptuous quadrilles" and "mazy gallopades" to the accompaiment of a horn and violin.[21] The yearly ball of the Perseverance Company, on the other hand, was sponsored by leading figures in New Orleans society. During the summer months the Fireman's Charitable Association held or sponsored public concerts and displays of fireworks. Individual companies went on outings to Carrollton, Algiers or Milneberg and at least once a year companies hoped to save sufficient funds for an over-the-lake trip to one of the many summer resorts. Throughout the year companies entertained "brothers" from other companies and were entertained in return.

Certainly all of these actions: the concerts, outings, dances, parades, gay uniforms, ornamented fire engines, and frequent and spectacular fires made the firemen one of the most colorful and popular elements in New Orleans. It is no wonder that a visiting Italian should remark: "Louisiana boys play firemen the way our boys play soldier."[22]

THE MILITIA[23]

The main military body in New Orleans throughout the antebellum period was the militia. Units had been formed under the French domination and continued under Spanish and American rule. The local militia had fought with honor and distinction against the British in the campaign of 1814-1815 and against Mexico in 1846; but in spite of the past glories of Louisiana and New Orleans militia units, it was obvious by 1853 that a reorganization of the state militia was necessary. The number of men in the militia had declined rapidly and even existing units were at far less than full strength. Furthermore there was no regularity in the size of the units, nor was there a clear-cut line of command between officers in volunteer and regular militia companies.

According to a law passed in 1853, the regular Louisiana militia was to be composed of all free white males between eighteen and forty-five years of age. The militiamen who resided above Canal Street were in the First Brigade and those below Canal Street were in the Second Brigade. Each brigade was subdivided into two regiments and they in turn into two battalions. The law was not very clear and about the number of companies in a battalion, but every ten companies would comprise a regiment. An infantry company was to have three commissioned officers, eight non-commissioned officers, and "if possible" sixty-four privates. An artillery company was to be sligthly larger with two more officers plus two buglers and two artificiers. The duties

Canal Street, New Orleans — 1858 (From an old print)

French Market, 1860.

of the officers were those of a similar grade in the United States Army. This was also true of the manual of training and the militia uniform.

Volunteer companies were to be organized under the same rules as the regular militia. They were allowed to retain their distinctive uniforms subject to approval by the governor. Voluntary companies could be disbanded by the governor for faulty attendance at musters and, like militia units, could be called up by the chief executive of the state and forced to serve three months if necessary. The troops of the Louisiana Legion, a unit composed of volunteer companies, were exempt from this act provided they entered the First Division.

The law provided the ideal; it was seldom realized in New Orleans. The number actually enlisted in the regular militia was far smaller than the eligible local population—there were never more than a few hundred regular militia in the city. Volunteer units often represented paper soldiers; companies organized and dispersed with amazing frequency. For example, in the mid-fifties even such a well-known unit as the Washington Artillery had dwindled to twelve men. In 1858 the actual volunteer and regular militia units in New Orleans were composed of three brigades. The Legion Brigade consisted of the Orleans Battalion of Artillery with six companies—two without officers—and the Regiment of Light Infantry with seven companies of which six were German volunteer units. The First Brigade included the Washington Artillery (company strength), the Washington Regiment (less than Battalion size), a company called the Louisiana Greys (without officers), and a Regiment of National Guards composed of five companies. Added to the above volunteer units were four regiments of regular militia. The Second Brigade consisted of the Fourth Regiment of regular militia. Since the militia regiments were often only token units and the voluntary companies were seldom at full strength, the above militia force probably did not number over 1,500 active soldiers.

The pride and joy of the New Orleans citizenry was not in the regular militia but in the volunteer units. Many of them, for example, the Spanish Cazadores, Volantes, and Catalanos, the German Jaegers (or Yagers), Rhinegold Rifles and Fusileers, the Irish Emmett Guards and Emeralds, the Swiss Carbiners, and the French Chasseurs of 1814-1815, Voltiguers, Mameluke de la

Garde, Éclaireurs, Sapeurs de Genia, and Trailleurs d'Orléans represented ethnic units. The Washington Artillery and some of the companies of the National Guards had a definitely upper class character, with important positions held by wealthy Creoles and Americans. Perhaps some volunteer companies had the support of political parties; the Continentals, at any rate, were the favorite sons of the American Party press.

Unlike the rather drab garb of the regular militia the volunteer units were attired in a natty manner. A group formed in 1855 determined that their uniform "shall be that of the 'Continentals of 1776'." And it was. The seventy-six soldiers and five officers paraded in white knee breeches, buff vest, blue coat, white cross belt, white gloves, and three-cornered hats with a red, white, and blue plume. After observing this "unique uniform" one newspaper man rhapsodized: "The historical accuracy of their dress so vividly calls upon the olden time when that uniform bore the brunt of revolutionary battle that the heart bursts with a higher pulsation as we gaze upon their marching column."

The German First Company of Fusileers wore "green frocks with looped up hats, in the Kossuth-style, and small green feathers; the officers had white ones." The Second Company dress was similar except for their large scarlet plumes in place of the First Company's green and white fathers. The German influence affected the "beautiful and unique" uniform of the Southern Rifles formed in 1858. They dressed in green hunting shirts, buff leather knee britches, buff top boots and black felt hats looped-up at the left with plumes. Hunting rifles and horns completed the costume of this Gulf Coast *Scharfschutzen*. Just before the Civil War a newly organized company of Zouaves wore "red fez caps with blue tassels, blue kilts faced with red, baggy red breeches, and guttapercha 'leggings.' They [had] light blue sashes around the waist, and their grey blankets [were] hooped over the left shoulder and under the right arm." At the same time a Garibaldi Legion affected wide-brimmed black hats, red shirts, and bottle green pantaloons.

Volunteer soldiers had to furnish their own uniforms, but the state and city aided in providing some of their equipment. But right up to the Civil War the local militia was poorly equipped. Reports from the state arsenal in New Orleans revealed a chronic shortage of rifles and small arms, though the shortage might perhaps have been considered a blessing in disguise, for many of the guns were unsafe, if not positively dangerous to use. The Federal government gave the state of Louisiana between 200 and 300 muskets yearly—an insufficient number to meet the demands of an expanding militia.

The artillery of the city were the elite units, but even among them parade ground spit-and-polish did not always equate with efficient arms. In 1856 for example, the Battalion of Artillery had six six, two twelve, and two twenty-four pound guns; the Washington Artillery had only two six-pound guns. By 1860 the Washington Artillery had four more six-pound guns, but two of them were useless, four cassions were in poor condition, and their ammunition included neither cannister nor grape. The Battalion of Artillery, 216 strong, were in somewhat better order.

The militia was mustered out several times in the fifties to maintain order. They patrolled the city for a short time in the spring of 1850 after the police was unable to prevent a wave of arson cases. A breakdown of civilian authority forced the militia to quell the anti-Spanish riots in 1851, the Know-Nothing Party induced political riots in September, 1854, and the pre-election fighting which centered around Jackson Square in 1858. A handful of militia were also called out during a bogus Negro insurrection in 1853. The militia met these calls to duty in a fairly effective manner except in 1858 when most of the companies refused to turn out.

Like the local firemen, the militia entertained as well as protected the citizenry. Four times a year military reviews were conducted in which units, held in step by marching bands, paraded through the most populous parts of the city and gathered for review at one of several city squares, usually Place d'Armes. Frequently the governor or the lieutenant-governor graced the procession and utilized the event to orate on the condition of the nation, state, parish, and city. Because officers were fined for missing reviews, while no penalty accrued to the soldiers in the ranks, the parades were officer-heavy. After the quarterly review companies would retire either to a nearby saloon, to their armory, or to join another unit in a social affair; in all cases the newspapers recorded that "substantial refreshments" and "general hilarity" were common practice.

In addition to quarterly reviews the militia, or parts of it, might parade on patriotic holidays or other special occasions. On January 8, the anniversary of the Battle of New Orleans, there was a general turn-out of volunteer units. The Continental Guards, usually supported by a few other units, paraded on Washington's Birthday and on the Fourth of July, while the Battalion of Artillery marched and then attended church service on the feast of St. Barbara, patroness of cannoneers. Various units also paraded in honor of visiting celebrities and for funerals of well-known political and military personages.

The most popular community function of the militia companies centered around their military balls held during the winter social season. Probably none was quite so plush as the Washington Artillery ball sponsored by the upper class of the city. In the ball of 1859, Odd Fellow's Hall

> was filled to its utmost capacity by an assemblage of eager pleasure seekers, arrayed in all the varied styles of costume which impart such a glittering chameleon-like aspect to military and fancy dress balls. The Hall was decorated in the tasteful and elegant style for which this gallant Company is distinguished. Over the platform, from which the band discoursed most eloquent music, was suspended a splendid picture of WASHINGTON, and above it spread in graceful festoons rose the American flag. From the platform itself a pair of handsome brass cannon commanded the hall in a manner exceedingly threatening but altogether harmless, imparting to the scene an imposing military appearance, while the stacked arms that ornamented the windows, and the gleam of epaulettes on manly shoulders that moved through the dance, rendered the laconic invitation 'Try Us,' printed on the front wall, very acceptable in a festive sense. . . . Every section of the city, and every style of beauty were represented by the ladies, who shed the lustre of their presence on the 'noble troops that waited on their smiles.'

Among themselves military units engaged in competitive target practice on holidays. During the summer months they made excursions to resort places near the city or over Lake Pontchartrain and on the lower Gulf Coast. At these watering places they paraded for the local inhabitants, shot off their guns, listened to their bands play marches, and drank innumerable toasts. Individual units also participated in funerals of their members and collected funds for several charitable enterprises in the city.

In general the New Orleans militia, especially after the modest revival of interest in the mid-fifties, was probably on a par with military units in other urban centers. If the local soldiery lacked equipment and numbers, there appeared to be no loss of *esprit de corps* or discpline in the ranks. In spite of an elective officer class court martial records indicate few and only minor infractions of military rules by officers. Criticisms of the militia were mild and usually tempered; elements of the press occasionally cavilled about clumsy marching, target shooting and parading on the Sabbath, or small attendance at military reviews; and there is some evidence that a few merchants were piqued because their clerks were called out for frequent parades.

Military units probably reduced class conflict by serving as a favorable community-wide symbol. The militia companies did not of course enable the rich and the poor to stand on an equal basis, but they did enable them to belong to similar organizations; and certainly the high prestige of the military units were reflected on the humblest private. From the vantage point of the soldier on parade, a silk handkerchief waved by a white-frocked young lady from a balcony was as much for him as for his mounted leader. Furthermore the common duties and entertainments of the military companies provided some primary group contacts between several social strata in New Orleans society. The Washington Artillery, once a symbol of Creole-American conflict, became in the 1850's an upper class unit staffed largely by Creoles and Americans. The Regiment of National Guards, "composed of the elite of the young men of the city," drew members of its companies from all sections of New Orleans. Undoubtedly, hostility toward the newer immigrants was lessened by common participation on the parade ground and target field of various ethnic units. German companies, in particular, were praised for the dapper character of their dress, precision in marching, and accuracy on the range.

To the New Orleans citizen of 1861 the protection of his life and limb was only a little better than it had been ten years previously. There had been improvements in the quality of the police force in this decade, but they were slight. Perhaps the upper and middle class really did not care. Heads cracked, lives taken, money and goods stolen usually concerned a group distant in status and communion from the city's rulers. If police protection broke down completely, the militia could be called out to maintain order; it was a form of insurance. Far more important was protection from costly fires and here the city respectables were determined, by political pressure if necessary, to obtain the best qualified fire department. It is also interesting to note the high prestige of the fire and militia companies whereas the police, who did not even have a benevolent society until 1888, wrere reviled and frequently treated with contempt. The idea of a trained civil service to perform essential duties impersonally and honestly was not current among American city dwellers in the mid-nineteetn century. Only organizations like the militia and the fire companies which combined community services within a rural democratic pattern of voluntarism and fraternity could bridge the gap between the agrarian past and the urban present.

NOTES

[1] *Louisiana State Republican*, September 16, 1854.
[2] Sanitation will be discussed in Chapter six.
[3] *Message of Gerard Stith, Mayor of the City of New Orleans, to the Common Council*, October 11, 1859 (New Orleans, 1859), 19. Stith dismissed 269 policemen in his first year in office.
[4] Police Department, Records of Messages Received and Sent, 1860-1863, (MS) Public Library Archives, New Orleans.
[5] Stirling, *Letters from the Slave States*, 140.
[6] *General Message of Mayor C. M. Waterman to the Common Council of the City of New Orleans, October 1st, 1857* (New Orleans, 1957), 87.
[7] Dorothy Stanley, ed., *The Autobiography of Henry Morton Stanley* (Boston, 1909), 82.
[8] *Daily Crescent*, June 12, 1858.
[9] Mackay, *Life and Liberty in America*, 173.
[10] *Weekly Delta*, October 31, 1852.
[11] *Weekly Mirror*, September 18, 1858.
[12] *Weekly Delta*, February 20, 1853.
[13] *Ibid.*, July 4, 1853. After 1858 all executions were made private.
[14] Stanford Chaillé, "Insane Asylum of the State of Louisiana," *New Orleans Medical and Surgical Journal*, XIV (January, 1858), 112.
[15] There were also seven elected justices of the peace in Orleans Parish; they handled criminal and civil cases involving less than $100, performed marriages, issued orders to expel tenants, and through their constables seized and sold property involved in litigation.
[16] *Daily Crescent*, June 25, 1858.
[17] *State v. F. Bruneto* (1858), 13 La., 45-51.
[18] Thomas O'Connor, *History of the Fire Department of New Orleans from the Earliest Days to the Present Time; Including the Original Volunteer Department, the Fireman's Charitable Association, and the Paid Department Down to 1895* (New Orleans, 1895), 36.
[19] Fire Company No. 21, Record Book, 1850-1853, p. 28, (MS) Archives of the Howard-Tilton Memorial Library, Tulane University.
[20] C. G. Rosenberg, *Jenny Lind in America* (New York, 1851), 156.
[21] *Daily Orleanian*, February 22, 1852.
[22] Guilo Adamoli, "Letters from America, 1867," *Louisiana Historical Quarterly*, VI (April, 1923), 278.
[23] With minor changes and less footnotes this discussion of the militia originally appeared as "Militia in New Orleans, 1853-1861," *Louisiana History*, III (Winter, 1962), 33-42.

Chapter VI

AN UNHEALTHY CITY

> New Orleans has been an unhealthy city, not only during epidemics, but also when free of them . . . not only for whites, but also for the blacks. . . .[1]

In the 1850's New Orleans had the "unenviable character of being the most unhealthy [city] in the world."[2] Illness and death were ever present and uncomfortably familiar spectres, as yellow fever, cholera, typhus, and lesser plagues scourged the city with terrifying frequency. Travellers who came to New Orleans were convinced of the "proverbial sickliness of the great city of the south," and that no one was safe from the "annual visitation of the dreadful epidemic."[3] It was no wonder therefore that many New Orleanians undertook a yearly hegira to escape the summer epidemics, while outsiders were deterred from taking up residence in the city; or, if they did, with the notion that their abode would be only temporary.

The city's health was entrusted to Providence and the medical profession. Providence seems to have been unkind, but the local doctors did their best to lower the death rate. Indeed, considering the small number of physicians in the city — seventy-five in 1860 — there were several remarkable men who were responsible for significant contributions to medical science. Dr. Warren Stone was a nationall-known figure for his pioneer work in vascular and arterial surgery. In the latter field he was the first to apply a silver ligature to an artery, a practice which eventually became universal in arterial operations. Dr. Stone led the movement in New Orleans for the use of anesthesia and he performed the first operation in Louisiana in which sulphuric ether was used. He converted other surgeons and after 1849, when the safer chloroform was available, it became inconceivable that an operation would be conducted without anesthesia. Dr. Alexander J. Wederburn, professor of anatomy and clinical surgery at the Medical College of Louisiana from 1843 to 1856, was famous for his operations involving the removal of bone chips and malignant tumors. Dr. Samuel Choppin in 1861 successfully performed a vaginal hysterectomy that was for the age an extreme rarity. Dr. Charles Faget, who like Drs. Choppin and Armand Mercier, was as well known in France as in the United States, did important work in the field of early diagnosis of yellow fever cases.

That the city had more than its share of brilliant medical innovators (only a few are mentioned above) is probably because New Orleans represented an unique meeting place of English and French medicine where graduates of the Sorbonne and the medical colleges of London and Philadlphia could interchange ideas — and occasionally curses and shots. For example, from the Anglo-American influence came anesthesia, from the French came newer techniques in surgery and early suggestions about blood transfusion. The French-educated carried with them the image of the physician-intellectual, the doctor who wrote poetry and theatre criticism, who participated in the literary life of the community, while the Americans and English stressed the role of the physician-scientist. It is not without significance therefore that the New Orleans Academy of Science was composed almost entirely of medical men and that some of the most literate writing in the city during the 1850's should be found in the local medical journals.

There was, to be sure, also a full quota of quack doctors, who, in an atmosphere where legitimate physicians were seldom able to arrest epidemical diseases, found a ready audience for their nostrums. "Doctor" C. P. Crane used the appeal of the little-known phenomenon of electricity in his Electro-Chemical Institute where he treated the diseases of his patients by means of "electro-chemical baths," "galvinism," and "electro-magnetism." According to Dr. Crane, sufferers who visited him found relief for all types of maladies from general debility to paralysis. The kindly healer even recorded cases of restoring hearing to the deaf and sight to the blind after one of his treatments. An elderly Negro combined magic with medicine to attract clients: "This miserable old African is worshipped as an oracle by many who would be angry if we called them fools," complained a local medical journal.[4] Along the same lines were Madam La Blanche, "The only natural and true Clairvoyant, Spiritual Medium and Female Physician Known at the Present Time," and Madam Caprell, a "Second-Sight Seeress" who had accomplished "many wonderful cures," and offered to send "horoscopes of life" and medicines to all parts of the United States.

For those unable, or unwilling, to afford any type of medical advice, there were hosts of patent medicines available which promised that nearly all diseases of man or beast could be cured by "secret" remedies. A typical example was the popular Dr. Vandeveer's Medicated Gin and Genuine Scheedam Schnapps, "a wholesome beverage, and an invaluable FAMILY MEDICINE particularly beneficial in all cases of Dysentery, Dyspepsia, Diarrhea, Rheumatism, Gout, Fever, etc. etc. etc." The good doctor's gin and schnapps was "peculiarly adapted to the use of females and children." A handy medicine was John Bull's Fluid Extract of Sarsaparilla which could be taken internally for such ailments as headaches, female disorders, and syphilis, or administered externally as a cosmetic. Speed was the appeal of Radway's Ready Relief, which was guaranteed to cure a toothache in one second, diarrhea in fifteen minutes, influenza in one hour, and the stony problem of rheumatism in four hours. The medical profession ignored — or used — some of these patent medicines; only in the case of some "female pills" that produced miscarriages if used during pregnancy did medical authorities protest.

Patients who could not be treated at home by local doctors were transferred to one of several hospitals. The largest and most famous of these was Charity Hospital, which had its origins as an almshouse infirmary in the eighteenth century and had operated as a free hospital under the Roman Catholic Sisters of Charity since 1834. In the fifties the hospital was composed of three attached buildings: a large handsome three-story structure which contained the hospital proper, a "death house" where unclaimed cadavers were stored for use by the city's two medical colleges, and a three-story building which had been constructed in 1844 as an insane asylum, but after 1848 it primarily housed isolation wards. The hospital had room for over 650 patients (one thousand in times of epidemics) arranged according to disease and language in thirty-nine wards. Between nine and twelve thousand patients, ninety per-cent of whom were foreign born, were admitted to Charity yearly. Caring for these patients was a resident house physician, an assistant surgeon, a staff of fifteen doctors, and forty nurses.

Though Charity Hospital was supported by direct appropriations from city and state governments and by proceeds of special taxes and fines, there was almost no questioning of the management or of the ability of the Catholic nuns in charge. A local Protestant minister considered the Sisters of Charity the "most perfect exemplification of a Christian spirit,"[5] and a Protestant

The Charity Hospital, New Orleans — (Ballou's Pictorial XVI, August 16, 1859)

layman who worked closely with the nuns compared them to the "Vestal Virgins of old."

> I have seen the Sisters of Charity in the silent rounds of duty, in the infirmaries, hospitals, and rickety tenements of the poor, comforting their own sex of all religions, castes, and conditions, fearless of contamination, dressing loathsome wounds and inhaling the most nauseating odors. Sinner as I am, I hold them too holy and sacred to disturb them by any remarks from me.[6]

There were a few local rugged individualists who opposed the principle of a "charity" hospital which, they felt, treated lazy foreigners by taxing hard-working Americans. There was also criticism of the use of Charity Hospital as an almshouse and old age home for the indigent.

The other major New Orleans hospitals and infirmaries were: Maison de Santé, founded in 1839 by Dr. Warren Stone and leased by the Sisters of Charity, and Hôtel Dieu a small hospital opened in 1859 by the same order of nuns; Luzenberg Hospital, a small institution with a staff of two physicans in the Third District, and Touro Infirmary, established by the famous philanthropist, Judah P. Touro. Among other such institutions was the Franklin Street Infirmary, Southern Medical Dispensary, a free dispensary connected with the New Orleans School of Medicine, and the Circus Street Hospital operated by Drs. Mercier and Chaillé, which was closer in function to a clinic than a hospital. For special care there was Dr. Anfox's Small Pox Hospital, an eye infirmary, and an orthopedic clinic. Less savory, but perhaps a lucrative institution, was an infirmary operated by a Dr. James who offered cures for "Old Chronic, Mercurial, Syphiletic, and all Private Diseases without Mercury, hinderances from business, or exposure to friends. . . ."[7] On the West Bank, in the small community of McDonogh, the federal government operated a United States Marine Hospital, treating nearly two thousand seamen yearly. A major break in the levee in 1858 forced the removal of patients to the United States army barracks below the city; plans were drawn and a building begun for a new marine hospital in New Orleans, but before it could be completed the Civil War intervened.

Despite the sometime herculean efforts of the medical community, New Orleans had a phenomenally high mortality rate, though the exact percentage depended on the medical statistician and varied from 6.93 to 46.3 per thousand. The following figures, collected by the Louisiana Board of Health for the year April 27, 1855, to May 1, 1856, indicate the major causes of death.

Cause of Death	Number of Deaths
Yellow fever	2760
Cholera	1029
Tuberculosis	652
Infantile convulsions	383
Stillborn	307
Diarrhea	262
Teething	223
Tris mascentum	200
Enteritis	195
Typhoid	187
Inflamation of lungs	168
Congestion of the brain	156
Infantile marasmus	113
Debility infantum	112
Congestive fever	106
Apoplexy	106

Cholera, like yellow fever, was an epidemical disease, but unlike yellow fever, it made almost yearly visitations. In a rare year like 1860 when the city was spared the scourge of yellow fever and cholera, the leading causes of death were tuberculosis (826), infantile convulsions (409), stillborn (334), and scarlet fever (200).

New Orleans had a reputation as a grave of young men, and the statistics bear out this fact; again for the period April 27, 1855, to May 1, 1856:

Ages	Number of Deaths
Less than one year	1474
1-2	699
2-5	443
5-20	1142
20-25	1156
25-30	1136
30-40	1411
Over 40	1604

Calculations from these figures show that twenty-eight percent of those who died were less than five years of age and two-thirds less than thirty. Keeping out of a New Orleans cemetery before one's alloted three score and ten was no mean accomplishment.

The high mortality rate was certainly related to, and aided by the wretched sanitary conditions in New Orleans. Drainage was on a primitive level with canals often hardly more than "muddy ditches of stagnant and putrid water,"[9] draining the city's waste into the swamp, "that great cesspool of the metropolis."[10] In some sections of the city the canals did not even provide minimal drainage and troughs of water and waste remained. The largest of these, Gormley's Basin in the First and Fourth Districts, was described in vivid terms by a contemporary medical writer.

> The appearance of the hot sun, after a rain, speedily covers [Gormley's Basin] with a deep green mantle, which in a few hours of solar action converts into an elevated black foam. As the evaporation goes on, nearly the whole space becomes uncovered, the basin yields up its dead, and the whole necropolis of departed animal and vegetable life lies naked to the rays of the sun. To crown all, the whole district is occupied by a series of soap factories and tanneries, which no precaution can prevent from exhaling an offensive odor....[11]

Nor did the streets offer adequate drainage; few streets in the city were paved and, despite ordinances, hogs, goats, cows, horses, and dogs ran loose in the city, leaving the streets and gutters a quagmire of stagnant green mud and offal. Dead animals were often simply left to decompose in the streets — at one time twelve dogs rotted on the streets of a few square blocks in the French Quarter. The condition of the streets was not improved by the methods of collection and disposal of garbage. In 1856 the Grand Jury of Orleans Parish reported that the "garbage and refuse of kitchens is often left on the banquettes to decompose and fester in the broiling sun till eleven, twelve, or one o'clock, which should be removed before eight in the morning."[12] Refuse was hauled in open carts to nuisance wharfs in each district and dumped; however after 1853 the city employed nuisance barges which carried the city refuse and garbage to mid-stream before jettisoning it. It is no wonder a local paper complained that the "effluvia which

Sick Wards, Charity Hospital (*History of the Yellow Fever in New Orleans, Summer, 1853*)

"Sister of Charity". (History of Yellow Fever in New Orleans, Summer, 1853)

at times arises from the rich compost of manure, offal, garbage, and the sweepings of paved streets, is so offensive as to annoy whole neighborhoods, compelling them to close their doors and windows to escape its influence."[13] Or as an English traveller superciliously remarked, New Orleans drainage, "affects painfully the olfactory nerves of all who prefer the odours of the rose to those of a cesspool."[14]

The inadequate water supply of New Orleans only worsened sanitary conditions. For those who could afford the luxury, home cisterns provided water (and breeding places for mosquitoes), but the poor had to rely on public hydrants. The water supply came from a not very efficient privately-owned company which pumped water from the river into a tank whence it flowed by gravity to various parts of the community. At times this water supply stopped entirely as dead animals, which had been dumped in the river, clogged the intake valves of the water system. No attempt was made by the company to purify the water; it came directly from the Mississippi, "the purest water in the world."[15]

The existing sanitation problem was further intensified by widespread sub-standard housing for the city's poor. On the edge of the swamp there were a number of shanty towns, where

> tenements jostle[d] each other and [were] graced with innumerable stores of empty barrels, delapidated wash tubs, remnants of ancient costumes, and old and new garments flaunting from the clothes' lines — children and dogs . . . clustered around the gateways[,] and from within the yards, alleys, open doors and windows issued fragmentary specimens of every language spoken under the Canopy of heaven.[16]

These "miserable shanties," wrote a local physician, "are the disgrace of the city;" here

> the poor immigrant class cluster together in filth, sleeping a half dozen in one room, without ventilation, and having access to filthy wet yards which have never been filled up and when it rains are converted into green puddles.[17]

Most of the poor however lived along the waterfront in boarding houses and tenement buildings. There was hardly a city in Europe, one observer contended, that 'could show as many wretched destitute poor crowded together in the same place as that part [waterfront] of New Orleans."[18] In these crowded, filthy tenements sanitation was almost unknown; a family might use a single room to raise together children, dogs, and fowl; privies were seldom cleaned, and streets and levees were often used in their stead.

Of all the diseases in New Orleans, the most serious was yellow fever; about 25,000 people died of it during the fifties and in three years, 1853, 1855, and 1858, yellow fever reached epidemical proportions. It is not necessary to describe each of these epidemics; a brief study of the 1853 epidemic, the most severe of the three, will suffice to illustrate the effect of these epidemics on the community and the forces which attempted to deal with it.

When the first yellow fever case of 1853 was reported is debatable, but it was sometime in late May or early June. At first the general tendency was "to ignore and discredit the existence of the fever," and when the original cases were announced they were passed off as a "slight sickness among sailors and poor laborers who eat bad food."[19] The reason for official reticence concerning yellow fever was that such news would have an adverse effect on the city's commercial development.

> "Commerce is king" and it is no more permitted to any physician to report cases of fever with impunity in the absence of an epidemic, than to foretell and "encompass the king's death."[20]

On June 22, at least two weeks after cases of yellow fever were reported, the *Crescent* optimistically insisted that "yellow fever has become an obsolete idea in New Orleans." The *Orleanian* did not admit the existence of yellow fever until July 13, but declared that there were "no prevalent diseases or epidemics." This at a time when 204 people had died of yellow fever in the previous week and country newspapers had long reported the epidemic! It was not until July 24, that the *Delta*, and on July 26, the *Crescent* and *Commercial Bulletin*, were "bound to admit" the existence of a yellow fever epidemic. And as late as July 27, when one hundred persons a day were dying, the New Orleans Common Council timidly announced that yellow fever "may spread and become epidemic."[21]

The death rate from yellow fever rose through July. Fifty-nine died during the week ending July 9, 204 during the week ending July 16, 429 during the week ending July 23, and 692 during the week ending July 31. The treatment of the growing number of sick strained all of the community's resources. The doctors tended to what patients they could, but were almost helpless against the disease. Some suggested taking quinine and avoiding the night air or the sun's rays; others kept the patient dosed with liquor or drugged with opium. A few doctors died. Charity and other hospitals filled rapidly and floors and corridors were pressed into use. Temporary infirmaries were opened throughout the city; even the workhouse, the city insane asylum, the parish prison, and the notorious Globe Ball Room were utilized. Nurses and nuns in charge of the sick themselves fell victim to the fever, and patients hardly recovered from the disease were called upon to serve. Th clergy, particularly the Catholic priests, brought whatever sol-

Family Scene — Yellow Fever in New Orleans, 1853
(History of the Yellow Fever in New Orleans, Summer, 1853)

ace they could to the ill and dying, and for their devotion at least fifteen clergymen lost their lives of the fever.

The city government proved itself incompetent or absurd during the epidemic. At one time the city fathers had cannon fired regularly and tar burned in the streets,[22] and when this did not ward off the evil spirits of yellow fever, the mayor requested the aid of the Almighty and declared a day of public prayer. In a more practical vein the city bought eight wagons and placed two of them in each district to carry the poor to the hospitals free of charge. On July 29, the Common Council established an official Board of Health composed of fifteen men, who were entrusted with enforcing rules of sanitation through health inspectors appointed for each ward, securing burial returns from cemetery sextons, and establishing a quarantine station below the city for all ships coming up the river. The board was soon roundly criticized for allowing unsanitary conditions to continue and for maintaining a bootless quarantine after the disease had broken out. But this criticism did not bother the Common Council; its members had fled the city for the summer.

Local benevolent societies, fire and military companies, and fraternal lodges gave money and time to treat the hordes of sick, but of all the local agencies to comfort the ill, none was quite so valuable or so dramatic as the Howard Association. This organization, founded during the epidemic of 1837 to work among the sick and dying, was limited to thirty individuals, mostly clerks, who prided themselves on being of all nationalities and religions. In mid-June, 1853, the Howard Association was mobilized and on July 13 began treating the sick. It printed lists of pharmacies where patients might obtain free medicines; provided a panel of forty physicians paid by the Association; established eight temporary infirmaries and three orphan asylums; and distributed emergency funds and foods to the needy. Individually, members were assigned a specific section of the city where, aided by their wives, auxiliary members, and hired nurses (often Negro), they visited the indigent sick. At each fever-ridden home they offered medicine to the ill and acquainted other members of the household with methods of treatment; they arranged for drugs and a doctor's care, occasionally left a nurse at the dwelling, and if necessary had the patient removed to a hospital or infirmary. In all too many cases they took care of funeral arrangements. At least 10,000 patients came under Association care during the epidemic. In support of the Howard Association the city government contributed a paltry $2,000 while private donors from New Orleans and elsewhere gave over $200,000.

How valuable these amateur male nurses were it would be difficult to ascertain. They relied upon quinine therapy which was probably as good as any treatment used. Certainly their care was of value to the sick and saved many lives. One can imagine the feelings of a lonely immigrant family living in a tenement or shanty with two or three stick, crowded in a single bed, when a member of the Association appeared to offer concrete aid and comfort. More important they provided a focus of hope and responsibility in the community; under plague conditions panic could have developed. The Howard Association radiated confidence, whereas the city government merely spread burning tar.

The epidemic raged through the month of August. Death tolls from yellow fever increased daily. During the first week of August the Board of Health reported 967 persons died; during the second week, 1,288; during the third week, 1,346; and during the fourth week, 1,243.

The city by now was a "huge lazar house, the abode of the dead or dying."[23] Death dominated New Orleans. "The city offers a very sad view," wrote the Catholic editor, Abbé Perché. "Everywhere it presents a picture of funereal dress."[24] All roads led to the graveyards.

> Funeral processions crowded every street. No vehicles could be seen except doctor's cabs and coaches, passing to and from the cemeteries, and hearses, often solitary, taking their way toward these gloomy destinations. The hum of trade was hushed.[25]

At the worst stage the number of dead increased so rapidly that the cemeteries were unable to handle all of the dead. The macabre spectacle that resulted at one cemetery was vividly described by a *Crescent* reoprter.

"The Little Coffin Bearers"
(*History of the Yellow Fever in New Orleans, Summer, 1853*)

At the gathering point carriages accumulated, and vulgar teamsters, as they jostled each other in the press, mingled the coarse jest with the ribald oath; no sound but of profane malediction and of riotous mirth, the clang of whip thongs and the rattle of wheels. At the gates, the winds brought intimation of the corruption working within. Not a puff but was laden with the rank atmosphere from rotting corpses. Inside they were piled by fifties, exposed to the heat of the sun, swollen with corruption, bursting their coffin lids, and sundering, as if by physical effort the ligaments that bound their hands and feet, and extending their rigid limbs in every *outre* attitude. What a feast of horrors! Inside corpses piled in pyramids, and without the gates old and withered crones and fat huxter [sic] women, fretting in their own grease, dispensing ice cream cones and confections, and brushing away, with brooms made of bushes, the green bottle-flies that hovered on their merchandise, and then anon buzzed away to drink dainty inhalations from the green and festering corpses. . . . .

[Inside] Long ditches were dug across the great human charnel. Wide enough were they to entomb a legion, but only fourteen inches deep. Coffins in them showed their tops above the surface of the earth. On these was piled dirt to the depth of a foot or more, but so loosely that myriads of flies found entry between the loose clods, down to the cracked seams of the coffins, and buzzed each hour their new hatched swarms.

But no sound was there of sorrow within that wide Gehenna. Men used to the scent of dissolution had forgotten all touch of sympathy. Uncouth laborers, with their bare shock heads, stood under the broiling heat of the sun, digging in the earth; and as anon they would encounter an obstructing root or stump, would swear a hideous oath, remove to another spot, and go on digging as before. Now and then the mattock or the spade would disturb the bones of some former tenant of the mould, forgotten there amid the armies of accumulated victims, and the sturdy laborer, with a gibe would hurl the broken fragments on the sward, growl forth an energetic d--m and chuckle in his excess of glee. Skullbones were dug up from their long sepulture, with ghastliness staring out

'From each lack-lustre, eyeless hole'

without eliciting an 'Alas poor Yorick," and with only an exclamation from the digger of 'room for your betters.'

Economy of space was the source of cunning calculation in bestowing away the dead men. Side by side were laid two of gigantic proportions, bloated by corruption to the size of Titans. The central projections of their coffins left space between them at their heads and heels. This was too much room to be filled with earth. How should the space be saved? Opportunely the material is at hand, for a cart comes lumbering in, with corpses of a mother and her two little children. Chuck the children in the spaces at the heads and heels of the Titans, and lay the mother herself, out there alone! A comrade for her will be found anon, and herself and babes will sleep not less soundly from the unwonted contact.

The fumes rise up in deathly exhaltations from the accumulating hetacombs of fast-coming corpses. Men wear at their noses bags of camphor and odorous spices — for there are crowds there who have no business but to look on and contemplate the vast congregation of the dead. They don't care if they die themselves — they have become so used to the reek of corruption. They even laugh at the riotings of the skeleton Death and crack jokes in the horrid atmosphere where scarcely they can draw breath for utterance.

The stoical negroes, too, who are hired at five dollars per hour to assist in the work of interment, stagger under the stiffling [sic] fumes, and can be kept at their work by deep and continued potations of 'fire water.' They gulp deep draughts of the stimulating fluid, and reeling to their tasks, hold their noses with one hand, while with the other they grasp the spade, heave on the mould, and rush back to the bottle to gulp again. It is a jolly time with these ebon [sic] laborers, and with their white co-workers, as thoughtless and as jolly, and fully as much intoxicated themselves.

And thus, what with the songs and obscene jests of the grave diggers, the buzzing of the flies, the sing-song cries of the huxter-women [sic] vending their confections, the hoarse oaths of the men who drive the dead carts, the merry whistle of the boys, and the stifling reek from sources of blackened corpses, the day wears apace, the work of sepulture is done, and night draws the curtain.

The brunt of the deaths occurred among the unacclimated immigrants. Crowded together and lacking the simple sanitary safeguards, they died like flies — in one boarding house alone forty-five died in thirteen days. In their wretched quarters the dead, dying, and convalescent often occupied the same beds. Entire families were wiped out or left a single survivor. The native-born had considered themselves immune, but by early August it was obvious that yellow fever was making inroads on the Creole population. Even Negroes, who were thought to be not at all subject to yellow fever, contracted the dread disease.

The epidemic continued into September, but the deaths decreased with each week after the end of August, amounting to 749 during the week ending September 4; 421 during the week ending September 11; 221 during the week ending September 17; 125 during the week ending September 24; and eighty-five during the week ending October 1. By mid-October the number of deaths from yellow fever had dropped to forty-two a week. On October 8, the *Commercial Bulletin* announced rather optimistically that "We can now safely say that New Orleans is as healthy as any city in the Union. . . ." Five days later the Board of Health declared that yellow fever no longer existed as an epidemic in New Orleans. However, the last yellow fever death of the season was registered late in Dcember.

When the final tabulation was made it showed around 29,000 cases of yellow fever and 8,100 deaths. This total was an estimate only, for cemetery statistics were inaccurately kept by the sextons, people were buried clandestinely, and doctors listed yellow fever deaths under other causes. By one account the mortality rates in the heat of the epidemic were only about seven-tenths correct. According to Dr. E. H. Barton the mortality rate for the city during the epidemic was 111.91 per thousand with at least one in every five Irish and better than one in every eight Germans residing in the city dying of yellow fever. And Barton was probably guilty of under-estimating the total!

With the abeyance of the fever a degree of normality returned to the city. On October 8, the *Price Current* noted a "re-opening of business within the past few days." Outsiders poured into the city as the fever was forgotten and the commercial year began.

> Everywhere the note of preparation for the approaching commercial campaign is heard. Renovation, reconstruction is the order of the day. . . . Everything presages a business season of great activity and brilliancy. Already the city is beginning to assume the appearance of bustling, stirring life it is wont to wear in the winter season. It is surprising how rapidly and with what unbounding elasticity New Orleans regains her erect position, after bending momentarily before the blasts of misfortune. A stranger visiting it to-day for the first time, could scarcely realize that within a period of a few weeks it had been the scene of a scourge unparalleled in the history of the country. Everyone we meet seems full of business, of hope and confidence. The momentary depression that seized upon the minds during the ravages of the epidemic has passed away. . . . Nobody even talks of leaving New Orleans. The idea has seized fasthold of the public mind that the yellow fever in the future can be warded off.[26]

One result of the epidemic was to establish a semi-permanent ship quarantine. The city Board of Health set up a quarantine station at Slaughter House Point (present day English Turn) below the city, but the Board and the quarantine were discontinued in December, 1853, and were not reinstituted the next summer. The state government ignored the question of quarantine until 1855 when the legislature provided for a state Board of Health, one-third of whose members were to be named by the New Orleans Common Council. The new Board operated, from May 1 to November 1 in 1855 and subsequent years, three quarantine stations, one on the Mississippi, one at the Rigolettes, and one in Atchafalaya Bay. These city and state quarantines were attacked by elements of the medical profession who argued that yellow fever was indigenous and noncontagious, and by merchants who considered delays at the quarantine stations a deterrent to the New Orleans economy. The *Picayune* complained that the quarantine "has been a prolific source of delay, annoyance, loss and expense without accomplishing anything for the public good, that we are aware of."[27] In George Cable's bitter words:

> The merchants, both Creole and American, saw only the momentary inconveniences and losses of quarantine and its defective beginnings; the daily press, in bondage to the merchant through its advertising columns, carped and cavilled in two languages at the innovation and expanded on the filthiness of other cities, while the general public thought what they read.[28]

The disastrous epidemic led the New Orleans Board of Health to form a Sanitation Commission composed of prominent medical men to investigate the causes of the epidemic and prepare ways and means of preventing future catastrophes. The chairman of the commission was Dr. Edward H. Barton, a long-time resident of New Orleans, and when the report appeared in 1854 it was largely his handiwork. Yellow fever, according to Barton, was not contagious, but was contracted from a contaminated atmosphere breathed by the citizens. The air became impure as a result of the natural warm humidity of the lower Mississippi delta and the surface filth accumulating from poor sanitation and the turning over of the soil in construction work, canals, and ditches. In the words of one of Barton's advocates:

> The theory . . . of the etiology of yellow fever, may be thus stated: From the accumulation of filth in large cities (chiefly night-soil and the animal matter of urine) putrefaction must necessarily take place, and from this putrefaction, *under certain meteorological conditions*, there is generated a poison, which, either in the form of a volatile oil, or other organic mat-

ter, held in solution by ammonia, floats in the atmosphere; is inhaled during the respitory movements; is taken into the circulation and poisons the system.[29]

Only rigid sanitary devices, Barton insisted, could prevent the recurrence of yellow fever. Because Barton did not believe yellow fever was contagious, he expressed little faith in preventing fever through a quarantine system, but urged its continuance as a precaution against bringing into the city infected persons and ships which might propagate fever in the hot, humid atmosphere of New Orleans.

The report of the Commission unleased a Pandora's box of conflicting opinions expressed in articles, pamphlets, and books. The Great Yellow Fever Debate — always smouldering in New Orleans — erupted; and "quelle diversité, quelles contradictions, quels tâtonnements, quel empirisme avengle, quel chaos!"[30] Barton's report was roundly criticized — one physician said it was a "tedious book, abounding in absurdities, extravagances, and self glorification"[31] — and new theories were presented. Far and away the most fantastic thinking on the problem of the cause or prevention of yellow fever was done by Drs. John McFarlane and Samuel A. Cartwright. McFarlane presented a "filth" theory, that is, he contended that by spreading about the streets mud, night soil, offal, and allowing it to decompose in the heat and moisture of the city, the causative agent of yellow fever would be eliminated. He supported his theory with statistics purporting to indicate that the areas of greatest filth had a relaitvely low yellow fever rate. The theory was attacked in medical circles, McFarlane being pronounced "either a fool who deserved pity, or a knave who deserved the severest punishment."[32] Cartwright in 1853 affirmed that the main cause of yellow fever was the hot sun. It was simply too torrid in New Orleans for the "master race of men," and Negroes should be forced to do all of the outside work during the summer. Lesser causes, he thought, were impure water, lack of green vegetables, excessive number of "grop shops," faulty home architecture, and overcrowding of the poor. In 1859, after experimenting with Professor John L. Riddell's new binocular microscope, Cartwright expanded on this theme. Yellow fever, he pontificated, was caused by unacclimated immigrants just off the boat who had "scorbutic blood" and the contagion of European typhus or ship fever on their clothes; these medical conditions, combined with physical labor on the waterfront and the rays of the summer sun, generated "the yellow fever in their systems," and released "zymnotic germs" which were "not slow to seek a nidus in other unacclimated persons." He was not quite sure why the "acclimated" also suffered in 1853, 1855, and 1858, but suggested that it might have been due to "some terrene poison forced into the atmosphere by terrene dynamics, or brought up by the electricity of the earth by deeply wounding the earth with mattock and spade in the hot season of the year."[33]

One of the most violent of the yellow fever controversies took place between Dr. Charles Deléry and Dr. Charles Faget. This quarrel, which extended over twenty years, hinged on the question of the immunity of Creoles and Negroes to yellow fever. Faget insisted that what Creoles and Negroes occasionally contracted was not yellow fever but "fièvre paludeéne." Deléry was equally insistent that they could acquire yellow fever like any other inhabitants. It became a point of honor with Deléry and he challenged Faget to a duel. The latter refused on the ground that his Catholic belief did not allow for either murder or suicide. Besides, pamphleteering was easier and more enjoyable. For each tract one wrote, the other followed with a blistering "réplique." After an estimated seven exchanges, Dr. Faget weakened and in 1877 wrote a "Dernier Réplique."

The yellow fever debate continued year after year with New Orleans physicians continuing to analyse the causes and cures of yellow fever, whether it was imported or endemic, whether it was contagious, and whether quarantine was a justified practice. But perhaps the most honest of the medical scribes of the 1850's was Dr. M. Morton Dowler, who simply stated that the discovery of the causes of yellow fever was far in the future; all theories thus far advanced were "rubbish." And near the end of the decade, after three epidemics, the editor of a local medical journal sadly admitted that "many points connected with yellow fever are almost as undecided now as they were twenty-five years ago."[34]

Effective sanitation, the *sine qua non* of successful eradication of most epidemical diseases, had hardly progressed during the fifties. Differences among physicians, divided counsels in City Hall, fear of losing business, above all indifference on the part of the merchant class to the life and death of the poorer citizens made a concerted program of sanitation impossible. It remained for the hated Union army of occupation to enforce sanitary measures which led to the first significant decline in the city's mortality rate in the nineteenth century.

Since this chapter has discussed mortality, it may be appropriate to consider funeral and burial practices in the Crescent City. In case of the average working man preparations were simple; the body was washed, a short wake was held (the city required burial within forty-eight hours), a religious service was conducted, and a hurried interment followed. Even simpler was the fate of the corpse of a pauper which could look forward to an unceremonious ride on the Street Commissioner's cart to Potter's Field or to go under the dissecting knife of a medical student. For the wealthier, more elaborate dispositions were made. Because embalming was, by modern standards, crude, the main hope of preservation was in the purchase of ponderous metal, mahogany, or cypress caskets. The local "undertaker stores" sold the caskets, performed whatever embalming or preservation they were able, and displayed the body at the home of the deceased.

Newspaper obituaries were often embellished with lengthy eulogies on the departed testifying to his "numerous manly and endearing virtues," or concluding, "May the clod rest lightly upon him, and may flowers forever bloom over his grave." Now and then the obituary took the form of a poem. "Consolation" was the title of the following verse:

> The barrier which we all at last
> Must leap! How blessed the lot so cast —
>   Thus to go
> Without a stain of sin or wo[e]
> From the dark journey here below.

The high point of the funeral was the procession, which by the fifties, due in part to the influence of a free Negro undertaker, Pierre Casanave, had become extremely elaborate and ceremonial. The hearse, a large bulky conveyance, ornately carved and draped, was drawn by caparisiond horses — undertakers also operated livery stables. Over the hearse and horses streamers of black crepe were hung for adult funerals, while white crepe was used for children. The hearse was dispensed with if the deceased was a member of a fire or militia company, in which case the body was rested on a fire truck or artillery caisson. When the deceased belonged to a fraternal, benevolent, military, or fire company or-

New Orleans Burial Vaults — the "Dead Ovens."

ganization his brothers marched in mourning to the cemetery. Accompanying these organizations, and indeed in private processions as well, were military-type marching bands. The bands played lugubrious dirges on the way to the cemetery, but often on return they played quick-stepping tunes, "a type of music more suitable for a festive occasion than one of a mournful interest."[35]

The city's seventeen cemeteries were unique among American graveyards; because the water level was so close to the surface, conventionally-dug graves were impossible, and burials were made above ground. A slightly amazed traveller gave the following description:

> the cemeteries of New Orleans differ from other spots where the dead rest, in the peculiarity that the latter are all above ground. For tombs in the literal sense of the word receive them. In some instances there are merely brick receptables admitting a single coffin; in others, they are large structures rising thirty and forty feet from the ground, formed into compartments, and frequently decorated with much architectual embellishment. Between these extremes, every variety is to be met with, but the greater efforts are the result of societies; and therefore it is a common practice for individuals to combine, to obtain a decent place of rest when they cease to be. . . . The appearance of the cemetery is therefore striking in the extreme. As you walk among these last homes of your

fellows, you feel indeed that you are in the company of their remains. . . . The tombs are . . . dilapidated; many are fallen in; and in the record which affection, or compliance with custom has traced, has in no few instances long since faded to nothingness. Rank grass grows around these receptacles of the dead. But you come to spots where affection has raised tributes to those who had [sic] passed away, in the shape of flowering shrubs, and in the French taste, garlands and mementoes are hung on many a tomb.

The tombs and "ovens" (rows of graves, four to six tiers high along the walls of the cemetery) often displayed carved statuary or bas-relief. Poetry could be found on some tombs — traditional stanzas from the Book of Psalms, lines from Goethe in German, verse taken from a pious church publication, and a few which appear to have been written by friends or relatives. Following are examples of what is probably home-spun verse found on tombs in Lafayette Cemetery No. 1:

> Our Darling babes have gone to rest
> Their souls to God are given
> We mourn, though think t'was for the best
> As they are now in Heaven

American or Protestant Cemetery — New Orleans - 1853

Potters Field (New Orleans, 1853)

>Farewell dear Ma and Pa weep not for me
>For my sweet Saviour call[s] me away from thee
>Afflictions sore a long time she bore
>>Physicians were in vain
>Till God did please to give her ease
>>And rid her of her pain
>
>This lovely bud so young and fair
>Called hence by early doom
>Just came to show how sweet a flower
>In paradise would bloom

Other tombs revealed in a laconic fashion the cause of death, "Mort victime de l'honneur," or "Died of Yellow Fever." and still others capture the contemporary sentiment toward the deceased with "Our Angle Myrthee," "Our Peerless Robert," "Our little Henry," and this enigmatic line: "May her son, so live, that he may be worthy to write her epitaph."

The cemeteries became the focus of community interest every October 31, the Feast of the Poor Souls in Purgatory, and November 1, the Feast of All Saints (Toussaint), when many citizens visited graveyards, sang funeral chants, and decorated the tombs of the departed. Though Toussaint was a Roman Catholic feast day (Protestantism has no concept of Purgatory), the Protestant cemeteries were also decorated on the two religious days. Like Mardi Gras, Toussaint was a French-Catholic institution adopted by Americans and foreigners; "it will remain," declared the *Delta* editor, "one of the beautiful customs of *our* people." A holiday spirit was lent to the occasion by street vendors who hawked real and artificial floral pieces bearing such titles as "Eternal Regrets," "A Mon Bon Ange," and "Tears for the Dead," while Catholic orphans and members of several benevolent societies stood at the gate soliciting funds for orphan asylums. Only the stony-hearted could have refused a wistful ophan's bequest in such an atmosphere.

NOTES

[1] Stanford Chaillé, *Life and Death in New Orleans from 1787 to 1869 and More Especially During the Five Years 1856-1860* (New Orleans, 1869), 10.
[2] Cunyhghame, *A Glimpse at the Great Western Republic*, 220.
[3] Charles Mackay, *Life and Liberty in America*, 254; Alexander Mackay, *The Western World*, II, 87.
[4] "Quackery Rampant," *New Orleans Medical News and Hospital Gazette*, VII (July, 1860), 394.
[5] Theodore Clapp, *Autobiographical Sketches and Recollections During a Thirty Five Years' Residence in New Orleans* (Boston, 1957), 240.
[6] [William L. Robinson], *Diary of a Samaritan By a Member of the Howard Association* (New York, 1860), 195-196.
[7] *Daily Crescent*, January 11, 1859.
[8] Louisiana Board of Health, *Report*, 1857 (New Orleans, 1857), 25-31. Included in the cholera total were 144 deaths listed as "cholera infantum."
[9] *Weekly Picayune*, July 14, 1856.
[10] *New York Daily Tribune*, April 2, 1861.
[11] M. Morton Dowler, "On the Reported Causes of Yellow Fever and the So Called Sanitary Measures of the Day," *New Orleans Medical and Surgical Journal*, XI (July, 1854), 44.
[12] Grand Jury of the Parish of Orleans, *Report*, 1856 (New Orleans, 1856), 8.
[13] *Daily Creole*, July 12, 1856.
[14] Charles Mackay, "Transatlantic Sketches. The Crescent City," *Illustraed London News*, XXXII (April 10, 1858), 377.
[15] Samuel A. Cartwright, "The Influence of Floral, Hydro and Terrene Dynamics on Health, Agriculture and Commerce," *Medical and Surgical Journal*, XVI (March, 1859), 183.
[16] Wharton, diary, June 12, 1854.
[17] "History and Incidents of the Plague in New Orleans," *Harper's New Monthly Magazine*, VII (November, 1853), 798.
[18] Samuel A Cartwright, "Prevention of Yellow Fever," *Medical and Surgical Journal*, X (November, 1853), 315.
[19] "History and Incidents of the Plague in New Orleans," *Harper's New Monthly Magazine*, VII, 797.
[20] Dowler, "On the Reported Causes of Yellow Fever and the So Called Sanitary Measures of the Day," *Medical and Surgical Journal*, XI, 55.
[21] "History and Incidents of the Plague in New Orleans," *Harper's New Monthly Magazine*, VII, 798.

[22] One elderly dissenter from the cannon-and-tar technique urged the city to hire a band to parade through the streets; "the genial strains . . . will tend to elevate the minds and raise the spirits of the suffering patient [more] than the firing of all the cannon in the arsenal." *Weekly Delta*, August 28, 1853.

[23] "New Orleans—The Yellow Fever," *Illustrated London News*, XXIII (September 24, 1853), 244.

[24] *Propagateur Catholique*, August 13, 1853.

[25] "History and Incidents of the Plague in New Orleans," *Harper's New Monthly Magazine*, VII, 798.

[26] *Commercial Bulletin*, October 20, 1853.

[27] *Weekly Picayune*, December 10, 1855. The *Picayune* followed a have-your-cake-and-eat-it-too policy by urging a rigid quarantine law, providing it did not hold up any valuable cargoes.

[28] George W. Cable, *The Creoles of Louisiana* (New York, 1885), 305.

[29] John Harrison, "Speculations on the Cause of Yellow Fever," *Medical News and Hospital Gazette*, II (August, 1855), 246-247.

[30] Charles Deléry, *Précis Historique de la Fièvre Jaune* (New Orleans, 1859), iv.

[31] M. Morton Dowler, "Review of the Report of the Sanitary Commission of New Orleans on the Epidemic Yellow Fever of 1853," *Medical and Surgical Journal*, XI (January, 1855), 526.

[32] "The Great Yellow Fever Epidemic in 1853," *De Bow's Review*, XV (December, 1853), 600.

[33] Cartwright, "The Influence of Floral, Hydro and Terrene Dynamics on Health, Agriculture and Commerce," *Medical and Surgical Journal*, XVI, 186-187.

[34] "Editorial," *Medical News and Hospital Gazette*, VI (September, 1859), 559.

[35] "Music at Funerals," *The Masonic Review*, VI (March, 1851), 183.

[36] [William Kingsford], *Impressions of the West and South During a Six Weeks Holiday* (Toronto, 1858), 58.

Chapter VII

RELIGION

"New Orleans . . . was not an eminently religious city."[1]

ROMAN CATHOLICS

Rising high above the slate roofs of the Vieux Carré was the Roman Catholic Cathedral of St. Louis. The late eighteenth century church (modified and remodeled in 1850), built with funds provided by the Baron de Pontalba, was flanked by the impressive Cabildo and Presbytere and faced the flowered walks of Jackson Square. Together with the nearby chapel of the Ursuline Convent and the mortuary chapel of St. Anthony on Rampart street, it symbolized colonial Louisiana and its French-and-Spanish-speaking population. It was the Bishop's church; from its massive wooden altar he celebrated mass and issued pronouncements; in its chancery office the birth, marriage, and death records of New Orleans old families were meticulously kept; under its lofty nave slave and free worshipped and its excellent professional choir sang the time-honored liturgy. Even visiting Protestants, immersed in music, spectacle, and incense, found the experience awe-inspiring. In this one church much of the history and sociology of early nineteenth century New Orleans could be recorded.

Catholicism in New Orleans might have remained Gallic, easy-going and ritualistic, if it had not been for the large scale immigration of Irish and German Catholics. As early as 1837 St. Patrick's Church on Camp Street was begun for use by Irish Catholics, and between 1845 and 1860 fourteen additional churches were constructed to meet the needs of the new immigrants. These congregations were often formed to serve several ethnic groups entering the city which in turn created overlapping parish districts. For example, many Creoles, regardless of the part of the city in which they resided, worshipped at the St. Louis Cathedral. In the Fourth District, where French, Irish, and German immigrants lived in the same area, there were three Catholic churches—St. Alphonsus, Notre Dame, St. Mary's—within a few blocks of each other. The same pattern was found in the Third District and, to a lesser degree, in the central districts of the city. Occasionally a church which was geographically isolated served several ethnic groups and employed more than one language in devotional

William Mure, British Consul
at New Orleans, 1860

uel Horton Kennedy, banker
prominent business man,
ident of the Boston Club—
(From a painting in the
ession of the Club by
ge P. A. Healy, famous
erican portrait painter)

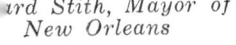

rd Stith, Mayor of
New Orleans

John T.
Monroe,
Mayor of
New Orleans

A. D. Crossman
Mayor of New Orleans

John Slidell, U.S. Senator from Louisiana

Rt. Rev. Bishop Polk, of Louisiana

Pierre Adolphe Rost, Associate Justice of Louisiana Supreme Court — 1853

Ben De Bar

Paul Morphy, Chess Player

exercises. To a German who might have accidently entered the confessional box with a French speaking priest this must have involved some theological difficulties.

Though separate churches were formed for the major ethnic groups, no parishes were established for the city's twelve to fifteen thousand Negro Catholics. Reflecting perhaps the liberal racial views of the French population, the Catholic Church did not sanction segregation of the races at religious services. There was, recorded an English traveller, "no distinction as to colour of skin, all knelt side by side."[2] Negroes received sacraments indiscriminately with whites, they sang in mixed choirs, and were buried in Catholic cemeteries alongside whites. Free Negroes were, like any other group of Catholics, held responsible for the upkeep of their parish churches. At St. Augustine's church free Negroes raised part of the funds to construct the church and rented about one-half of the pews. It should be pointed out however that integration of Negroes and whites in the Catholic church did not extend beyond worship services. Catholic authorities sponsored separate benevolent and religious associations for Negroes. Parochial schools for free Negro children were small and segregated.

In order to provide religious leadership for the growing number of Catholic schools, charitable institutions, and churches, Bishop Antoine Blanc invited several religious orders to open houses in New Orleans. Among the orders which entered the diocese in the fifties were the Christian Brothers, Brothers of St. Joseph, the School Sisters of Notre Dame, and the Sisters of Mount Carmel. Their schools and orphanages supplemented the older facilities of the Ursulines and the Sisters of Charity. The demand for priests was met by Vincentians, Redemptorists, Jesuits, and secular fathers drawn from assorted European countries. The Bishop hoped to obtain new priests from the Vincentian seminary in Jefferson Parish and the diocesan seminary in Plattenville, but vocations were few and the seminaries seldom had more than a dozen students.

By 1860 there were an estimated 65,000 Roman Catholics gathered in the city and its suburbs. New Orleans was thus the principal Catholic center in the South. Undoubtedly this fact prompted the Pope in 1850 to make the city a Metropolitan See and to create the Province of New Orleans which included the dioceses of Little Rock, Galveston, Natchez, Mobile, and New Orleans.

The rapid growth of the Catholic population engendered a conflict between the Creole and immigrant Catholics, a conflict already evident in the class system and in local politics. Of the two groups, Church officials preferred the immigrants. In 1844 Bishop Blanc reported to the Holy See: "It is highly important to the interest of religion in New Orleans to uphold especially the influence of the Catholic portion which speaks English [i.e. Irish]. That portion will always sustain the Bishop." In the same year he wrote to a fellow prelate: "The Irish and Americans have always sustained us and will be always in [sic] the side of authority."[3] The Irish, coming from a nation where Church and nationality were synonymous, militantly supported the local hierarchy. Though not always examples of angelic purity, the Germans and Irish never doubted the validity of the faith or its officials. They were docile children of Mother Church.

Not so devoted were the French Catholics. Thomas J. Semmes, a Catholic from Maryland, declared in 1855 that the "men among the native population are generally infidels, tho' the woman are pious Catholics. [The men] are what may be termed liberals, and a vast number of them are Catholics in sentiment, tho' not, I am sorry to say, in practice."[4] This liberalism was reflected in such Creole Catholics as P.G.T. Beauregard, who denied that miracles were manifestations of God's will; "men will more readily believe what is un-natural than what is perfectly simple and natural." If a man were good and obeyed the Ten Commandments, Beauregard tolerantly declared, the matter of his religious affiliation was of minor concern.[5] Alexander Dimitry, a Creole graduate of the Catholic Georgetown University, felt that all talk of conscience was "twaddle;" an enlightened conscience was possible only for the educated few, but the majority must be kept in line by informing them that "if you steal, they'll send you to the penitentiary; if you don't say your beads, the Blessed Virgin won[']t beg her Son for you; if you don't read the Bible . . . you shall surely go to hell." The Divine Presence, Dimitry contended, was found in nature and divine laws were the "law of mildness, the law of kindness, the law of love, the law of brotherhood."[6] Whatever validity Beauregard and Dimitry's ideas might have, they were certainly not inspired by Catholic theology.

To Creole males religion was the duty of women and children; a man had to appear in church only for his wedding and his funeral. They cheerfully ignored church rules on attendance at mass, on reception of the sacraments, and even on dueling. Furthermore French immigrant and Creole Catholic newspaper editors at times vehemently castigated the Church for being reactionary, anti-republican, Machiavellian, ultramontane, and abolitionist. In turn, the Catholic newspaper, *Propagateur Catholique*, accused the editors of being infidels, socialists, and even Albigensians. "Catholique vous même! Cher Courrier!" Abbé Napoléon Perché caustically wrote, "Vous etes maladroitement hypocrite, et voila tout."

Creole Catholics came in direct conflict with the hierarchy and with the immigrant Catholics by their support of the trustee system, by membership in the Masonic order, and by adherence to the American Party. The first of these, the trustee question, had been settled by 1850. After a protracted conflict during which the lay trustees (Marguillieurs) of the St. Louis Cathedral kept the Bishop out of his own church the Prelate had finally gained control. No schismatic Hoganites arose from among the lay trustees, as happened in Philadelphia, but the struggle had evoked a great deal of bitterness. During the 1850's the trustees, shorn of their power, continued to serve, but in the newly constructed churches Bishop Blanc refused to allow a lay trustee system. He preferred opening small churches accountable to and owned by himself in order to counter whatever influence the Cathedral trustees might still exert.

Though American Catholic participation in the Masonic order was not expressly forbidden by the Papacy until 1869, membership was never regarded as the sign of a devoted son of the Church. It was with the Masons (and Odd Fellows) in mind that Archbishop Blanc proclaimed in 1860:

> ... you cannot take part in those societies which are based on naturalism, or rationalism, or an imagined natural religion, and which regard as uncertain or unnecessary the revelations which God has made to man. ... You are likewise bound to keep aloof from societies which require an oath of initiation of members, that they may more effectively conceal the purposes for which the associaiton is designed.[7]

The Archbishop might have added that open anti-Catholic attitudes on the part of elements in the local Freemasonary were not unknown. The Scottish Rite ritual used by Spanish speaking Masons was rabidly anti-clerical, fulminating frequently against the "Intolerancia, la Supersticion y el Fanatismo" of the Roman

Catholic Church.[8] Violent anti-Catholics speeches at major Masonic affairs were known to be given, and the "Masonic baptisms" held at the Foyer Maconique must have struck Blanc as a sacrilege second only to the hated Black Mass. Nonetheless, in spite of the secret oaths and the covert anti-Catholic disposition of the Masonic order, French Creoles were important in the development and membership of New Orleans Freemasonry. In 1850, for example, three of the Cathedral trustees were members of the Masonic order, and one was an Odd Fellow. The Parfaite Union and the Polar Star Lodges contained many Creoles, most of whom were associated with the Catholic Church. This dual allegiance of the Creoles to the Church and to Masonry probably did nothing to convince the hierachy of their true Catholicism. In contrast, Irish and German Catholics were seldom Masons or Odd Fellows.

The major conflict between the doctrinally correct immigrant Catholics and the Creole Catholics arose over the latter's membership in the American Party. As noted earlier the Louisiana Know-Nothing movement welcomed the votes and leadership of Creoles and in turn removed the anti-Catholic plank of the national party from the state platform. But it continued to degrade immigrants and urged their limitation which to Irish and German Catholics only seemed to prove the lacklustre character of Creole Catholicism. They reasoned that in view of the large-scale Catholic immigration, the Creoles were in reality attempting to curtail the growth of the American Catholic Church; "war against foreigners is little more than a pretext," declared the editor of the *Southern Standard*, "War to Catholicism is the true aim and object" of the American Party. In Abbé Perché's words, "proscription of Catholicism is the principal object of the Know-Nothings." Certainly the secrecy of the party's councils and the rabid anti-Catholicism of the organs of the American Party in New Orleans gave validity to this argument.

Though the rift in the Church between Creole and immigrant Catholics remained pronounced throughout the decade, it became less intense in the late fifties. Creoles began to participate in city-wide Catholic affairs along with their immigrant co-religionists. Antagonism was further reduced as the nativism of the American party waned. And on the eve of the Civil War Creole and immigrant Catholics became more united in face of the increased threat of the slavery question to the city and the South.

PROTESTANTS

The problems that faced Protestantism in New Orleans were manifold. Many Protestants belonged to a seasonal merchant group, a fact which meant that churches were nearly empty and poorly financed four to five months of the year. "The flock is scarcely gathered before it is scattered" complained a local minister.[9] Religious lethargy was almost endemic among Protestants who felt no kinship with the local churches or who were captivated by the more secular entertainments of the Cresecent City. According to an Eastern magazine, New Orleans churches were "like missionary stations on the edge of barbarism."[10] Militant Protestants viewed themselves akin to early Christian martyrs surrounded by the fleshpots of a New Rome. Or as one embattled editor saw it, New Orleans Protestants were

> a Spartan band, for our city is a Thermopylae. A small body of heroic spirits, composing a forlorn hope and representing some four or five denominations, occupying the pass—contending manfully against the vast waves of vice, dissipation, corruption, error and crime.[11]

Despite the adverse condition and the pessimism of local church people, there was a significant increase of Protestant churches. Of thirty-seven white Protestant churches and missions listed in the 1860 city directory, twenty-seven had been founded since 1844. As the non-Catholic middle and working class became more stable and permanent, they renewed the intimate associations with church bodies they had known before moving to New Orleans.

The Protestant Episcopal Church claimed to be the oldest Protestant denomination in New Orleans. Its Christ Church congregation, dating from 1805, for many years was the only Protestant church in the city. St. Paul's was added in 1838 and between 1844 and 1853 seven more churches opened; in 1857 there were 734 communicants and 875 Sunday school pupils on the church rolls. The Episcopalian Church drew many of its members from among the wealthier Anglo-Americans. Some of them were Anglicans before arriving in New Orleans; others undoubtedly joined becaues of its superior prestige, an attraction that doubtless counted also with a certain number of well-to-do Creole and French and German immigrant families who entered the church. The fact that the Episcopalian theology (low church) was not as demanding as the Catholic, as harsh as the Presbyterian, as cold as the

Unitarian, or as vulgar as the evangelical sects, made it a comfortable religion for the merchant princes of New Orleans. Its "chastened conservatism," to use Bishop Leonidas Polk's phrase, must have had a special appeal to this class.

The Episcopal clergy could boast of no outstanding leader in philanthropy and none noted for his sermons. Leonidas Polk, Bishop of the Diocese of Louisiana and later a Confederate General, spent very little time in New Orleans. For years he preferred the solace of his library, paintings, and flower gardens on his Bayou La Fourche plantation. His idyll was destroyed by his failure to make a profit raising sugar and in 1854 he moved to New Orleans where he became pastor of Trinity Church. In spite of Polk's occasional perigrinations (an assistant pastor managed Trinity Church) he conducted his diocese with a fair degree of pomp and efficiency.

A Methodist church had been founded in 1825, but this early and rather auspicious origin proved misleading; the Methodist cause withered on the vine until the Protestant upsurge of the forties and fifties. During the 1850's white membership in the Methodist Episcopal Church, South, increased from 590 to 1,037; in 1860 it was the largest Protestant church body in New Orleans. The local Methodist churches—thirteen of them in 1860—appealed primarily to lower middle class Americans in the First and Fourth Districts. Their pastors were not among the stellar lights of New Orleans Protestantism and they were even denied the importance of having a resident Bishop. However what the Methodists lacked in ability, prestige, and finances they compensated for in zeal. Theirs was the most elaborate Sunday school program in the city with 138 teachers and 1,070 pupils in 1858. Indeed the Sunday schools grew so rapidly that the church had to rent halls; in the Third District the German mission held its Sabbath school in the very un-Methodist surroundings of a beer garden. Each church had an annual Sunday school anniversary and once a year a city-wide celebration was held in one of the larger churches. On these occasions proud parents and helpless visitors were regaled with lengthy convocation sermons and stuttered student recitals of such moral and sentimental favorites as "My Mother's Dead," "I'll Never Use Tobacco," "Temperance Boy," and "Farewell Mother."

Like the Methodists, New Orleans Presbyterianism opened its first church in the 1820's and then remained almost moribund until the Protestant revival two decades later when between 1843 and 1860 eight more Presbyterian churches were started. A separate New Orleans Presbytery, covering the southern part of Louisiana, was established in 1854.

The local Presbyterian body had the support of wealthy merchants and enjoyed a prestige nearly equal to that of the Protestant Episcopal Church. Much of the Presbyterian status arose from its ministers who were the best known and the ablest in the Protestant community. Of these, the Reverend Benjamin Morgan Palmer, a "strict calvinist," was the most outstanding. Though a young man he had been lured in 1855 from Charleston, South Carolina, by an offer of the pastorate of the impressive new First Presbyterian Church on Lafayette Square at the incredible salary of $6,000 a year. His sermons attracted large audiences and he was extolled in the press. "Seldom," wrote an awed editor, "have the people of this city been permitted to listen to discourses delivered with so much earnestness, eloquence, and power." As the Civil War approached Palmer's unqualified advocacy of slavery—it was he declared the "providential destiny" of the South—and his unflinching advocacy of military means to maintain the peculiar institution made him far and away the leading figure in New Orleans Protestantism.

Itinerate Baptist Missionaries visited New Orleans early in the century, but the first known church, organized with thirty-two Negroes and sixteen whites, was not formed until 1818. It lasted only two years, but in 1826 a Negro Baptist church was opened and in 1843 and 1851 two white congregations were started. These Baptist churches had few members, seldom totalling more than two hundred souls, but they seemed to have the characteristic zeal of that faith. The very fact that they constructed the thousand-seat Coliseum Place Baptist Church with less than one hundred members on the rolls attested to their religious optimism whatever doubt it might have cast upon their wisdom. Support for the Baptist cause came almost entirely from a body of working and lower middle class Americans with the result that the local congregations were almost continuously in financial difficulties—they even lost one church when its mortgage was foreclosed. So small and so poor were the local Baptists that the parent Southern Baptist Church considered New Orleans missionary country and its churches proper objects of support by national missionary societies. "There does not exist a more important missionary field domestic or foreign than this great city," a Baptist official proclaimed in 1853.[12] He could see no reason for sending missionaries to Shanghai when New Orleans was at hand. The only local benefactor was a merchant, Cornelius Paulding, who bequeathed the church a valuable building and property; even here the benefit was limited since the trustees through collusion or stupidity sold the bequest for $21,000, only to find the purchasers reselling it almost immediately for $35,000.

The history of Unitarianism in ante-bellum New Orleans was really the biography of the Reverend T. S. Clapp. Originally a Presbyterian, Clapp came to the Crescent City in 1822 to preach for that denomination. After much soul searching, he became convinced that the trinitarian doctrine was not valid, publically renounced his old faith, joined the Unitarian Association, and in 1834 began preaching in what he called the First Congregational Unitarian Church of New Orleans, but more commonly known as the Strangers' Church or simply Reverend Clapp's Church. In many other Southern communities Clapp's actions might have meant a form of social and financial suicide, but in New Orleans, with its many New Englanders, it did not prove harmful to the Parson. His sermons, considered masterpieces of that difficult art, and a choir that added color to the normally simple Unitarian services, drew not only New Englanders, but other persons as well. Clapp's personality also contributed to the popularity of his church. In times of crisis such as the yellow fever epidemics he courageously worked among the city's sick and dying. Unlike most Protestant servants of God, who were firmly assured of the damnation of their Catholic religious counterparts, Clapp showed an amazing tolerance. Finally Clapp's very theology was attuned to the optimistic business philosophy of New Orleans; "this age," he declared, "is more glorious than any of its predecessors." His Unitarianism demanded of its followers only a certain reasonableness, and its vague transcendentalism was romantic enough to appeal to an age which had forgotten its Hume but remembered its Scott. At the same time Clapp, in contrast to his New England confreres, refrained from disturbing his wealthy congregation with demands for social reforms.[13]

Evincing the missionary complex so characteristic of American Protestantism, several faiths made efforts to establish churches for seamen, immigrants, and Negroes. A walk down Gallatin Street would have convinced all but free thinkers that visiting mariners needed soul-saving. Accordingly the Episcopalian Young Men's Missionary Society opened a Seamen's Bethel on Esplanade Street which after several years evolved into St. Paul's Church. The Methodists' Seamen's Mission had a rather fitful existence from 1843 to the Civil War. Hardly more successful was a Presbyterian Seamen's Bethel near the docks on Esplanade Street. Though begun as early as 1836 it was never more than a small, rarely attended, mission. The New Orleans churches failed to dent the waterfront palaces of sin.

Immigrants have always been fair prey for American Protestant denominations and the Europeans who landed in New Orleans in the 1850's were no exception. The Irish however seemed impervious to Protestant prayers and appeals, but the Germans and French offered what seemed to be unbounded possibilities. The Protestant Episcopal Church formed a missionary society to preach the Gospel to French and German immigrants. Their labors in the vineyard went almost for nought. The more militant Methodists formed a tract society in 1855 to deliver religious leaflets and pamphlets among the unchurched immigrants and they established four missions for Germans. The local Teutons perhaps found American Methodism a bit confusing, but the missions provided services in their own language and by 1860 there were 224 church members. The Presbyterians, whose theology was close to that of Calvinist denominations found in parts of France, Switzerland, and Germany, were able to gather a small following among the immigrant population. There were two German churches established in the fifties and a handful of Germans and French attended the regular Presbyterian churches. The Baptists, with their frontier background, were so totally alien to European immigrants that it was not until the late fifties that they could open a small German mission.

The majority of the non-Catholic Germans belonged to the Lutheran churches which had sprung up with the immigrant waves after 1840. Initially the Lutheran churches were affiliated with the Texas Lutherans in a common synod, but in 1853 C. F. W. Walther, the great religious leader associated with the Missouri Synod, sent representatives to New Orleans, and by 1856 three of the four Lutheran churches in the city has joined the Missouri Synod. These Lutheran churches were social as well as religious institutions for the Protestant German population; indeed they were the principal force in maintaining a German feeling among the immigrants. The pastors were German, services were in German, German customs were encouraged, and as a result the Lutheran impact on the Protestant community was negligible.

Most of the Protestant missionary endeavors were expanded on seamen bethels and German-language churches; few efforts were made to contact Negroes, make them welcome, furnish separate churches, provide pastors, and train Negro church leaders. Only the Methodist Episcopal Church, South, might be considered an exception. The Methodist Church excluded Negroes from white congregations, but instead established separate chapels for their worship. In 1860 there were three chapels—Wesley, Soule, and Winans—with 1,174 members, mostly slaves. The preachers were themselves slaves, who according to a newspaper account could "read, and though colored, preach a fair sermon." The Louisiana Conference appointed over each church a white pastor whose duty was to preach on Sunday afternoons, administer the sacraments, and maintain a "wholesome discipline." Sunday schools were open to Negro children who were taught by the "oral system" in order to offer religious instruction without facing legal restrictions on teaching slaves how to read. There is no record of slaves' opinions, but the Negro chapels certainly met the approval of the white community; a contemporary observer reported that the chapels "are large and orderly and enjoy the good will and protection of the city authorities. They are spiritually prosperous also, and do much good."[14]

The Protestant Episcopal Church had free and slave Negro communicants and Sunday school scholars at several of its churches and opened a short-lived, one year to be exact, mission for Negroes; by 1860 there were no more than 150 colored adults and children in the Anglican churches. The Presbyterian Church U. S. made only nominal efforts to bring Negroes into the fold— a handful attended regular services until 1859 when the lecture room of the First Presbyterian Church was used for services to Negroes. The Baptist Church, with a greater tradition of work with Negroes, formed three Negro congregations in the 1850's.

All of the above church bodies set aside separate sections of their churches for Negroes or formed mission churches affiliated with white congregations which provided pastors who in turn occasionally employed Negro assistants. This white domination and the everlasting sermons on St. Paul's admonition to the servant to return to his master were undoubtedly resented. Therefore some Negroes sought religious organizations which were independent of white influences. The most important of these all-Negro bodies was the African Methodist Episcopal Church which had been chartered in 1848 by ten free Negroes and within a few years membership had increased and two more churches were added; by 1858 the African church boasted of 1,500 members. Services were conducted by free Negro ministers, one of whom was appointed by the Missouri Conference of the national African Methodist Episcopal Church. Although the churches had an excellent reputation for proper conduct, their doom was sealed by a city ordinance in 1858 declaring all Negro religious bodies illegal. After the police closed their churches, representatives of the Negroes went to court seeking to prevent continued enforcement of the ordinance. The District Court sustained their plea, but the State Supreme Court held that the "African race are strangers to our Constitution and are subject of special and exceptional legislation." There are indication that services were continued on a clandestine basis in rented rooms and houses, but they were subject to suppression by the police and it was not until after the Civil War that the African Methodist Episcopal churches were legally re-established in New Orleans.

The semi-religious Voodoo cult also found Negro adherents in the city. The Voodoo mysteries were of African origin, but came to New Orleans from Haiti, where they had been partially mixed with elements of Catholicism. Following is a description of their rites:

> When they meet a sort of altar is erected in the middle of the room, and on it they burn a peculiar kind of gum, and in a state of entire or partial nudity, circle round and round in a dance which, to them, proves strongly fascinating. Other indescribable rites are then proceeded with, and spells, for good and evil, are woven for friends or enemies as the exigency of the times may require.[15]

At these meetings, held on the lake shore or in isolated homes (one was a dilapidated mansion in the middle of a raquette field along Elysian Fields Avenue), "queens" and "witch doctors" unfolded the mysteries of the cult to an audience composed of slaves, free Negroes, and some white women. The Voodoo cult had a certain amount of social acceptance in spite of its ceremonies and secrecy. At one time Voodoo practicioners threatened to sue the Third Municipality for having its police break up one of their religious observances. Maria Laveau, a Voodoo "queen," was unmolested in her nocturnal rituals and "Doctor John," a cult medicine man, was popularized by whites as much as by Negroes.

The Protestant religious boom in New Orleans in the last two decades before the Civil War brought in its train the usual host of non-denominational societies. These inter-church groups seemed to proliferate where Protestantism was sizable and militant and provided therefore the best indication of a viable and self-conscious Protestant community. At least five of these agencies were national organizations with a local sphere of operation. The Southern Aid Society, a non-denominational organization originating in New York but without the open or tacit anti-slavery views of the American Missionary Association, and the American Home Missionary Society sent missionaries and poor relief to New Orleans. In 1854 the American Tract Society opened in New Orleans a Southwestern branch to facilitate distribution of the Word of God. Less well known was the local representative of the American and Foreign Christian Union, an agency to convert Catholic immigrants to Protestantism. The Young Men's Christian Association founded a New Orleans center in 1854 with the ardent support and cooperation of leading Protestant churches. It provided a healthy religious atmosphere for single young men and a social center for many activities varying from polite lectures to a series of winter dances. Members supplemented the tract and Bible distribution of the city's churches; they administered charity to the needy, operated an employment service, and cared for the sick and dying during the yellow fever epidemic of 1858.

The only local organization designed to convert the heathen through inter-church cooperation was the New Orleans Bible Society. This agency, founded in 1840, was concerned with "such measures as will best increase and multiply copies of the Holy Scriptures, the Book of Life . . . in the City."[16] In one year it distributed 9,700 Bibles in thirteen languages and an estimated 430,000 religious tracts. The Society was instrumental in establishing Bible House, a center for their operations, the headquarters of the local branch of the American Tract Society, a temporary chapel for small congregations, a lecture hall, and a free library sponsored by the Y. M. C. A.

The labor of these inter-denominational societies revealed a great deal of harmony among Protestants, but such fraternal sentiments did not always extend to Roman Catholics. A militant anti-Catholicism may have arisen in part out of a feeling of insecurity in an environment where Catholics outnumbered Protestants. The two decades of anti-Catholic agitation in the United States which preceded the fifties had insured that it would take little to kindle the always-smouldering anti-Popery feeling of many American Protestants. Anti-Catholicism was probably accentuated by several minor irritants. Among them were the presence of a large number of Catholic priests (including Jesuits!) and nuns who were believed to keep their immigrant followers in a state of ignorance and subserviency; the adverse effects of Lent on business; open religious parades and services; the public proclamation by the Bishop of the doctrine of the Immaculate Conception and an extensive church ceremony connected with the pastoral announcement, the superior attitude taken by Catholic speakers like Orestes A. Brownson, editors like Abbé Perché, and even the common immigrant laymen (one Irishman bodily threw a Protestant coleporteur out of his shanty); and the belief that the Catholic Church was opposed to the Bible, the source of Christian morality and Republican virtue.

The major form of anti-Catholicism was stimulated by the view that the Catholic Church was somehow responsible for the city's indifferent observance of the Sabbath. Certainly to the devout American Protestant, nurtured as he was in a rigid adherence to the Sabbath, a New Orleans Sunday had all the fascination of a box seat on the edge of the Inferno. One Protestant minister mourned:

> Think of Paul in Athens! how his spirit was stirred there! Were he to rise in this century and take a walk through this metropolis, would there be nothing to stir his spirit? Let him go about of a Sunday night. The few churches tolerably full to be sure, but room for more. There is Fowler, the phrenologist giving the religion of bumps at Odd-fellows Hall; Christie's or Campbell's Minstrels, laughing and singing in burnt cork at the Armory; grand opera at the Orleans — perhaps "Les Hugenots" on the bill; horse-riding at the Ampitheatre by Miss Somebody; St. Charles full from pit to gallery; Varieties ditto; and so for a full page. The world is not saved yet. These civilized heathen are hard to pluck from the burning; easier to save Chinese or Mexicans.[17]

In the eyes of the stricter Protestants not only operas, plays, concerts, dances, and lectures, but also parades, balloon ascensions, open coffee houses, lodge anniversaries, cricket matches, bull and bear fights, and horse races were inadmissible on Sunday. Such Sabbath amusements seemed to "blunt the moral sensibilities of our citizens."[18] Since both by tradition and doctrine the Catholic (and the Lutheran) Church had no opposition to harmless pleasures on the Lord's Day, it was only logical to assume that the Sabbath breakdown in New Orleans could be attributed to Catholic and Lutheran attitudes.

> This disregard of the Sabbath is not of American [i.e. Protestant] origin. It cannot date back to the time when stern, indomitable men planted the seeds of empire in the wilderness, or heroes nurtured its growth in the times of revolutionary struggle.[19]

Anti-Catholicism in New Orleans, as elsewhere in the nation, took the form of nativism. There had been nativist agitation as early as 1835, and in 1849 an anti-Catholic mob destroyed the office of the *Propagateur Catholique*. In the following year the ubiquitous E. Z. C. Judson ("Ned Buntline") visited New Orleans with the hope of fostering anti-Catholicism. Failing to do this he returned north and published, for the times, a salacious novella entitled *The Mysteries and Miseries of New Orleans*. The Know-Nothing movement of the fifties offered another opportunity for nativists. While it is true that the Louisiana American party included Creole Catholics and it quarrelled with the national party over exclusion of Roman Catholics, it did display nevertheless its own brand and breed of anti-Catholic polemics. Without criticising the sacramental side of the Roman Catholic Church, press and party officials belabored aspects of the Church that were vital particulars of the faith. The Louisiana American party was especially concerned with the temporal claims of the Catholic Church and the "sacerdotal interference" of its priests which, if expanded, would lead to a "spiritual and civil despotism."[20] In other words, Know-Nothing spokesmen accepted the supposed Gallican position of the Creole Catholics (a heretical point of view!), but sternly denounced the "ultramontane" beliefs of the Papacy and its American representatives. The institution of the Papacy, an essential element of Catholic doctrine, was subject to bitter Know-Nothing attack. The Papacy, insisted the *Crescent*, "has always lived on bayonets — on those of Charlemagne, or Francis, or Charles, or Napoleon." The *Semi-Weekly Creole* was even more virulent: "The papal power throughout the world may be traced in lines of blood." This paper contended that the Pope's temporal power was a challenge to the American legal system; a papal conspiracy threatened the existence of American freedom. "The Pope is the *presiding general* of the army . . . the archbishops, priests, and curates are the subordinate officers, and that includes the whole body of Catholic Irish [who] could be moved by a nod and made to act in any manner by a wink of the *General*, the Pope..." The American hierarchy who led these "superstitious Catholics" were charged with "opposing our public school system — absorbing all church property, contrary to the genius of our laws, and accepting titles and receiving investitures unknown to republican usages." Meanwhile the Jesuits were readying their ignorant flocks for the day of "universal domination." It is no wonder that the Catholic press never doubted that the American Party was anti-Catholic!

While anti-Catholicism raged, other forces in the community tended to counter-balance it. Most important was indifference toward religion. In a society whose fundamental drive was the accumulation of wealth, theological wrangles were bad business and dull reading. The transformation of the American Party from a vehicle of nativism in the mid-fifties to a mere political machine by the end of the decade removed a major source of anti-Catholicism. The actions and attitudes of the Catholic Church also reduced tension. Catholic charitable institutions and the self-sacrifice of nuns and priests during the yellow fever epidemics, a time when Protestant ministers were roundly criticised for leaving the city, broke down antagonism to the faith. T. S. Clapp, admittedly more tolerant than most Protestant clerics, warmly applauded the Catholic clergy; they were, in his words, "Models of clerical wisdom, decorum, and propriety."[21] Furthermore Roman Catholic officials, with their stress on "fixed conservative principles" were in accord with the dominant Southern viewpoint. There was no fear that the Catholic Church harbored abolitionist sentiments; slavery was sanctioned by religious authorities, and priests and religious orders owned slaves. In 1860 at a provincial council the wrath of God was called down on John Brown and like-minded fanatics, and loyalty to the Southland was affirmed. The Catholic Church was safe.

JEWS.

The number of Jews in New Orleans was small, probably not over 2,000 in the 1850's. The first Jews had entered the city in the colonial period and their numbers were augmented in the decades that followed by the arrival of isolated traders and merchants from the Sephardic settlements in Rhode Island, New York, South Carolina, France, and the West Indies. Not until the German migration of the 1840's and 1850's was there a noticeable increase of Jews in New Orleans.

The first synagogue in the city, Gates of Mercy, was founded in 1828 by German and Sephardic Jews. The latter group, dissatisfied with the German ritual used in the synagogue, formed their own Portuguese rite Congregation Dispersed of Judah in 1846. Judah P. Touro, a fellow Sephardic Jew, gave the Congregation a building at the corner of Canal and Bourbon Streets which had formerly held an Episcopalian church; late in the 1850's the Congregation moved to a new location on Carondelet Street. Touro, it should be added, also contributed to the support of the German congregation. A second German rite congregation, Gates of Prayer, was organized in Lafayette in 1850; after utilizing temporary buildings, including a Methodist meeting house, they moved into their own synagogue on Jackson Avenue in 1860. Polish Jews in 1857 founded The Right Way, a congregation so poor and with so few members that it was several years after the Civil War before they constructed a house of worship. All of the city's Jewish congregations were orthodox; however, except for the Polish Jews, the ideas of reformed Judaism, associated with Rabbi Issac M. Wise of Cincinnati, found many sympathizers in the New Orleans Jewry. When a reformed synagogue (Temple Sinai) was established in 1870 its first Rabbi was James Koppel Gutheim who at various times in the 1850's had served as Rabbi of Dispersed of Judah and Gates of Mercy.

The local Jewish population showed little religious militancy. Membership in the synagogues was always small and Zionist organizations disbanded for lack of support. Jews like Judah P. Benjamin and Lieutenant Governor Henry Hyams were only ethnically Jewish; they took no part in religious observances and in Benjamin's case at least were totally ignorant of their Jewish heritage. Even those Jews who felt some attachment to their kinsmen and to the synagogue were closely assimilated into the community structure. The diary of Clara Solomon, daughter of a prominent Jewish merchant, presents a picture of indifference to traditional Jewish separatism. She took only a minor interest in the synagogue, ignored Jewish holidays and dietary laws, and paid no heed to taboos on intermarriage as she periodically fell in love with Gentile boys. She thoroughly, one could say breathlessly, approved of the marriage of Henry Hyams with Judith Ann Spriggs in the First Presbyterian Church. Isaac Marks, merchant and president of the Fireman's Charitable Association, was the author of most of the first platform of the nativist American Party; he named one of his sons after Henry Clay and another son became an Episcopalian minister after the Civil War. Theodore Moise, a portrait painter, married a Catholic and two of his sons eventually entered Roman Catholic religious orders. Then there is the story, possibly apocryphal, of an early Rabbi who married a Catholic and only by the earnest pleading of synagogue members did his wife desist from burying him with a crucifix.

Catholic Masons, unchurched Protestants, Christian Jews, and a sizable number of free thinkers (there was at least one rationalist society in the city) provided New Orleans with more religious variety and less zeal than perhaps any other metropolis in the

Street Railroad Car, New Orleans

United States. The religious revival of the fifties — Catholic and Protestant — dented, but hardly shook, the vast edifice of religious indifference in the Crescent City.

NOTES

[1]Klein, "Social Interaction of the Creoles and Anglo-Americans in New Orleans," 78.
[2]George Rose, *The Great Country; or Impressions of America* (London, 1868), 191.
[3]John Gilmary Shea, *History of the Catholic Church in the United States from the Fifth Provincal Council of Baltimore, 1843, to the Second Plenary Council of Baltimore, 1860* (New York, 1892), 268, 270.
[4]Quoted in Henry F. Brownson, *Orestes A. Brownson's Middle Life from 1845 to 1855* (Detroit, 1899), 608.
[5]P. G. T. Beauregard to Major J. G. Bernard, November 16, 1853, Beauregard Papers, Archives of the Howard-Tilton Memorial Library, Tulane University, New Orleans.
[6]Alexander Dimitry to N. R. Jennings, February 20, 1851, Hennen-Jennings Papers, 1840-1859, Louisiana State University Archives, Baton Rouge.
[7]*Catholic Standard*, February 5, 1860.
[8]*Grado Vigesimo de la Mazoneria Escocesa Y Segundo del Consejo de Kadosch* (New Orleans?, n.d.), 371.
[9]Charles B. Galloway, *The Editor-Bishop Linus Parker; His Life and Writings* (Nashville, 1886), 63.
[10]"Editor's Easy Chair," *Harper's New Monthly Magazine*, VII (November, 1853), 846.
[11]*Semi-Weekly Creole*, April 28, 1855.
[12]Southern Baptist Church, *Proceedings of the Convention*, 1853 (Richmond, 1853), 62.
[13]Clapp, *Autobiographical Sketches*, 254. The church censuses of 1850 and 1860 do not include three additional Protestant churches which by other evidence had followers in the Crescent City. The 1856 director lists the First Christian Church; its most conspicuous member was the *Picayune* editor, A. C. Bullitt. A few blocks away was the Church of the New Jerusalem associated with the local Swedenborgians. There are also indications that the semi-religious Spiritualist movement had a few table-rapping adherents in New Orleans.
[14]*Semi-Weekly Creole*, October 27, 1855.
[15]*Weekly Mirror*, April 23, 1859.
[16]Meeting Notes of the New Orleans Bible Society, 1841-1850 (MS), Louisiana Historical Society Library, New Orleans. In 1850 this organization was renamed the South Western Bible Society.
[17]Galloway, *The Editor-Bishop Linus Parker*, 57-58.
[18]*Semi-Weekly Creole*, February 21, 1855.
[19]*Ibid.*
[20]*American Exponent*, January 5, 1856.
[21]Clapp, *Autobiographical Sketches*, 235-241.

Chapter VIII

EDUCATION

In New Orleans the public schools have been growing in favor, although they have not yet led to the establishment of the higher institutions for academic and collegiate education. . . .[1]

PUBLIC SCHOOLS.

Before 1841 it can hardly be said that public schools existed in New Orleans, but in that year a group of Second Municipality merchants and lawyers, almost all of whom were northern-born, secured the passage of a state law establishing independent school districts in the New Orleans municipalities and obtaining a small subsidy from the state government. Under the leadership of Samuel J. Peters and Joshua Baldwin, president of the school board of the second Municipality, the noted Massachusetts educator, Horace Mann, was consulted about the means of forming a free public school system. At Mann's suggestion, his "excellent friend," John A. Shaw of Bridgewater, Masachusetts, was appointed first Superintendent of Public Schools in the Second Municipality. He was, Horace Mann testified, "an excellent and successful teacher of youth"; he had operated an academy in Bridgewater and as a state legislator led a successful struggle to prevent closure of the normal schools and dismissal of Horace Mann.[2] Shaw was thoroughly aware of the newer American and foreign pedogogical currents and was a confirmed exponent of Mann's basic belief that free public education was essential in a democratic society.

With Shaw's background, and the ardent support of the Board of Directors of the Public Schools of the Second Municipality, it is no surprise that upon his arrival in 1842 he proceeded to develop a New England school system on the shores of the Mississippi. Teachers were obtained from the North, so many that by 1851 a Yankee school marm could write that "With few exceptions, the teachers are natives of New England."[3] Teaching techniques, the division of elementary schools into primary and intermediate divisions, rules governing daily life of the pupils, and curricula were borrowed directly from Massachusetts public school systems. Textbooks from the beginning were purchased in Boston and were the same as those used for the corresponding grades in Massachusetts. The authors were themselves frequently

Bay Staters and their books reflected a New England outlook. Thus children who pondered over William Goodrich's popular Peter Parley histories and geographies were acquainted with the Puritans and hardly at all with Virginia settlers and they were required to answer such provincial questions as "How far is Bellows Falls from Boston, and in what direction?" In addition to textbooks, school apparatus, furniture, and library books were purchased in the Northeast.

From the Second Municipality the public school idea spread to the rest of the city and the neighboring suburbs. First Municipality officials worked with a committee from the Second Municipality school board and borrowed Shaw to establish their schools. For their English-language schools they brought in northern teachers and textbooks; even the first Superintendent of Schools was a Yankee teacher, Franklin Sawyer. Charles Gayarré, who served on the First Municipality school board, and Alexander Dimitry, who set up the Third Municipality school system, were ardent advocates of Horace Mann's teaching and attempted to propagate — unsuccessfully — the New Englander's ideas when they served as State Superintendents of Public Schools.[4]

The public school systems established or influenced by Shaw and his cohorts were highly successful. The number of public school pupils in the Second Municipality increased from 840 in 1842 to 3,155 in 1850 to 3,550 in 1859; in the First Municipality from 615 students in 1844 to 2,010 in 1850 to 2,557 in 1859; the Third Municipality school population rose from 230 children in 1844 to 1,120 in 1850 to 2,326 in 1859. No figures are extant on Lafayette schools but by 1852 it had 1,936 students enrolled and seven years later it had 2,164. Not only did the schools grow in number, but they introduced practices which, according to the Boston *Common School Journal,* "will not injure our New England schools to imitate." These included free textbooks and stationery, phonetic reading, free lecture series, a central school library, free copies of the *Common School Journal* to each teacher, and an active adult education program. Indeed New Englanders lavished praise on the local school systems; one woman stated that she had visited many Massachusetts schools "yet never have I witnessed any schools better ordered and disciplined, where classes were better taught, and where there existed such a friendly feeling between the teacher and the taught."[5] Henry Barnard, the famed educator, reported to Horace Mann that the Second Municipality schools would "compare favorably in point of discipline, thoroughness, & methods of instruction, regularity of attention &c with the schools of the East."[6] And Samuel Goodrich informed a New Orleans audience that some of its schools "would be deemed excellent in any part of New England—nay in Boston itself."[7]

The average elementary school pupil entered a neighborhood school at the age of six and, if like many students he did not drop out, he would spend the next six years in school. The children, divided by sex (except in two small schools in the Third District), attended class six hours a day, five days a week, for two five-month terms. In the primary years (grades one through three) they were taught the rudiments of reading, writing, spelling, and geography; the intermediate grades (four through six) were devoted to advanced geography; United States history (and ancient history in the Second District), grammar (in French and English in the downtown schools), elements of composition, and, of course, the favorites of the day, elocution and declamation. Singing classes, using Lowell Mason's *The Boston School Song Book*, were offered in all of the schools.

High Schools for boys and girls were opened in the Second Municipality in 1843 and by 1852 each district had publically supported secondary schools. The schools were supervised by special high school committees composed of three men from the district school board and three residents of the district. Like the elementary schools each high school had a principal responsible to the district superintendent. Only those children who proved themselves academically superior were eligible to enter the high schools; in addition, the need in many families for the income their adolescent children might earn, kept enrollment at a minimum. In the First District, which had the largest high schools, there were never more than 223 students.

The high school student entered the three-year course at the age of twelve or thirteen. During these years he was exposed to a rigid and demanding curriculum. Following is a list of subjects taught at the First District Boy's High School in 1856; with a few variations it is similar to that offered in the Girl's High School and the high schools of the other districts.[8]

First Year: Analytical Grammar, Rhetoric, Universal History, Algebra, French Pronounciation and Orthography, Latin, and Weekly Select Reading, Composition, and Declamation.

Second Year: Rhetoric, Physical Geography, Chemistry, Geometry and Trigonometry, French, Latin, and Weekly Composition and Declamation.

Third Year: Physical Geography, Intellectual Philosophy, Surveying and Navigation, Natural Philosophy, Astronomy, Outlines of Bookkeeping, French, Latin, Weekly Composition and Declamation and General Review.

The textbooks used in some of these courses were often remarkably advanced. For example, Abercombie's *Intellectual Philosophy* (psychology) and Boyd's *Elements of Rhetoric and Literary Criticism* demanded an excellent reading and cognitive ability for a lad of fifteen. Francis Wayland's *Elements of Moral Science*, which was used in the Second Municipality high schools, required a high level of philosophical sophistication from its juvenile readers.

Each year the district public schools held an annual examination in the schools or in a public hall. A committee of teachers and school board members quizzed students on their proficiency in various subjects. The examination was enlivened by a program prepared by the school children which included a medley of songs and a host of uplifting student orations. Over the years the annual exams and the high school graduations came to be popular social events; politicians, prompted perhaps by the presence of so many parents and newspapermen, gave speeches and presented prizes of books and medals to special students. There was also a sizable number of young blades present whose attention it was reported was focused not on intellectual or political topics but on the young lady teachers. It may be assumed that these maidens, bored with their charges and windy politicians, were well aware of the eligible bachelors.

The graduates of the high school were frequently employed as teachers in the school system and by the mid-1850's a few had become principals. To provide further teacher training a one-year normal school was established in 1858. Funds for the operation came originally from the city and First District school board, but in 1860 the state government assumed control of the normal school. Classes were taught by four teachers, themselves graduates of eastern normal schools, in the Girl's High School of the First District. The students were given an intensive program of studies, primarily of a pedogogical nature, and engaged in practice teaching throughout their training period. By 1861 the normal school had 116 pupils enrolled and had become, a New Orleanian bragged, "a *crowning feature* of our system of public education."[9]

The public schools while unquestionably successful — sensationally so in comparison to the rest of the state and the South in general—were not without problems and critics. There was, for example, the persistent issue of financing. Funds came from state property taxes—about $85,000 in the mid-fifties—and from sale of certain public lands. The city government appropriated funds from general revenues at an average of twenty dollars a student and it granted general appropriations for school construction, rentals, and repairs. By 1860 the common council was spending $259,960 for maintenance of the school system. In addition revenues were provided in the latter part of the decade from lands willed to the city by John McDonogh and an insignificant sum came from night school and high school tuition. But in spite of increased revenue, schools were overcrowded and badly in need of repair. Worse, teachers were poorly paid; in 1854 the average primary school teacher in the Second District received forty-five dollars a month, or less than a dock worker. Pay was slightly higher in the other districts with primary teachers paid $600 a year, intermediate and high school teachers between $600 and $1,320; principals received from $1,200 to $1,800 and the district superintendents $2,500. Even these meagre salaries, which often forced teachers to supplement their incomes by offering private lessons after school hours, were subject to cuts by the common council and penny-pinching school boards.

Teachers were not given appointment with tenure; they had to be elected each year by the school board. This "annual farce," as the *Picayune* termed it, undoubtedly made teachers insecure and fostered political acuteness rather than academic proficiency. The system was criticised in the press, though it must be entered in its favor that according to the diary of Thomas K. Wharton, a First District school board member, politics was not a factor in selection.

There were also critics who contended that the northern teachers were "warm admirers and apologists of that libelous publication known as Uncle Tom's Cabin."[10] The *Delta* derided the practice of employing Yankee female abolitionists and insisted that the First District school board dismiss them. Other uptown newspapers castigated the *Delta* for introducing sectional animosity into the school system. In the latter fifties state school superintendents constantly harped on the need of insuring "soundness in Southern sentiment" among teachers and eliminating Yankee teachers who were "mischievous spies and agents of those mortally hating us and our institutions." They fondly hoped that the normal school would provide teachers who were *"Southern born* and *Southern educated."*[11] In New Orleans these stern warnings of state school officials were totally ignored.

Occasionally the curriculum offered in the high schools was subject to critical scrutiny. Thus in 1853 a school board committee in the First District favored an increase of science classes, the substitution of Greek for Moral Science and bookkeeping for astronomy, and improvements in the teaching of English and French. Newspapers occasionally questioned the wisdom of teaching girls bookkeeping and requiring Latin and French, but no changes were made.

A far more burning issue was the question of Bible reading and prayers in class. Because of political pressures religious observances had been removed from the First and Second Municipality schools by 1850 and under the directorship of the freethinking Alexander Dimitry they had never been introduced in the Third Municipality. But in the Fourth District daily readings from the King James Bible were required and in 1854 as many as seven hundred Catholic children were removed from the district public schools. However, probably out of fear of enraging Protestant sentiment further, the Church relented and the children returned to school. The issue was not raised again in the ante-bellum period.

Separate school districts, which developed out of the tri-municipal system, were not abandoned with the unification of the city in 1852. Each district, including the Fourth, had its own school board and its own superintendent who were appointed by the common council and required to make quarterly reports to that body. The school directors had the power to make rules and regulations for the government of the schools, to suspend and hire teachers, and to apportion the funds allotted to the district by the state and city governments. Though the district schools came to reflect the customs, language, and politics of the separate districts, the divisions were more apparent than real. Shaw's plans had provided a fair degree of pedagogical unity throughout the city and in the fifties regular meetings were held between superintendents and school board members to discuss common problems.

With the Union occupation came the dissolution of the district school boards and the unification of the school system under a single set of directors and one superintendent.

The public school in New Orleans did more than provide its pupils with the usual three R's. It also served as an instrument of social change. Since it was free and public, and generally offered a better training than the private schools, it became a vehicle for upward mobility; it educated such lower middle class Americans as George Washington Cable, and many first generation and immigrant Irish and Germans, products of the public schools, turned up in leadership roles during the last third of the nineteenth century. Of equal significance the public school system tended to provide a unified set of symbols and to a great degree a single language for the city's conflicting ethnic elements. A French journalist considered the public schools "la gloire de la Nouvelle-Orléans" and an Anglo-Saxon editor contended:

> The prosperity of our public schools has secured for them general favor. Under their healthful influence the population of this city, divided as it is in race, language, and opinion, may be made homogeneous in its future character. Americanism will be imbibed—a love of country will grow up under a wise system of popular education.[12]

In other words the public school system served as an unifying element in the community; it created cultural homogeneity in place of cultural diversity.

PRIVATE SCHOOLS.

The largest network of private schools in New Orleans were operated by the Roman Catholic Church. The Ursuline schools had provided a religious education for the upper class for over one hundred years, but Bishop Blanc was much more interested in establishing schools for the immigrant which would be free, or with a nominal tuition. The prelate therefore encouraged teaching orders to open schools in the city. The School Sisters of Notre Dame were brought in to open parish schools at St. Alphonsus and St. Mary's in the Fourth District. The Christian Brothers opened an academy in 1851 attached to St. Patrick's Church and added another academy in St. Mary's Parish and a grade school at St. Stephen's in Jefferson City during the decade. In the Third District the Sisters of the Holy Cross and the Tertiary Carmelite Sisters opened parochial schools. Most of these schools were supported by the parish and by tuition. To aid Catholic children whose parents were unable to meet the costs of a religious education, the Catholic Free School Society (Association Catholiques de la Nouvelle-Orléans pour l'Érection d'Écoles Gratuites) was formed "sans distinction de denomination" in 1851. Under its sponsorship the Christian Brothers began a free school in St. Patrick's Parish and by 1853 it had grown to 350 students. In addition the Sisters of Charity operated a free grade and high school for girls in the heavily-immigrant Third District and the Ursuline nuns had a small free school just below the city. By 1860 over 2,500 Catholic children were attending parochial schools, the majority enrolled in Fourth District. Despite a rapid growth in the parochial school population, the Archbishop near the end of the decade declared that more educational institutions were necessary. "Unhappily," he stated, "the number of our Catholic schools is far from corresponding with the wants of our numerous population."[13]

For the rich who felt the public schools were too vulgar and the parochial schools too narrow, there were numerous private non-denominational schools in New Orleans. In 1860, for example, there were fifteen private schools in the Second District alone. Among the better-known private schools in New Orleans in this decade were: Madame Desrayaux's, Jefferson Academy, Boyer's School, New Orleans Female Collegiate Institute, High School for Young Ladies, St. Louis Institute, Mrs. D'Aquin's School, New Orleans Female Seminary, School of Madame M. D. Giraud, Goubault School, Franklin High School, Bellegrove Institute (Carrollton), and the Orleans Academic Institute. If parents wished to send their children out of the city, the rural parts of Louisiana and Mississippi were sprinkled with academies, female institutes, boarding schools, and day schools. Louisiana alone had over 150 private schools in the 1850's. Tuition at these schools varied from eight to ten dollars a month for the primary grades to fifteen to twenty dollars in the secondary. Certain schools with prestige value, such as Madame Desayraux's School, charged sixty-five dollars and above per month.

Intellectually the private schools, with rare exceptions, were inferior to the New Orleans public schools. Boys were given a basic background in the classics with occasional musical training. Science was seldom offered; even less often were they exposed to commercial courses. Judging by the subjects offered in the academies the girls were wretchedly educated. The ideal was to provide the young ladies with the essentials of a foreign language, reading, writing, arithmetic, and music, along with such wondrous subjects as tapestry, sewing, mythology, needlework, embroidery, guitar, accordion, harp, artificial flowers, lace work, drawing, painting, shell and chenille work, and beadwork. Most of the schools gave religious training and there was an occasional concern with belles-lettres. By far the best girl's school in New Orleans was the St. Louis Institute, "Female Literary and Scientific Institution," which taught grammar, rhetoric, composition, "prosody," elocution, history, geography, arithmetic, astronomy, philosophy, zoology, botany, logic, music, and French. But this school was an exception; it was obvious that social poise only slightly tempered by intellectual acumen was the aim of education for upper class southern women. These schools were to provide, one teacher insisted, "various branches of refined education" which would

> form a limited number of Young Ladies to virtue, enrich their minds with useful and agreeable knowledge and to cultivate in them whose qualities and talents which render young persons both amiable and good in the family circle, as well as in society.[14]

It was no wonder therefore that Madame de Grandfort found the graduates of these schools to be frivolous and boring.

Unlike white children, free Negro students had to chose private over public education, though their parents paid taxes to support the public schools and John McDonogh's will specifically stated that "all Classes and Castes of Color" were to be freely educated. A few wealthy free Negroes were able to educate their offspring in Paris where, in most cases, they remained. About two hundred free Negro children were enrolled at the Couvent School which had originated in 1832 when a wealthy free Negro woman donated a sizable fortune in her will toward the erection and maintenance of a school for indigent free Negro pupils with, however, some allowance for tuition students. Additional funds were gathered by other wealthy free persons of color who organized the Société Catholique pour l'Instruction des Orphelins dans l'Indigence. Funds were tied up in the courts for a number of years so that the school did not officially open until 1848. The quarrelsome but able Armand Lanusse was named principal in 1852 and on its staff were leading free Negro intellectuals, Paul Trevigne, Joanni Questy, Adolphe DuHart, and Madame Nathalie

Populus. Most of the 1,008 free Negroes who attended school in 1850 were educated in small institutions conducted in private homes in order not to arouse the fear and hostility of the white population. In spite of their caution, state laws and city ordinances were passed in the mid-fifties making it a legal offense to open a free Negro school. According to the federal census of 1860 only 275 free Negroes attended school, but the figure may have been higher since classes were held surreptitiously. As for slaves, whatever schooling they received was obtained through masters who hired tutors to increase their bondsmen's value or were secretly taught by whites and free Negroes. During the 1850's stringent laws were passed and enforced against educating slaves and by 1860 there were only a handful of literate slaves in New Orleans.

HIGHER EDUCATION.

In ante-bellum New Orleans the success of public elementary and secondary schools was not correlated with impressive gains in higher education. In 1805 the College of Orleans was established, but it was hardly more than an academy and it closed in 1824. Twenty-one years later the University of Louisiana was founded by the state government; it consisted of an already existing medical school begun in 1834, a law school (1847) and a collegiate branch. Because state aid was meagre, private endowments few, and students rare, the latter division by 1850 had been closed. The impressive collonaded college building on Common Street housed only a private grammar school. Later in the decade high school and college departments were opened, with most of the students enrolled in the preparatory school; by 1857 it was reported that there were no college students for the faculty and the appointed but unpaid teachers simply dispersed. The sad state of the college aroused consternation in the local press; the state's reaction was to close the collegiate branch and until well after the Civil War the University of Louisiana was, except for the schools of medicine and law, a paper organization.

The law department of the University in terms of enrollment could hardly be considered a success; the student body in the 1850's varied from twenty-one to thirty-six young men. The faculty was small (three or four), but it included three of the outstanding jurists in the Crescent City; Theodore McCaleb, Randall Hunt, and Christian Roselius. They forced their charges into a dawn-to-dark routine of lectures, preparing of briefs, and conducting cases in moot courts. From these superbly trained students came lawyers who later attained outstanding recognition in politics and at the bar. The prestige of the law school was such that in 1855 the state legislature ordered the Louisiana Supreme Court to grant law licenses to any graduate of the law school "who shall produce evidence of good character."

The most prosperous branch of the University of Louisiana was the medical school. In 1851 it had 165 students and eight years later it had 402; much of the growth coming in the four years before the Civil War. The faculty, generally between seven and nine in number, was probably on par with that found in any medical school in the nation. Students, most of whom came from Louisiana and Mississippi, boarded at private homes and attended classes at the University and in a special class room at the Charity Hospital. A wide variety of disease and accident victims were available at Charity Hospital for students to observe and treat; furthermore the large number of paupers who died there gave a boundless supply of cadavers for medical and surgical study. In addition the student was encouraged to use the anatomical museum at the University; it was, Dr. Josiah C. Nott proclaimed, "unrivalled in this country."[15] After three school years (October through March) the student was granted his doctor of medicine.

The expansion of the University of Louisiana medical school prompted the formation of another medical school in this decade. In May, 1856, a small group of doctors announced in the *Medical News and Hospital Gazette* their intention to form the New Orleans School of Medicine. They contended that another medical school was practical because of the "clinical advantages unsurpassed, if equalled in the world, and with opportunities for the study of pathology and anatomy in all its phases, such as are elsewhere unknown. . . ." The school's proponents argued that competition of another medical school would not cause both institutions to decline; rather it would lead to the development of New Orleans as a major medical center and it would, they affirmed, end the "annual pilgrimage of Southern young men to the medical schools of the north. . . ."

The School of Medicine was housed in an "elegant and commodious" building opposite the Charity Hospital and on November 17, 1856, its first class, a surprising total of seventy-two students, began their studies. The original faculty was chosen from the ranks of the city's doctors, but in 1858 it hired Dr. Austin Flint, a New York physician already famous in international circles, as the first professor of clinical medicine and auscultation and precussion in the United States. Classes were conducted in the medical school and with the cooperation of the Charity Hospital Board of Administrators, the School of Medicine students were granted the same rights and privileges as the medical pupils at the University of Louisiana. To take best advantage of facilities offered in the hospital and a free clinic operated by the School of Medicine, a chair of clinical medicine, the first in the United States, was established in 1857. This school pioneered the modern method of clinical teaching through the policy of assigning each student a patient on whom he had to make a report for the instructor's analysis and criticism. If the patient died, the body was dissected by the students. The School of Medicine was also the first institution in the city formally to train pharmacists.

With its excellent faculty of ten men, the medical college progressed rapidly—the number of students increased from seventy-six in 1856-1857 to 216 in 1859-1860. At the same time, as noted above, the University of Louisiana medical school also grew in size and by January, 1859, the *Medical News and Hospital Gazette* could honestly consider New Orleans the future " 'Medical Metropolis' of the South and West;" the city would "ere long rival Philadelphia" as the nation's leading medical center. On the eve of the Civil War the University of Louisiana ranked fifth and the School of Medicine seventh in size in the nation, and New Orleans was exceeded only by Philadelphia and New York in total number of medical students.

Catholic higher education in New Orleans was represented by the College of the Immaculate Conception. Founded in 1849 with funds furnished by the Bishop and the Ursuline sisters, it was maintained by the Catholic Society for the Diffusion of Religious and Literary Education, which was a sort of collective *non de plume* assumed by the Society of Jesus. Thus, under guise, the Jesuits returned to New Orleans sixty years after their expulsion; appropriately they purchased property on the scene of the old Jesuit plantation. By the latter half of the fifties the College averaged 250 students consisting chiefly of local born Irish, Creole, and Anglo-Saxon Catholic youth. The curriculum followed the traditional Jesuit *ratio studiorum*, that is, classical languages, basic sciences, mathematics, grammar, and rhetoric; a small obeisance was made to the nineteenth century by offering a few commercial courses.

For the student who desired a more practical form of higher education there were two business colleges in New Orleans. Dolbear's Commercial College taught Latin, a modern language, algebra, geometry, navigation, bookkeeping, and penmanship. George Soule, a Yankee like Rufus Dolbear, in 1856 opened Soule's Commercial College; his institution provided training in mathematics, science, and languages as well as the strictly commercial subjects. Under Soule's aggressive leadership the school grew in size and by 1860 Soule could contemptuously insist that students had left Dolbear's to enter his college because "This is the only Commercial School in the city where the branches of a thorough commercial education are taught practically, and as practised in New Orleans business houses."[16] Dignity was not a hallmark of business schools in that age.

The paucity of institutions of higher learning in New Orleans is not entirely an index of college attendance, as many sought an education outside the city. A few upper class Creoles and Americans were educated in France or Germany, after which the young men made the required "grand tour" and returned home to assume their favored place in the professional or commercial world of New Orleans. Wealthy Anglo-Americans more commonly went to Harvard or Yale while the Catholic colleges of Georgetown (Washington D.C.), St. Mary's (Maryland), and St. Joseph's (Kentucky) were often chosen by upper class Creoles. As the sectional controversy increased in intensity there was a determined effort to dispatch students to a southern school where their virtue and sectionalism would be unspoiled. This sentiment is expressed perhaps best in the efforts of the Episcopal Bishop of Louisiana, Leonidas Polk, to form the University of the South in Sewanee, Tennessee. Opened in 1860, Bishop Polk modestly predicted that the new school would be an "Oxford or a Gottinger [sic], or a Bonn, or all three combined."[17] But the good clergyman's main appeal was not for the school's intellectual character but for its unalloyed southernism.

ADULT EDUCATION.

New Orleans was one of the first cities in the nation to offer a program of public adult education. The idea was spawned and nurtured by Joesph Landis, a native of Pennsylvania and a member of the school board in the Second Municipality. By 1853 the movement had spread to the Second and Fourth Districts and by 1860 there were about 1,400 students enrolled in the night school program. In these schools adults without benefit of an earlier education, working children, and immigrants desiring an English schooling, were taught the basic elements of spelling, arithmetic, reading, writing, English grammar, United States history, and modern geography. The classes, taught by instructors recruited from the regular school system, must have presented a pedagogical challenge; for example, the First District night school in 1856 had 455 pupils, male and female, representing forty-eight trades, and natives of nine countries.

Informally education was presented in the community through lectures, learned societies, and libraries. Lectures on diverse subjects were sponsored by organizations such as the Mechanics Society, the Lyceum and Library Society, the Catholic Institute, the Young Men's Christian Association, the Masonic Grand Lodge, and the Mercantile Library Society. There were also lecturers who were not sponsored by a group, but arranged through an agency to rent a hall and handle details. Others simply hired themselves a hall and spoke to the masses who might hear—and pay. The chief lecture centers were the Armory Hall and the Odd Fellows Hall.

Though the *Picayune* admitted that "popular lecturing has never thriven in this latitude," there were a considerable number of famous individuals who bored or captivated New Orleans audiences during the decade. Lectures on science were given by Louis Agassiz in geology, B. A. Gould and Ormsly M. Mitchell in astronomy, and George R. Glidden in Egyptology. The pseudo-science of phrenology was represented by Orson Squires Fowler, and spiritualism by Thomas Gales Foster, who lectured "in a trance state." There were outstanding speakers from the field of religion; the Roman Catholics brought in Bishop John Spalding of Kentucky and Jesuit theologian R. P. Adams S.J.; Protestants were delighted with the Rev. Van Arsdale, the Rev. Orville Dewey, and the querulous Parson Brownlow. Local celebrities also took to the lecture podium to enlighten their fellow New Orleanians; among these were Christian Roselius, Charles Gayarré, Thomas J. Semmes, M. M. Cohen, Edward Bermudez, Abbé Napoléon Perché, Alexander Dimitry, the Rev. Benjamin Morgan Palmer, the Rev. Dr. D. D. Bolles, Professor W. P. Riddell, Dr. I. L. Craw-

James H. Caldwell

John McDonogh

Glendy Burke

Rev. Theodore Clapp

Abbé Adrienne Rouquette

*Abbé Rouquette's Chapel at Lacombe, Louisiana
(From the collection of Stuart O. Landry).*

cour, and the Rev. Dr. William T. Leacock. Of all the lecturers the most noted were the Catholic convert and magazine editor Orestes A. Brownson and the English novelist William Makepeace Trackeray. The former presented a series of five lectures on Catholicism and Liberty in the Odd Fellows and Armory Halls and despite the vituperation poured on him by every daily newspaper in the city he addressed capacity audiences. Less contentious, Thackeray in March, 1856, lectured on the safely-dead four Georges. These lectures, a reporter announced, were like a "graphically sketched panorama, the features of which passed before the eye in brilliant procession. . ."[18] Like Brownson, Thackeray spoke before applauding SRO crowds.

The only learned society worthy of note in the city was the New Orleans Academy of Sciences. Founded in 1853 with twenty-seven members, most of whom were local physicians, its first officers were Josiah Hale, M.D., President; J. S. Copes M.D., Vice-President; Albert W. Ely, Second Vice-President; I. L. Crawcour M.D., Corresponding Secretary; William B. Lindsay, Recording Secretary; Henry Hughes, Treasurer; Edward C. Bolton, Librarian; and D. F. Mitchell, Curator. These "men of talent and information" banded together to seek "the advancement of Science, properly so called, in all its various departments."[19] As the decade progressed new members were added and a system of "honorary" and "corresponding" membership was established which included such prominent figures as Louis Agassiz, William Humboldt, Elisha Kane, M. F. Maury, Ashbel Smith, Captain George McClellan, and Bishop Leonidas Polk. By December, 1854, *De Bow's Review* concluded that the Academy of Sciences "bids fair to become one of the most important institutions of the kind in this country."

Meetings were held monthly at which members presented papers in their specialties. These studies were published by the Academy and were occasionally reprinted by the local medical journals or in *De Bow's Review*. The Academy of Sciences served as an advisory board to the city government on problems of sanitation and drainage and in 1855 it undertook a tentative geological and scientific survey of Louisiana for the state legislature. Meetings were conducted the first year in private homes; later they met in the city hall and Mechanics Hall, and in 1855 the Academy was given a quasi-official status in the University and provided with a regular meeting room.

Two additional learned societies might be mentioned. The Physico-Medical Society, composed of local doctors, joined the Attakapas Medical Society in 1849 to form the Louisiana State Medical Society. Meetings were held yearly. The Louisiana Historical Society dated from 1836 (the historian François Xavier Martin was its first president) but it waned and in 1846 it was reorganized by such prominent New Orleanians as John Perkins, J.D.B. De Bow, Edmund J. Forstall, Charles Gayarré, General Joseph Walker, and Alfred Hennen. In the following year it was incorporated and a constitution modeled after the Massachusetts Historical Society was drawn up. The Louisiana Historical Society was very active in the late 1840's, but by all indications it was nearly defunct in the fifties. By 1860 the headquarters of the Society and the larger part of its membership was in Baton Rouge.

Library facilities in New Orleans were inferior to those of comparable cities in the North and West. Desultory endeavors were made to form a free public library after Abijah Fisk, a wealthy merchant, left a building and a private collection for that purpose. Interest lagged, the building was sold, and the books were transferred to the Mechanics Institute. Substituting for a free library were several subscription libraries which allowed members of the organization use of the book collection and charged non-members subscription fees. The subscription library fostered by the Catholic Institute, the YMCA, and the Masonic Grand Lodge offered a limited and specialized collection. The Mercantile Library Association, organized in 1857 to give "opportunities for self improvement" to clerks, began auspiciously having 633 subscribers and 3,485 books a year later, but the original enthusiasm waned and the Association failed in the Spring of 1859. The most impressive subscription library belonged to the Mechanics Society; in 1860 it boasted of 15,000 books available for its members.

The largest libraries in the city during the 1850's were connected with the public school system. Early in the previous decade Samuel J. Peters suggested that, rather than a library in each school, a central library be created in the Second Municipality. With initial funds provided by Peters, the Lyceum and Library Society was formed; it allowed school children for a nominal sum (twenty-five cents a year) to become members of the society. They could withdraw books from the library located in city hall and they were able to attend free lectures sponsored under the aegis of the Society. The program was a remarkable success; by 1850 there were 10,000 books in the library and the idea of a central school library and lecture series was copied in several northern communities. However during the 1850's the Lyceum Library added only two thousand more volumes as the common council, private individuals, and the school board were far less open handed than they had been earlier. On at least two occasions the lack of funds prevented the public school library from purchasing large private collections.

The other districts also established central school libraries and in 1859 the ones in the Third and Fourth Districts consolidated their holdings with those of the Lyceum and Library Society in the First District. An independent school library was maintained in Algiers and in the Second District, the latter containing 4,000 volumes and housed in the third floor of the Cabildo. Unlike the uptown library it was open to everyone, though books were not on a circulating basis and had to be used in the building.

The bulk of the books in the school libraries were in English with about two to three thousand in French and a few hundred in German and Italian. In addition the libraries subscribed to a number of popular magazines for children and adults. The school libraries possessed excellent collections of the standard classics of Western thought, but because they were often dependent on book gifts and because adults as well as school children used the books, the shelves exhibited a weird selection of works. Along with a host of sentimental, moralizing novels, books and unimportant poetry, and how-to-do-it manuals, New Orleanians were free to ponder over Comte, Confucius, Kant, Fichte, Boethius, Locke, Hobbes, Arian, Quinet, Constant, Condorcet, Vico, Spinoza, Humboldt, and many other philosophic and social thinkers. In the First District the readers' Whiggism was preserved by works of Daniel Webster and by the *American Review;* Jefferson and his ilk were unrepresented. On the other hand the Second District library contained the radical writings of Fourier, Louis Blanc, Proudhon, Cabet, and Blanqui. Citizens could be titillated by a fine selection of Restoration plays, by the works of Aristophanes, Benjamin de Musset, Rabelais, and an 1827 study with the entrancing title of *Prostitution dans la Ville de Paris*. To balance these profane works there was an abundance of religious material in both libraries.

By 1860 New Orleans could boast of an excellent public school system, many private schools, a few examples of higher education, and a fair library system. While perhaps weak in comparison to northern cities (public schools excepted) the city was a veritable bastion of learning surrounded by a southern forest of illiteracy. It is significant that the drive for public education, libraries, and lecture series was in large part the labor of a northern-born merchant and professional class. These men did not possess the aristocratic pretension toward educating the select alone; they saw nothing subversive in John A. Shaw's view that "Give men equal opportunities for mental culture and you do all that can be done toward equalizing their condition in life."[20] Nor did they have the immunity to the intellectual foment of the Northeast which chilled, where it did not disgust, the southern agricultural aristocracy and the intellectually backward Creoles. It is also noteworthy that the initial proponents of public education were almost entirely Whig merchants and lawyers whereas in the North the demands for public schools were a perogative of working class Jacksonian Democrats. Perhaps the Whigs fostered public schools in order to educate a population which, remaining illiterate, would fall prey to demagoguery; they might vote for Democrats and upset Whig domination of the city. As merchants they realized the necessity of a literate citizenry to staff a commercial economy. Whatever the reason, the formation of a viable public school system was the finest legacy ante-bellum New Orleans passed on to the post-Civil War generations.

NOTES

[1]"The Public Schools of Louisiana and New Orleans," *De Bow's Review*, IX (August, 1850), 239.

[2]Mary Peabody Mann, *Life of Horace Mann* (2nd. ed., Boston, 1865), 159.

[3]"The Schools of New Orleans," *Common School Journal*, XIII (June 1, 1851), 171.

[4]Dimitry in 1848 became the first state Superintendent of Public Schools; Gayarré held this position earlier as part of his duties as Secretary of State.

[5]"The Schools of New Orleans," *Common School Journal*, XIII, 171.

[6]Barnard to Horace Mann, March 26, 1843, in Edgar W. Knight, ed., *A Documentary History of Education in the South before 1860* (5 vols., Chapel Hill, 1953), V, 336-337. Barnard was asked in 1843 to assume the Superintendency of the First Municipality schools. He turned down the offer, but in 1850 he agreed to replace Shaw as Superintendent in the Second Municipality; however his wife's illness prevented him from assuming the position.

[7]Samuel G. Goodrich, *Recollections of a Lifetime or Men and Things I Have Seen* (2 vols., New York, 1857), II, 329.

[8]Board of Directors of the Public Schools of the First District, *Report*, 1856 (New Orleans, 1856), 11-13. Since instruction was partly in French in the two downtown districts, English was the "foreign" language required.

[9]Louisiana Department of Public Education, *Report*, 1861 (New Orleans, 1861), 59.

[10]*Weekly Delta*, August 7, 1853.

[11]Louisiana Department of Public Education, *Report*, 1861, p. 7, 63; Ibid., 1857 (New Orleans, 1857), 13.

[12]Emile Hiriart, "Guerre aux Écoles Publiques," *La Renaissance Louisianaise*, May 19, 1861; *Semi-Weekly Creole*, February 17, 1855.

[13]*Catholic Standard*, February 5, 1860.

[14]*Ibid.*

[15]Josiah C. Nott, "Medical Schools," *New Orleans Medical and Surgical Journal*, XIV (November, 1857), 355-356. J. J. Ampére, a visiting French scientist, took a dim view of the anatomical museum; by European standards he felt it was woefully inadequate.

[16]*Daily Delta*, September 30, 1860.

[17]Quoted in William M. Polk, *Leonidas Polk: Bishop and General* (2 vols., New York, 1915), I, 248.

[18]*Daily Picayune*, March 7, 1856.

[19]Wharton, diary, February 12, 1855; *Charter and By-Laws of the New Orleans Academy of Sciences Together with a List of Fellows, Honorary, and Corresponding Members* (New Orleans, 1887), 9.

[20]"Attempt to Abolish the Board of Education and the Normal Schools," *Common School Journal*, II (August, 1840), 240.

Chapter IX

THE GOOD TIMES

Everybody lives freer and spend their money more willing here.[1]

[For public amusements] there is no city in the country that has transcended it in attractions.[2]

To me everything had a holiday look. . .[3]

One hundred years ago, as today, New Orleans was billed as "the city care forgot." A combination of forces — French traditions, sea port town, frontier influences, wealth — gave New Orleans in the 1850's a reputation as the most glamorous, and most decadent, city in America. Here the New Englander, free from the restraints of church and community, lost his puritanism — or moved within a small uptown circle that railed against this modern Sodom. Here the Westerner could forget his rural boredom and soak up enough liquor and sin to keep him in stories for a dozen years. Here the European traveller found echoes of continental enjoyments and proof that not all American cities were similar and dull. It was the best place in the United States for a good time.

St. Charles Hotel, New Orleans
(Gleason's Pictorial V — July 16, 1853)

Probably the major social centers in New Orleans were the grandiose St. Charles and St. Louis hotels. The St. Charles, "an enormous establishment of the American type, with a Southern air about it,"[4] accommodated a thousand guests and had a large rotunda, an enormous bar room, various confectionary and cigar stores, a telegraph station, a steam bath, a barber shop, a bakery, a laundry, a richly decorated "ladies' ordinary" in one wing and a "gentlemen's ordinary" in another wing, and a large dining room. The St. Louis Hotel, which held "the same high rank as the St. Charles,"[5] covered an entire square bounded by St. Louis, Toulouse, Chartres, and Royal streets. While offering fewer services than the St. Charles, this hotel was more lavishly decorated and had a more cosmopolitan air about it.

Every day in the rotundas of the St. Louis and St. Charles hotels slaves were sold. Mounted on a platform the shouts of the auctioneer rose above the chat of dry goods wholesalers, retailers, commission merchants, sugar brokers and other traders as they engaged in business transactions. Add to this the appearance of hotel guests, hangers-on waiting for a tip or drink, and employees of the hotel dashing about on their many duties, and it is easy to imagine why one traveller compared the lobby of the St. Charles hotel to the noise and confusion of the Paris Bourse or the New York Stock Exchange.

If the domain of the merchant was in the rotundas, the politicians found a ready audience in the bar rooms. Meetings were sometimes held here, deals were made, and newspapermen, always eager for news and free drinks, were contacted. Political arguments were so common in such an atmosphere that challenges to duels, fights, and even a few murders hardly disturbed the equanimity of the crowd clutching their dime drinks and partaking of the sumptuous free lunch. The bar rooms also seemed to be a hang-out for local adventurers and more than one filibustering expedition was planned there.

The dining rooms at the St. Charles and St. Louis were immense — the St. Charles for example could seat four hundred persons at three long tables in a dining room dominated by five massive ornate chandeliers. Silverware, and even gold for special occasions, added to the opulence. The food, prepared by a *maitre de cuisine* from Paris, was, by all accounts, varied and excellent. A traveller declared that the daily printed menu was so extensive that it "bore resemblance to a miniature gazette."[6] That this was only a slight exaggeration may be deduced from one dinner menu at the St. Charles:

DINNER

Soups.—Ox-joint; vermicelli.
Fish.—Baked red snapper, with brown oyster sauce.
Boiled.—Leg of mutton, with caper sauce; sugar-cured ham; corned beef.
Cold Dishes.—Corned beef; roast beef; mutton; ham.
Roast.—Beef; loin of lamb; pig, with apple sauce; loin of pork; loin of mutton; loin of veal.
Entres.—Beef a la mode; calves head, with brain sauce; croquettes of rice, with lemon sauce; calves feet a la Pascaline; veal and ham scolloped with mushrooms; maccaroni, with Italian sauce; oyster patties.
Vegetables.—Irish potatoes, mashed or boiled; hominy; rice; beans; spinach; cabbage.
Relishes.—Worcestershire sauce; mushroom catsup; walnut and tomato catsup; pickled beets; mixed pickles; pickled cucumbers; Cumberland sauce; lettuce; cheese; Harvey sauce; beefsteak sauce; John Bull sauce.
Pastry and Pudding.—Gooseberry pie; bread pudding, with brandy sauce; Pethivier pie; Genoese perlies; biscuits Milanais; annisette jelly; English cream.
Dessert.—Raisins; filberts; almonds; pecans; oranges.
Coffee.[7]

It should be noted that one could order as many dishes from each course as he desired. A dinner like this, two other meals and a room, all, for three dollars a day!

There were, of course, regular restaurants in the city, the best known being Victor's, Moreau's, and McDonald's (the Delmonico's of New Orleans.) At these restaurants and at market stalls, though seldom at the hotels, Creole cooking could be savored. The thick chicory coffee, gumbo filé, bouillabaise, callas, congri, sagamité, patassa, sabotin, and jambalaya, products of Negro cooks who combined a French richness with an Indian flair for hot spices, were already internationally famous and did much to associate New Orleans with excellent eating.

During the winter season the local hotels were crowded with business men representing northern and European companies, visitors from southern towns and northern cities, and planters and their families. To the wives and daughters the social whirl at the hotel was especially pleasing. Thus the typical morning of

St. Louis Hotel

a woman guest at a New Orleans hotel was described by a female visitor:

> After making a fashionable toilette, breakfast is the next important event — and this is loitered over as long as possible, listening to proposals for the morning walk, the afternoon drive, or the evening *hop*-eration, and digest simultaneously scandal and scrambled eggs — a stroll to Chartres Street, to patronize those fashionable *modistes,* Olympe and Scanlon. . . .[8]

The afternoon might be sent in resting, a drive along the shell road to the lake shore, or a social visit with a New Orleans family.

Most evenings the young ladies could look forward to a formal dress, military, or costume ball, and on special occasions, such as Mardi Gras, Washington's Birthday, and the Feast of St. Joseph (Mi-Careme), several formal balls were held on the same eve. The St. Charles and St. Louis hotels witnessed weekly "racy grand and brilliant" cotillions sponsored by the hotels themselves or by local organizations. The management of the Orleans Theatre conducted during the opera season a series of exclusive society balls "in the style of the Grand Opera balls at Paris."[9] Such groups as the Odd Fellows, the Young Bachelors, the Y. M. C. A., the fire companies, the military units, the benevolent societies, the fraternal lodges, and the dancing studios held balls yearly at the Odd Fellows Hall, the St. Charles Theatre, and the Armory Hall. Prices at these dances varied from $1.50 a couple to the $6.00 charge for box seats at the Orleans Theatre. Dancing generally began at nine in the evening. At midnight with "Hail Columbia" or the March of the Druids from *Norma* as a musical signal, supper was served to the partners after which, with strength regained, the waltzes, quadrilles, polkas, mazurkas, and lanciers were continued until early morning.

Not all of the city's balls were characterized however by prestige and propriety. Scattered throughout the city were dance halls of a questionable nature. These "Brothel Ball Rooms," as one man called them,[10] were frequented by a rowdy and adventuresome lot, "the depraved portion of our population."[11] The bravos who entered these places were not without a flashy elegance, at least according to a police description of one of them:

> . . . he is about Twenty years old, he is a little bald headed [with] black hair auburn side whiskers mustaches & Flyhar [?] on a white shirt with gold sleeve buttons gray cahsimere [sic] pants with black stripes on each side, black coat morocco gaiters brown felt hat, has long finger nails very sharp, gold watch & chain, the chain is a long guard chain, black velvet waiste cat [sic] with gold buttons, a gold finger ring with the initial (J. G.) large black scarf and a gold breastpin with a black stone.[12]

Bowie knives, dirks, pistols, and brass knuckles were part of the normal attire of the dance hall clientele, though the management and the city government required them to park their arms at the door when entering. Fights still broke out and places like the Globe, Louisiana, Pontchartrain, Stadt Amsterdam, Homeward Bound, and Orleans Ball Rooms had an ugly reputation. But the police, whether from fear or bribery seldom closed them.

The women in these dance halls — "eager harpies and hungry harlots" — were generally furnished by the management.[13] In imitation of women at upper class balls they wore masks, but then the similarity ended, for by all accounts brazenness was more common than coquetry. Small rooms off the dance hall balcony or upstairs from the ball room gave proof that the girls earned their living in ways other than dancing.

In the romantic legend of New Orleans the quadroons were the most famous of the dance hall girls. According to sentimental interpretation these attractive and intelligent maidens danced demurely with wealthy Creole gentlemen who temporarily desired their charms. Nothing could be further from the truth — the quadroon balls were "interracial orgies."[14] Though Negro women were required to entertain on different nights than their white sisters, the rule was violated frequently. The quadroon was simply a *garce*, a woman of pleasure, and her partner was more often a transient riff-raff of the New Orleans docks than a conservatively tailored gentleman.

The high point of the winter season entertainment was the celebration of Mardi Gras. On this day merrymakers wandered about the streets in masks and costumes forming impromptu parades and pelting each other and general onlookers with flour. It was a type of joyous anarchy. But in the early 'fifties the daytime celebrations had fallen into disrepute owing to the tendency of youths to cover marchers with mud and lime besides flour. Fortunately for the future of Mardi Gras, a group of young blades in the Fourth District, impressed by the Cowbellians, a parading and fun-making association from Mobile, formed in imitation the secret Mistick Krewe of Comus with the Pickwick Club as its "front organization." In their first Mardi Gras parade (1857) the Mistick Krewe developed their float and marching themes from Milton's *Paradise Lost*. The parade was an instant success and became an essential part of Mardi Gras celebrations. In the following year at least 20,000 persons turned out to watch the parade. Each year a different motif dominated the parade. In 1859

> the procession started from Orleans Street toward Lafayette Square, accompanied by music, torches, and transparencies. It presented an appearance hitherto unsurpassed for the variety of grotesque and laughable figures of which it was composed. First came a knight in full armor, mounted on a white steed who led the way. He was followed by a transparency bearing the words 'Twelfth Night,' with the motley characters intended to represent the scene, including Trumpeter, Herald, Clown, Ensign, Crownbearer, Cards, Lords of Misrule, Dice, Chess, Abbot of Unreason, Draughts, Domino, Twelfth Cake, Snake, Billiards, Backgammon, Lotto, Nine Pins, Fox and Goose, Bilboquet.
>
> Next came 'May Day' the personages in which were designed to represent the characters traditionally associated with English merrymakings on May Day. They were as follows: Jack in Green, Tom the Piper, Tabor Man, Hobby Horse, Scarlet, Morris Dancers, Muck, Robin Hood, Maid Marian, Friar Tuck, Stokesly.

Comus Parade
(Illustrated London News, May 8, 1858)

The third division of the procession was made up of the characters representing 'Midsummer's Eve' and consisted of St. George and the Dragon, the giants Gog and Magog, the Bear, the Lion and Unicorn, Titania, Puck, and the Attendant fairies of her court. . . .

In the fourth and last division of the procession came Merry Christmas, with his Tree, richly covered with gifts from the good Santa Claus. Among his attendant dispensers of good things were Harlequin, Bell Man, Boar's Head, Wassail Flagon, Mince Pie, Plum Pudding, Beer Barrel, Music, Champagne, Port.

In this order the merry-makers reached the City Hall, where Mayor Stith, accompanied by his accomplished lady and her sister . . . together with a large number of invited guests, received them in the parlor. An immense bowl of champagne punch had been provided for his guests by the liberality of the Mayor, as well as a bouquet for each of the lady members of the procession. They remained but a few minutes, as the time had arrived for their appearance at the [St. Charles] theatre.

On their arrival there, the various tableaux enumerated above were represented successively, to the great delight of a large and brilliant audience, consisting of over two thousand persons.[15]

Mardi Gras night was the scene of continued revelry. Balls were held throughout the city with those at the St. Louis Hotel, St. Charles Hotel, the Orleans Theatre, and the Krewe of Comus ball at the St. Charles Theatre being the most important. Formal dress and costumes intermingled on the dance floor as the dancers celebrated until the early hours of the morning. One cosmopolitan observer stated that even the Mardi Gras balls of Paris were not equal to the New Orleans cotillions.

Over and beyond the parades, merrymaking, and balls, Mardi Gras has a deeper significance in New Orleans history, for it offers the clearest example of the adoption of Creole folkways by the American population. In the 1830's Mardi Gras was still a Creole celebration based on French custom and Roman Catholic theology, but during the forties a number of Americans became interested in the affair. In 1848 Lyell found both Americans who participated in and Americans who opposed the parades and revelry. By this time half of the dancers at the Mardi Gras balls at the St. Louis Hotel were Americans. "The encroachment of the Saxon," wrote a reporter, "[was] apparent, even in this far famed arena of Creole beauty and gallantry."[16] Creole couples, on the other hand, came to be found as regularly at the St. Charles as at the St. Louis Hotel; personal taste rather than ethnic considerations counted most in deciding which Mardi Gras ball to attend. The best proof of adoption of Mardi Gras by the American group may be seen in the formation of the Mistick Krewe of Comus. Not a single Creole was among its twelve founders, and out of eighty-three members of the Pickwick Club, only six were Creoles. The historian of the Krewe clearly understood this assimilation and transformation of Mardi Gras by the creators of Comus:

> It [1857] was the last year that the Creoles could call Mardi Gras peculiarly their own. Their press had disclaimed it, and in the following year the Saxons assumed leadership and, with organization, persistence, and good weather, brought the festival to a degree of perfection which the Creole soon acknowledged with pride, and in which his spirit and genius have remained predominant.[17]

Not all Americans, of course, were converts to Mardi Gras celebrations. A young law student wrote home in 1857 that he saw "tall swells round town, scaring children, dusting decent people & other foolish things." Significantly his brother four years later was less critical: "Three days ago was Mardi Gras — I saw some sights — some pretty, some ugly, heard some splendid music & at night the procession of the 'Mistick Krewe of Comus' was a splendid thing."[18] In general Mardi Gras was transformed in the twenty years after 1840 from an ethnic festival to a city-wide celebration that in the United States still remains peculiar to New Orleans.

For a few people in New Orleans entertainment and good company was found within the sanctum of their private clubs. The Boston Club—named after a card game, not the New England city — was the earliest (1841) and most famous of the private clubs. It included on its rolls many of the wealthiest citizens of New Orleans; indeed, in no other association is the Anglo-Creole upper class merger so obvious. Limited as it was to the wealthy and powerful, club "membership was desirable and few turned it down."[19] Occasionally a non-resident was made a member, but only after he was given the approval of the membership.

The Boston Club offered its members not the revelry and highjinks of other clubs in the city, but rather a quiet conservative center. It was a friendly association of resident citizens for mutual entertainment of sociable intercourse—gentlemen who desire to pass the leisure hours, when at their disposal, agreeably and pleasantly, in comparative privacy and retirement . . . it is almost needless to add that propriety of demeanor and proper courtesy are alone exacted within its portals.[20]

In its marbled halls merchants and lawyers gathered to talk business and politics. Here they were served elaborate dinners and occasionally treated to a quiet and orderly dance. For the more sporting, the club had domino sets, billiard tables, and card rooms wherein hands of boston, brag, whist, and other games were played.

Close to the Boston Club in prestige, though less well known, was the Pelican Club, a social organization founded two years after the Boston Club. It made a special appeal to bankers, lawyers, physicians, and to the British representatives of Liverpool cotton houses. Indeed, during the cotton season the Pelican Club had almost the character of a British outpost, a sort of Pall Mall refuge on Canal Street. Unlike the Boston Club, it did not survive the Civil War.

Most of the other social clubs in the city were primarily drinking and gambling clubs; "rather spendthrift and 'fast'" and characterized by a "wild hotel scramble for excitement."[21] The Pickwick Club, as noted above, drew its original membership from the organizers of the Mardi Gras association, the Mistick Krewe of Comus. The Orleans Club (founded 1850) was made up of the younger turf followers, newspaper men, and merchants excluded from the Boston Club. With a reputation for drinking and gambling, this club was for a time a very popular organization with four hundred members and a large club house on St. Charles Avenue. Its membership lacked cohesion however, and during the rise of the Know-Nothing movement, split asunder over politics and finally dissolved. In 1859 the Gaiety Club took over the role and much of the membership of the Orleans Club, with perhaps a heavier enrollment among race track enthusiasts. The Hiawatha and the Louisiana Clubs, organized at the end of the decade, were similar in character to the general run of social clubs.

Social clubs appealing to ethnic groups were common, but only the German *Turnverein,* with several local chapters, was of any size or importance. The local Turners stressed the usual choral groups and gymnastics, but apparently the free thinking and socialism associated with the *Turnverein* elsewhere was not found among the local Teutons. Starting in 1853 the *Turnverein* sponsored the annual *Volksfest* on May 1, and by 1858 the celebration had become so popular it was extended over two weekends. In that year the Turners began with a large and colorful parade to the Union Race Course where "waltzing and polkying," "youthful gymnasts," "valorous riders in high boots and fancy decorations . . . bearing off pendant hoops," "lager beer and eating tents," and even two "Ethiopian minstrel bands" attracted thousands of non-German visitors. Declared the *Crescent:*

> The Volkfest is a German institution — but hereafter the Germans will not be able to monopolize it. The thing is contagious, and the indications this year have been such [as] to warrant the prediction that the whole population, more or less, will join in the festival hereafter.[22]

Fraternal societies such as the Masons, Odd Fellows, Druids, Sons of Malta, Improved Order of American Red Men, and Good Fellows also played a major part in the recreational life of New Orleans. At lodge meetings comradeship was engendered by the ritualistic paraphernalia associated with lodge initiations, rites, and uniforms. The lodge was a temple into which the male could escape from the conflicts of the business world and the tedium of Victorian home life. A foreign traveller might think it a "trifle childish," but to many New Orleanians the lodge filled a real psychic need.

For the sports fan or participant, New Orleans offered as many opportunities as any city in the nation; and of the city's sports none was more popular than horse racing. The racing season at the four local tracks extended from the middle of autumn to the end of spring and drew turfmen and mounts from the entire country. On racing days crowds of planters, race track touts, professional gamblers, well dressed members of the exclusive Jockey Club, and innocent but excited onlookers milled about in the stands or saloons exchanging information and making bets. At the sound of a drum, betting stopped and the horses with the slave jockeys wearing the colors of the owner approached the starting point. Most of the races were a series of five one-mile heats over a grassy track (four mile post races were also popular), and the owner of the horse which captured the best of three of these heats took the complete purse. Additional interest was nurtured by stake races sponsored by local social clubs. Probably the most famous race in New Orleans history took place on April 2, 1855, when Lexington defeated Lecompte and set the world record for the four-mile run.

For wealthy blades interested in trotting races it was customary to take their favorite team and carriage out the wide and hard shell road that ran from the city to Lake Pontchartrain; it was, said one admirer, "the most beautiful track for fast driving in the world."[23] More formal racing was organized in 1850 by the New Orleans Trotting and Pacing Club and by 1857 harness racing at various race tracks had become extremely popular. In 1858 the Metairie Trotting Club was founded and in the following year opened the Creole Course designed solely for trotting races.

The wide expanse of Lake Pontchartrain and the many oceanside resorts near the city made a natural appeal to sailing enthusiasts. Regattas, sponsored by the Crescent City and Southern Yacht clubs, were held yearly on Lake Pontchartrain and at Pass Christian involving sailing craft from New Orleans and the lower Gulf Coast. Indicative of the growing popularity of the regattas was the formation of the Junior Yacht Club in 1858 to allow smaller craft to participate in the races. Rowing on the Mississippi had been popular in the 1830's and 1840's before a cave-in on the West Bank in 1844 washed away many of the boat houses and cast a damper on rowing enthusiasm in the city. After a fourteen-year period of inactivity, the Monoma Boat Club was started with a boat house on Lake Pontchartrain, and the following year the Pioneer Boat Club was organized. Each club had several boats which they used for pleasure and intra-club races.

A "sport" that had a certain backing among the more sedantary of the local populace was chess. The New Orleans Chess Club, founded in 1841, languished for lack of interest, but in the middle-fifties began a program of weekly tourneys and enjoyed an increase of membership. This revitalization of the Chess Club was due to the stimulus aroused by the fantastic career of Paul Morphy, a local Creole, who became the world's champion chess player by the time he was in his mid-twenties and was a legend by the time he was thirty. Certainly his was the greatest American contribution to the art of the ancient game.

For those financially unable to partake of the pleasures of horse racing and yachting, or intellectually at a loss in chess, other sports beckoned. Cricket was popular among adolescent whites and Negroes of the city who played the game whenever they could find a field. The sport has enough following to warrant the establishment of the Crescent City Cricket Club in 1858, the "pioneer association in the introduction of this manly game in the South...."²⁴ Matches were played both within the club and against invading teams from Mobile. Once removed from cricket was the game of baseball, which by 1860 was already spoken of in the

French Market Scene
(Emerson's Magazine and Putnam's Monthly, V, October, 1857)

local press as a "national game."[25] Large crowds watched the contests of the Empire Club, from Jefferson Parish, and the Orleans Club, a "scientific and wiry and long winded set of boys living in the Third District."[26] Probably closely related to cricket and baseball was "les quatres" which borrowed much of its terminology from these games. As in baseball, its outstanding players were chiefly Irish. There were two quatres clubs in the city, the Variety and the Apollo.

A popular sport played among the rowdier youths in the city was raquette. This game, supposedly introduced by the Choctaw Indians, closly resembled lacrosse. A leather ball, somewhat larger than a tennis ball, was picked up and carried or thrown with two spoon-like sticks toward an opponent's goal, a canvas target a foot and half wide placed on a tall frame. The side with the most hits won the game. In this decade it was considered the "Grand Old Game of the Ancient Third,"[27] the district in which the raquette ground, a huge field between Moreau and Claiborne Streets along the Pontchartrain Railroad, was located. The two teams usually mentioned in newspaper reports were Negro aggregations, the Bayous and the Lavilles. Games between them were played on Sunday afternoons and were widely attended by whites from the entire city. The teams, eighty and more men on a side, with the players shoeless, stripped to the waist, and wearing red or blue caps, made a colorful appearance. There were no sidelines and so the spectators themselves stood in the field of play. If the ball happened to fly among the refreshment stands nearby the hapless proprietors were run down by a host of athletes grubbing with their sticks for the ball. Considering this anarchy, it was no wonder that some games went scoreless for hours. So popular had the spectacle become by 1858 that groups of whites volunteered to police the field during the game. Whites also played raquette, though with less vigor and with more of a system of rules than prevailed in the Bayou-Laville matches.

Boxing had a devoted following in New Orleans with bouts attended by as many as two thousand "abandoned men and women."[28] Matches were held in the back of the city or in Algiers and though illegal, law enforcement officials rarely attempted to break them up. The fighters were local Irish toughs with an occasional out-of-town challenger. Fights were lengthy bare knuckle contests and paid the participants little—for one that went one hundred and sixteen rounds the winning pugilist received a stake of one hundred dollars. For "championship" matches however the successful prizefighter might take home as much as five hundred dollars.

Despite the viscosity of the waters, poorer citizens swam in the Mississippi and, more commonly, in the drainage canals. This practice aroused the ire of the city government because it was dangerous, and the opposition of many individuals who considered it immoral. The lake shore at Milneberg had an excellent beach with bath houses for Negro and white as well as rides, boardwalk entertainers, and cool drinks for the children. The swamp and lake, which were literally game and fish preserves at the doorstep of the city made hunting and fishing available to the masses. For the Dead-Eye-Dicks among the populace there were pistol galleries, and places in plenty catered to a rowdy crowd who preferred bowling and billiards. This same lot could also be found cheering and gambling with the spectators at the cockpits or at the illegal bull and bear fights in Algiers and dog fights in the Third District.

Plush gambling parlors catering to the wealthy also operated in open defiance of the law. Amidst carpeted floors and soft chairs, and the served drinks and free meals the chance wayfarer could play brag, poker, rondo, monte, boston, faro, roulette, and craps. The best-known places were those run by such famous gamblers—and gentlemen—as Price McGrath, Henry Perritt, James Sherwood, Charles Cassidy, Sam Levy, and "Count" Lorenzo Lewis.

Games of chance were also offered in bars and on street corners. Quite popular were the illegal keno parlors found in most parts of the city. A typical parlor was "a long room, dirty, dusty, dimly lighted, and redolent of beer, tobacco smoke . . . and other odors . . . furnished with rows of common deal tables . . . polished and grimy by common use." Keno cards could be purchased for five, ten, or twenty cents and when the "pool" was sufficient the game began. The person who covered a row of completed numbers with horn buttons and shouted "Keno" or "Gaque" won the pool—minus the house cut.[29] But the "big chance" for the common man was the popular lottery. Tickets for the Havana lottery were the most rewarding, but tickets of lotteries designed to aid higher education in Georgia and Alabama also found takers. Though lotteries were illegal in Louisiana, they were advertised in the newspapers and cards were vended everywhere in the city.

The one aspect of gambling that was treated with harshness by the press and the police was that involving slaves and free Negroes. Gambling was an important recreational outlet for the Negroes who gathered in vacant lots, street corners, or in unused houses to shoot craps and play cards. Often whites joined these ventures, and in turn Negroes might be discovered in bars or groceries dealing or rolling with their white compatriots. Such inter-racial gambling was subject to fines and imprisonment and the police enforced the ordinance with fair regularity.

The gamblers were a varied lot. The keepers of the elite gambling parlors were often gentlemen with a good deal of polish and prestige—one man, John Davis, was the first opera impressario in New Orleans. But every winter a slightly less respectable class of gambler drifted in from the North or came off the steamboats. "They may be seen," wrote a *Picayune* editor, "any day hanging about certain favored localities in the First and Second Districts, flashy vests and devil-may-care countenances being their chosen livery."[30] Honesty was not a hallmark with these "sharks"; marked cards, "partners," and pools soon divested the "sucker" of his money.

An evening's dalliance with a prostitute was one of the better-known recreational outlets in New Orleans. Street walkers were few (some doubled as beggars and flower vendors): more commonly, prostitutes operated from a house or tavern. How many dwellings of ill fame existed in New Orleans it would be impossible to determine, but they were considerable in number. Most of the houses were congregated in distinct red-light districts: Gallatin and Barracks Streets in the Second District; "Sanctity Row" on Elysian Fields, Moreau, and Frenchmen in the Third; and Girod, Basin, and Perdido in the First. There were, besides, isolated houses scattered about the city.

A few of the houses were lavishly decorated and their madams were solicitous of the health of their girls and the wealth of their customers. A half dozen or more prostitutes might occupy one of these establishments. Far more common were houses that were hardly more than "cribs" or rooms above a bar. The following is a description of a lower class den on Perdido Street, an area of ramshackle dwellings with more than its quota of "worn out, false eye-browed, sunken-eyed, disgusting . . . specimens of frail sisterhood. . . ."[31]

> . . . we find a place open 'contrary to ordinances.' We enter. A dull light flickers on the apology for a mantlepiece. . . . On a kind of 'settle' or sofa-bed one woman is lying, half clad, with a beastly look of evil passions and intoxication in her eyes. Five or six others are scattered around the room not larger than a prison cell. [There was] a black bottle or two filled with the poison of the neighboring tavern.[32]

Henry Morton Stanley as a young man entered one of these bagnios filled with "giggling wantons," "in such scant clothing that I was speechless with amazement."[33] Just how he expected prostitutes to dress, he does not say.

The girls were certainly not among the city's most docile citizens. They were, according to an irate taxpayer, "a set of worthless women, constantly drunken and disturbing the peace of the neighbors by their low swearing and indecent language."[34] The police were frequently forced to quell disturbances among the girls or with their patrons. Nor was the average prostitute much concerned about sanitary measures, for if Charity Hospital figures are an index, New Orleans had an extensive venereal disease rate. Furthermore these doxies and their associates were not above using drugged liquor and robbing visitors.

The *horizontales* came from many places. To the permanent dwellers were added an unholy host who drifted into the city from the North for the lucrative winter season. New ones were recruited from unscrupulous employment agencies or from newly-arrived immigrants by "fellows dressed in the garb of gentlemen, who offered highest wages, and represent their houses as most respectable."[35] By this technique girls as young as eleven and twelve were brought into the profession. White prostitutes, the great majority of whom were of Irish and native American origin, shared honors with a considerable number of the "frail daughters of Ethiopia."[36] Though most of the bordellos were segregated, the local press noted white and Negro women working at the same place, even with a Negro madam. "Undue familiarities" between white prostitutes and free Negroes and slaves were not unknown.

The public attitude towards prostitution in the city was generally one of apathy. "The impunity with which such establishments have theretofore been kept open in the immediate vicinity of private and respectable residences has created no little surprise," wrote a midly shocked editor.[37] Though prostitution was illegal throughout most of the decade, the police closed houses of prostitution only during an occasional show of righteousness. Even when arrests were made the penalties were so light as not to deter the profession. If times became difficult in one district the girls simply moved to another district where the police were both tolerant and lethargic. Only for fighting, disturbing the peace, intoxication, robbery, or murder did the police interfere.

A concerted attempt to deal with the problem of prostitution was made once in the fifties. In 1857 the city fathers passed "An Ordinance Concerning Lewd and Abandoned Women" that legalized prostitution. All prostitutes were to be kept within a restricted area (an area including most of the populated parts of the city). No single story building nor first floor of a house was to be used for a bordello. The girls were not allowed to walk the streets, stand in front of their dwelling, alley, gate, or door, to drink in coffee houses, to be indecently attired, or to beckon in any manner from their windows. Strict segregation of the races in separate houses was required. Upon petition of three "respectable" citizens in the neighborhood of a house, asserting that it disturbed the peace, the prostitutes could be evicted. The police were to make periodic investigations of the places, though no health standards were established. In order to operate legally, every house had to purchase a one hundred dollar license and pay an additional two hundred and fifty dollars fee for each girl. The law was a failure. Since the houses had openly operated when their existence was against the law, the madams logically concluded that an expensive license was not needed because of a mere ordinance issued from city hall. Very few licenses were purchased and the police did not enforce the law.

There was another form of prostitution rare but highly romanticized. This was the use of Negro mistresses, coffee-colored Camilles who corresponded to the mid-nineteenth century French women of the *demi-monde*. A young quadroon or octoroon was given to a white man, generally by her mother, as his mistress. The arrangement was called a *plaçage* and he became her *mari* and she his *placée*. The man set up housekeeping with the woman —one Frenchman even had his "mother-in-law" sharing his love nest—or he maintained her in addition to a legal wife who lived elsewhere in the city.

For Negro women the *plaçage* was desirable. While their lovers were not always as rich as pictured in romantic fiction, they were nonetheless able to keep a woman in room and board. In a few cases the man provided his mistress a slave or an Irish girl as a servant, and not infrequently the mistress' affection was rewarded with financial security or if she was a slave, by manumission. There was, moreover, hope on the part of the *placée* that by a sort of *usurpation ethnologique* her children might pass the color line.

To the men who indulged in it this system of concubinage was both pleasant and flattering—"Un bon plaçage est mieux qu'un mauvais mariage" was an old Negro expression in New Orleans. The quadroon girls were by all accounts "plus voluptueuse" and had a reputation for being faithful and considerate "spouses." For northern men and Europeans, faced with a shortage of women of their own backgrounds, the *plaçage* offered an ideal life. Even the crusty puritan, Frederick Law Olmsted, was convinced of its enjoyable utility. The practice was, furthermore, so institutionalized and conducted with such propriety that a man who engaged in it "was blamed but not ostracized either in society or business."[38] The only group that despised the situation were the white wives who held, according to Gayarré, a bitter enmity toward the colored women who shared their husbands' affections. The free Negro males also may have looked upon the system with a jaundiced eye; there is record of at least one wealthy free man of color who clubbed a French immigrant for trifling with his sister.

Last but not least among the popular entertainments was sharing a convivial glass in some public drinking house. There were multitudes of such places going under the title of saloons, gardens, groceries, oyster houses, and coffee houses. The common council estimated in 1854 that there were over two thousand liquor dispensaries in the city, while a mathematically inclined minister declared that if each of New Orleans' "coffee houses, cabarets, and tippling houses," were given a space thirty feet wide and placed in a line they would extend a total of over thirteen miles.[39] Whatever the truth of the statistics the fact is that no citizen had to search far for a drink. According to one critical visitor:

> In New Orleans drinking seems to hold its chief abiding place in the New World, and I should suppose that more spurious liquor and more genuine brandy was [sic] sold and consumed in this city than in any other portion of the Union.[40]

The high rate of intemperance with its attendant alcholism would seem to give credence to this conclusion; in the five years, 1856-

1860 a phenomenal 610 deaths during delirium tremens were recorded. With some justice a traveller wondered if it was yellow fever or drinking that caused the citizens to die in droves.

The best drinking parlors in the city, like the Gem, Ruby, Sazerac, Arcade, and Orleans, had all the comforts of a luxurious home. Costing several thousand dollars to furnish, they featured thick carpets, easy chairs, immense gilded mirrors, large gas-lit chandeliers, and "all that damask and velvet can do for comfort and gilding and mahogany for splendor."[41] Nor were the things of the mind and soul forgotten; a full rack of local, national, and European newspapers were available, and paintings, including the ever-present reclining nude over the bar mantle, covered the walls. In such pleasant environment the patrons could smoke their El Cruzadas, Donna Primas, Tres Gracias and other choice Havanas while drinking mint juleps, cherry cobblers, sazeracs, glasses of Old Bourbon or Monogahela, and the best cordials, brandies, and wines. They could talk of business and politics or engage in time-honored "toast, song and sentiment."[42]

The more common drinking places were generally called oyster houses or coffee houses, though "nobody ever saw anything drunk in these 'coffee houses' except spirits."[43] These establishments were found in every part of the city from the waterfront to the almost inaccessible sections of the swamp. They were often crude structures which served the primary function of providing alcohol without many frills. As an astonished German wrote to his countrymen, "There are taverns here but you seldom see a table in them, for they are furnished like a store. You go in, drink a glass of beer or wine without sitting down, and then go on your way."[44] Most of the cheaper drinking spots were friendly gathering places for the working classes, but at the more notorious of the establishments the customers were "an uncouth-looking company, who had all the appearance of being either borderers from Texas, or disappointed gold-diggers from California."[45] The bartenders in these rougher saloons were not above using strong arm tactics. One spoil sport complained:

> James Maglone keeps a disorderly coffee house in New Levee st. between Lafayette & Girod sts[.] he is in the habit of assaulting [sic] persons with Brass-Knuckles which he is in the habit of carrying[.]
>
> David   his X mark   Fennessy [46]

As a result the coffee houses were main ports of call for the police, who arrested several thousand persons yearly for intoxication or brawls that arose out of excessive drinking. Of even more concern to the state and city governments was the tendency of tavern owners to ignore licensing and closing hour requirements.

Most enjoyable of the working class drinking establishments were the German beer gardens. While chiefly associated with the local Teutonic population, they became increasingly popular with all ethnic groups. Within their friendly confines families gathered to eat heavy sour German foods, drink steins of foaming lager beer, and dance the waltz or polka to band music. The beer gardens were centers of old country *gemütlichkeit* where the immigrant escaped for a time at least the toils of a life in a new and not always hospitable surrounding.

The greatest concern to the city authorities arose over the sale of liquor to slaves. It was not extraordinary to see whites drinking with Negroes, free and slave, at "these dens of iniquity, where liquor of the most villanous compound is sold to slaves in all parts of our city, where the vicious of all colors congregate."[47] Groceries were especially guilty of selling liquor to slaves. The common council and the state passed laws increasing in severity through the decade in order to meet this problem but the laws were not always enforced.

The excessive drinking and the sordid character of many of the drinking places were countered by local temperance agitation. Strangely enough the Protestant clergy ignored the temperance movement, but Irish Catholic prelates brought over from Ireland the temperance movement which had begun there in the 1840's; they succeeded in establishing several temperance societies and inviting the Rev. Theobald Mathew, the most famous Irish crusader against the liquor traffic, to preach at St. Patrick's Church in 1850 where he urged his audience to take the pledge. Father Mathew probably had no more lasting success however than P. T. Barnum who combined his management of Jenny Lind with moral lectures on the evils of drink, or "Professor" Orson Squires Fowler who correlated the mysteries of phrenology with "cold water principles."

In the mid-fifties the *Semi-Weekly Creole* militantly campaigned for restrictions on the sale of liquor. The coffee houses were, according to the editor, a blight on the community. "They stimulate to excess—increase crime—absorb the earnings of the weak and create destitution and pauperism in the city. They destroy the honesty and work of our negroes, and lead to loss, suffering and demoralization." They were "dens of vice and fomentors of riots, rowdyism and drunkenness." The paper advocated "closing all coffee-houses in the city on the day recognized as the Christian Sabbath and set apart for rest by the fiat of the God of nature. . . ."[48] Most of the other papers ignored the issue. The *Delta* treated the temperance movement as a joke and the *Deutsche Zeitung* strongly opposed it. On the other side, a speaker for a local temperance organization accused members of the press of possessing "free tickets to the grog-shops of the city."[49] The *Creole* however had the support of the Moral Reform Society, the Sons of Temperance and the Knights of Jericho, lodge organizations whose members combined fraternal and benevolent features with the noble cause.

The efforts to save the local citizenry from the clutches of John Barleycorn came generally to naught. A few seldom-enforced ordinances dealing with closing hours, dancing in bars, and licensing provisions were all the temperance people could show for their agitation. The Sons of Temperance which had 2,400 members in Louisiana in 1850 declined to a paltry 258 in 1858 and the Moral Reform Society never attained popularity—at one of its meetings it was estimated that over one half of those attending were curious coffee house keepers. Its newspaper, the *Southern Organ*, ceased publication after two discouraging years. By 1860 the temperance movement was defunct in the Crescent City.

In spite of the wide variety of entertainments noticed in this chapter—to which later will be added theatre, opera, and concerts—boredom faced many people in New Orleans. The summer months were exceptionally difficult because the city's normal entertainment facilities were greatly curtailed. But even throughout the year many of the younger boarding house dwellers felt isolated; they had no kinship with the local churches and were too inhibited by rural puritanism or too poor and afraid to avail themselves of the popular entertainments. More than one clerk was similar to Ellwyn Manceville who could find nothing to do on Sunday but take walks. "There is nothing here of interest,"[50] moaned a homesick law student. The very glamour of the city had made it alien.

The Lighthouse at Lake Pontchartrain
(Harper's Monthly Magazine, XVII—December, 1858)

NOTES

[1] Frederick Law Olmsted, *A Journey in the Seaboard Slave States* (New York, 1856), 588.
[2] *Weekly Picayune*, May 26, 1856.
[3] Kingsford, *Impressions of the West and South*, 64.
[4] William Howard Russell, *My Diary North and South* (Boston, 1863), 335.
[5] *Appleton's Illustrated Hand-Book of American Travel. The Southern and Western States and the Territories* (New York, 1860), 296.
[6] Cunyghame, *A Glimpse at the Great Western Republic*, 217.
[7] David Macrae, *The Americans at Home* (2nd edition; New York, 1952), 391.
[8] Lillian Foster, *Wayside Glimpses, North and South* (New York, 1860), 154.
[9] *Weekly Mirror*, January 29, 1859.
[10] *New Orleans As It Is: Its Manners and Customs—Morals—Fashionable Life—Profanation of the Sabbath—Prostitution—Licentiousness—Slave Markets and Slavery, etc. etc. etc.* (Utica, New York, 1849), 46.
[11] Robinson, *The Diary of a Samaritan*, 159.
[12] Entry for February 14, 1861, Police Department, Record of Messages Received and Sent, 1860-1863.
[13] Robinson, *The Diary of a Samaritan*, 236.
[14] Tregle, "Early New Orleans Society: A Reappraisal," *Journal of Southern History*, XVIII, 35.
[15] *Weekly Mirror*, March 12, 1859.
[16] *Weekly Delta*, February 26, 1849.

[17] Perry Young, *The Mistick Krewe: Chronicles of Comus and His Kin* (New Orleans, 1931), 58.
[18] Thomas C. W. Ellis to Mrs. E. P. Ellis, February 24, 1857, E. P. Ellis [Jr.] to E. P. Ellis, February 16 1861, Ellis Collection, 1829-1856, Department of Archives, Louisiana State University, Baton Rouge.
[19] Stuart O. Landry, *History of the Boston Club* (New Orleans, 1938), xi.
[20] *True Delta*, May 10, 1857, Quoted in *ibid.*, 56.
[21] *Weekly Delta*, December 26, 1852.
[22] *Daily Crescent*, May 18, 1858. It should be noted that the Crescent was attempting to woo the German vote to the American Party.
[23] Edward Zane Carroll Judson, *The Mysteries and Miseries of New Orleans* (Philadelphia, 1851?), 32.
[24] *Daily Crescent*, March 19, 1860.
[25] *Daily Picayune*, November 1, 1860. The same term was applied to the game four years earlier by a New York publication. *Porter's Spirit of the Times*, I (December 6, 1856), 229
[26] *Daily Crescent*, March 10, 1858.
[27] *Ibid.*, August 16, 1858. Games were also played on the Delachaise grounds in Jefferson City.
[28] *Weekly Picayune*, March 17, 1856.
[29] Charles Desmais Gardette, 'Kino: A Mystification of the Crescent City," *The Knickerbocker or New-York Monthly Magazine*, LI (May, 1858), 470-476.
[30] *Weekly Picayune*, March 31, 1856. The editor might have added pistols to their attire.
[31] *Daily Orleanian*, April 21, 1852. Most of these places on Perdido and nearby Girod Street were owned by John McDonogh, the great New Orleans philanthropist.
[32] *Weekly Delta*, March 7, 1852.
[33] Stanley, *Autobiography*, 84.
[34] Entry for October 27, 1856, Mayor's Office, Complaint Book, 1856-1859, (MS) Public Library Archives.
[35] *Daily Orleanian*, February 14, 29, 1852.
[36] Grand Jury of the Parish of Orleans, *Report*, 1856, 9.
[37] *Weekly Picayune*, December 10, 1855.
[38] Charles Gayarré, "The Quadroons of Louisiana," in Mary Scott Duchein, "Research on Charles Étienne Arthur Gayarré," 140.
[39] J. Twichell, "The Sons of Temperance," in *The New-Orleans Book* (Robert Gibbs Barnwell, ed.; New Orleans, 1851), 206.
[40] Rosenberg, *Jenny Lind in America*, 156.
[41] *Weekly Delta*, October 27, 1851.
[42] *Weekly Picayune*, February 26, 1855.
[43] *Weekly Delta*, May 29, 1852.
[44] Karl J. Arndt, "A Bavarian's Journey to New Orleans and Nacogdoches in 1853-1854," *Louisiana History Quarterly*, XXIII (April, 1940), 493.
[45] Cunynghame, *A Glimpse at the Great Western Republic*, 226.
[46] Entries for July 10, 26, September 5, 1856, Mayor's Office, Complaint Book, 1856-1859.
[47] Grand Jury of the Parish of Orleans, *Report*, 1856, p. 8.
[48] *Semi-Weekly Creole*, February 7, 10, May 23, 1855.
[49] *Weekly Delta*, July 10, 17, 1853.
[50] Thomas C. W. Ellis to E. P. Ellis, February 10, 1857, Ellis Collection.

Chapter X

THE PUBLIC ARTS

"The theatre [in New Orleans] is middling."[1]
"Opera is probably more an *institution* in New Orleans than in any of our Atlantic cities."[2]

THE THEATRE.

The theatre provided a major source of public entertainment in New Orleans. For many citizens in search of pleasure the play was the thing. And its importance as entertainment was heightened by the high prices and esoteric character of opera.

In 1850 there were three theatres in the city which offered regular programs in the English language: the St. Charles and the New American which had been rebuilt after the originals had burned in 1842, and the Varieties which had been opened in 1849. Once-a-week performances in French were offered at the opera house and, as will be pointed out below, several other places in the city were the scenes of occasional plays.

The St. Charles was reputed to be the "largest and best located theatre in the South," though it was smaller than the first St. Charles Theatre.[3] It had a main floor, two rows of semicircular balconies, an upper gallery, and boxes on either side of the stage. The colors and the decorations varied, according to the observer, from gaudy to garish. Admission to the St. Charles could be had for as little as twenty-five cents in the gallery and fifty cents for the 'groundlings," while a chair in either the dress circle, parquette, or private box cost a dollar. Operated by a succession of able managers, Noah Ludlow, Sol Smith, and Ben DeBar, the St. Charles was a profitable venture.

The New American Theatre had its last and least successful season in 1850-1851 and for the next five years it was used sporadically for animal shows, amateur German productions, and political meetings. It was, by all accounts, an "ill looking barn of a place" patronized chiefly by hoodlum types.[4] After a backstage fire in 1854, a *True Delta* reporter declared that "It is an eye sore . . . and we presume some incendiary patriot intended to 'reform' it out of existence by a summary process." In the following year a wrecking crew "reformed" it and the unlamented New American was never replaced.

The Varieties Theatre had a checkered career. Constructed in 1849, and considered a "neat little thespian theatre,"[5] it had adequate room, reasonable prices, and under its manager, Tom Placide, was profitable until destroyed by fire in 1854. Placide moved his stock company into Dan Rice's Amphitheatre, a modified burlesque house and circus constructed in 1853, and renamed it the Pelican. In the same year a group of investors calling themselves the Variété Association built a theatre on the site of the old Varieties, hired the well-known actor-playwright Dion Boucicault as manager and opened the place as the Gaiety Theatre. It was plushly decorated even in an age of plush; private boxes on either side of the stage were "tastefully draped in crimson and green" and the first two rows of the box tier were furnished with "sofas with rounded ends and covered with cherry colored satin brocade," while the fronts of the balconies were "decorated with white and gold on a salmon colored grounds, with tops being cushioned with crimson damask, with a gold moulding on the edge." The proscenium was decorated with floral paintings and frescoes of Euterpe and Thalia, the proper muses for the Gaiety's usual fare of "comedy, comic opera, ballet, burletta, and farce."[6] The theatre opened under Boucicault for a season and was then managed by W. H. Crisp until 1858 when Placide purchased the Gaiety and renamed it the Varieties. Remodeled by the new proprietor and provided with an excellent stock company, it became the best theatre in the city; according to a boastful newspaperman, the Varieties could "be ranked among the most refined and best conducted establishments in the country."[7]

The Pelican Theatre, operated by Placide for two years with little success, was rented in 1856 to two circus and variety show promoters, G. R. Spaulding and Charles J. Rogers, who renamed it the Academy of Music. Perhaps its only distinction is that it was the first theatre in New Orleans to provide matinee performances.

Each theatre had a regular orchestra and a resident stock company to support visiting stars; an exception was the Théâtre d'Orléans and the second Varieties, whose stock companies were in fact repertory companies and not dependent upon theatrical celebrities. Stock company actors were usually drawn from thespians who had drifted into the city from England and the Northeast, or who were hired from French music halls. These latter insisted on contracts and at least one manager discovered to his dismay that he could not force a "seconde première danseuse" to "dance a parlor dance, in parlor dress, with the figurants of the theatre" if her contract did not call for such.[8] Pay for stock company actors was low in painful contrast to well-known American and European stars who were given the right to hold lucrative benefit performances for themselves.

In the fifties many English stars and virtually every major American actor trod the boards of one or more of the English language theatres in New Orleans. Junius Booth drunk or sober was the high point of the winter theatrical season. In fact the last theatrical performance of the veteran Shakespearean was made in New Orleans on November 19, 1852; he died shortly after leaving the city. The Booth tradition was carried on by his son Edwin who played bit parts with his father and in 1857 appeared as the lead in a mixed repertoire composed largely of Shakespeare's plays. On his return the following season the *Mirror* wrote of him: "Mr. Booth is an actor of the intensely emotional school; the throes of inward agony and the whirlwinds of excitement which are the lot of some natures find in his genius a powerful exponent." His acting, the editor declared, recalled "the efforts of his father in his palmiest days." Another son, John Wilkes Booth, made his first appearance in New Orleans in 1864 less than a year before he presented his most memorable performance in Washington D.C.

Female stars found an appreciative New Orleans audience. Charlotte Cushman, a famous figure in the history of the American stage, visited the city regularly during this decade. She was a pinch-faced, unattractive woman who reduced Victorian theatregoers to tears as the tragic figure in now happily forgotten melodramas. Two other famous women, Lola Montez and Adah Isaacs Menken, drew audiences less for their ability than for their beauty and their bohemian reputations. Lola Montez, a few years fresh from the bed of the King of Bavaria, appeared at the Varieties in 1853; she also managed to make three appearances on various charges in a recorders court. In one case Tom Placide accused her of striking him; she in turn claimed that Placide was usually half naked backstage. Needless to say she played to packed houses. Adah Menken, famous for her later role of Mazeppa, was a locally-born girl, daughter of a free Negro and a white mother. She had been in the chorus line at the Orleans Theatre in the early 1850's, but by 1858, when she appeared in a starring role, he had so obscured her past that local newspapers were unaware of the origins (racial or geographical) of the "pretty Mrs. Menken."

Plays offered on the city's stages varied greatly. The St. Charles theatre each season presented a number of Shakespeare's plays. The favorite was Shakespeare's *Richard III*, probably because the bloody, hunchbacked Richard satisfied the contemporary desire for the romantic, the gothic, and the melodramatic. Historical dramas based on Sir Walter Scott's novels, and others depicting the lives of Pizzaro, Richelieu, Brutus, Charles XII, Francis I, and Louis XI, also served to evoke romance and tragedy.

Far more common than tragedy and melodrama was the comedy of manners. Indeed, the Varieties and the Gaiety specialized in this genre. And of all of the comedies offered in the local theatres none was so popular as Tom Taylor's *Our American Cousin*, which came to New Orleans after a long New York run. In general the play was reviewed favorably, though one critic absurdly saw the play as a form of sociological realism—"a startling story of real life" — which he contended would ruin ("Tom Taylorize") the theatre. Taylor's *Sill Water Runs Deep* and *The Victims* were also perennial favorites in New Orleans. Comedies by Shakespeare, Congreve, and Sheridan were presented at various times during the decade. Of the lesser known comedies, many were hardly more than broad farces.

To divide up New Orleans theatrical productions into categories of tragedy, melodrama, and comedy would give a false impression. It was a rare evening when a single drama was put on the stage. The audience demanded five hour entertainment with an abundance of variety. Between the acts of tragedies and comedies the theatre-goer might be delighted with farces, ballet numbers, character sketches, and single acts from comedies; he might be thrilled by equestrian displays, tableaus, acrobatics, magic shows, marching Zouaves, and trained animals. After the clog dancer clumped off the stage Lady Macbeth would make her reappearance. Bills presented in the English language theatres on December 31, 1849, may be taken as typical examples. At the New American Theatre were two comedies, a farce called *My Sister Kate*, a "Highland Fling," and an Irish jig "In Wooden Shoes." The St. Charles offered two short comedies (*The Artful Dodger* and *The Irish Attorney*), a concert by the Heron family, and a comic opera, *The Waterman*. The Varieties advertised a "petite opera" entitled *Kate Kearney*, a dance number called "The

Flirtation Polka," a comedy entitled *Naval Engagements*, and something labeled "Grand Divertisement." Ten years later the play-bills were of a similar mixed nature. At the Spaulding and Rogers Ampitheatre the precocious Marsh Children were in their thirty-ninth triumphal night; they offered an "elegant comedy," *Faint Heart Never Won Fair Lady*, a "Comic Song," and a "moral drama" (a "boob shocker" as H. L. Menken called the type), *The Six Degrees of Crime*. The St. Charles featured the Ravels who performed a pantomine, a ballet, and an exhibition of horn dancing in wooden shoes. At the Varieties the Great Star Company acted out *Husband for an Hour*, a drama; "Toodles," a "laughable interlude;" "Pas de Trois," apparently a dramatic reading; and a concluding farce, *The Limerick Boy*.

It is quite obvious that the melange of theatrical offerings on a single night must have seriously impaired the dramatic effect, the essential unity, of a reputable play. According to a disgruntled writer for the *Mirror*, this vulgarizing of the theatre by a sort of P. T. Barunm mentality was a major factor in the "present and prospective depression of the drama here;" the citizens of New Orleans were "accessories to the murder of the legitimate drama." Such criticisms seem not to have affected theatre managers who could fall back on the cliche—and show financial records to prove their assertions—that they gave the public what the public wanted.

The star system and the wretched stock companies also came under attack by theatrical critics. The stars, according to one observer, were often failures elsewhere had looked upon New Orleans as a "sort of half-way house for outcasts on the road to ruin."[9] Still they were better than "second-hand stock performers" who, in the absence of a touring star, were unable to sustain either art or interest. After witnessing one stock company, an irate editor stated that he had seen better acting "in an English barn."[10] Since the stock companies were weak, and a manager found it hard to fill the theatre without a star, he turned to cheap crowd pleasures. According to the *Delta*:

> Our theatres are veryday approaching more and more to the delectable and fragrant character of booths for the exhibition of unnatural obesity or shocking live atomies [sic], of dwarfs and giants and infantile phenomena, of learned pigs and trained dogs and monkies [sic], etc.; a tendency that is mainly due to the disorganizing and emasculating effects of the starring system.

Apparently not all of the problems of the theatre (according to the critics) were the fault of the people (and animals) on the stage. New Orleans audiences talked during performances and drowned out actors' lines. The theatres reeked of stale food odors—and from high in the "peanutty precincts of the parquette" shells were showered on hapless folks below. The sensitive soul also had to face "tobacco perfumes" as city officials ignored an ordinance against smoking in theatres. Then, after surviving the above challenges, the good citizen still had to meet the taunts and shoves of "brawling idlers" who hung around the theatre entrances.[11]

However critical contemporaries might have been concerning the state of the English theatre in New Orleans during the 1850's, it was probably no better or worse than the theatre in Boston, New York, or Philadelphia. Though mediocrity dominated, the local theatres did manage to present the best thespians and many of the better contemporary and classical plays. This was a considerable accomplishment for theatres which found it necessary to appeal to the "hardy mechanic, with his wife and children, the boatman, the visiting stranger, the apprentice, the clerk . . . and others."[12] It is remarkable indeed that the theatre in New Orleans did step out of the wooden shoes of the clog dancer and into the buskin of the tragedian.

Stage plays in French were offered at the Théâtre d'Orléans each Sunday evening. The Orleans had a regular stock company which since the 1820's had been recruited yearly in France. The company offered surprisingly few productions from the classical period of Molière, Racine, and Cornielle; however the plays of Victor Hugo and Alexandre Dumas and dramas based on their novels and those of Eugene Sue and Henry Murger found an eager local audience. Most ccmon were light, frothy comedies interspersed with vaudeville numbers, ballet, and farces. Attendance at the Sunday plays were sparse and the programs were not very profitable, though this was probably of small concern since the popular operas held at the Orleans on week days undoubtedly assured a reasonably satisfactory return to the owners.

The local Germans labored to provide a national theatre in the city. Using amateurs and a few visiting professionals, they put on plays at the New American, the Gaiety, the Orleans, the Pelican, and the St. Charles theatres, and various rented halls. Finally in 1853 a special theatre for German plays was constructed, but it burned two years later and was not rebuilt despite a good deal of agitation from the German press. The plays of outstanding German dramatists as Schiller (Schiller festivals were presented in the late fifties), Grillparzer, Von Kleist, and Goethe were presented. The most popular productions were the farces of Kotzebue which did nothing to elevate the character of the German theatre in New Orleans. Not without reason an authority on the local German stage concludes that the "largest part of any German-American theatrical repertory was . . . composed of 'pot boilers'. . . ."[13]

In the latter part of May the theatres and the opera closed their portals and actors, like so many other citizens, fled the city in search of a cooler and healthier climate. There remained in the city however a sizable group of middle and working class people who desired to attend plays during the summer, and amateur theatrical organizations were formed to meet their needs. The Histrionic Association, founded in 1848, combined amateurs with a few professionals with some success until 1852 when their theatre burned. Their function was resumed in 1855 by a group called the New Orleans Can't-Get-Away Dramatic Association and later in the decade by the Crescent Dramatic Association. Both were strictly amateur organizations which used the stage of local theatres. There was also a French language amateur group that performed in the summer at the Orleans theatre.

Probably no discussion of the theatre in New Orleans would be complete without a discussion of the minstrel shows whose origin traces to the "Jump Jim Crow" routine "Daddy" Rice first presented on the stage of the Camp Street Theatre in 1835. By the 1850's when the minstrel show had evolved into a distinct medium, every season found one or more troupes in the city. Sometimes they played in the major theatres—they were popular and profitable—but more common they rented a hall for a short run. Of all the troupes that came into the city none was so popular as Peel's Original Campbell's Minstrels; for the grand price of twenty-five cents they delighted the local citizenry, young and old, with a wide variety of jest, song, and dance. "Their delineation of negro character, their burlesque, and their superior singing cannot be surpassed," wrote an enthusiastic follower of the group.[14] Members of the cast were even used in various church choirs which undoubtedly enlivened otherwise dull services.

Supplementing the theatre proper were numerous public entertainments offered in tents, rented stores, vacant lots, and, in the case of the ubiquitous Spaulding and Rogers, a "floating palace circus" docked at Canal Street twice in the 1850's. It was a rare time during the winter season when a curious New Orleanian could not find a seedy circus or tattered acrobatic group in a tent pitched on an empty lot. Vacant spaces and parks were used also for daring balloon ascensions, but since any one could watch a flight, promoters sought a paying public with bands, freak shows, free prizes, and lectures on skyway adventures. Normally balloon ascensions were brief, though one intrepid aeronaut floated from New Orleans to near Vicksburg. Appealing to less enlightened tastes were exhibits of human and animal freaks which solicited the public's change and taxed their credulity. The more elaborate of which called themselves "museums." The best known of such places, there were at least five during the decade, was Vanuchi's Museum which began as a travelling show and settled into a permanent three-story structure. "Open all hours during the day and brilliantly illuminated at night." Inside were found stuffed and bottled animals, "HUMAN CURIOSITIES" (dead and alive), wax figures chiefly of famous men from American and Biblical history, and an occasional pancrama. If nothing else, it was educational.

Last there was what might loosely be called a "theatre of the streets." The byways of the city bustled with "entertainers." Curious onlookers were accosted by men who operated "lung testing" or "strength testing" machines, while others offered to show the citizenry the mysteries of the stars through a telescope or the unseen world of "infusoria" under a miscroscope. To the less scientific a trained bear provided a few minutes of entertainment at the price of a picayune or two. Street musicians wandered about singing or playing for the edification of the crowd, hoping their musical offerings would deserve a small payment. Most popular of the street entertainers were Italian organ grinders whose Neopolitan tunes and pet monkeys delighted children and whose instrument frequently accompanied impromptu Negro street corner and courtyard dances.

THE OPERA.

New Orleans was the first city in America to have a regular opera season. As early as 1809 opera companies appeared on the

Le Nouveau Theatre de la Nouvelle-Orleans. D'apres une photographie. Known later as the French Opera House
(L'Illustration Journal University XXXIV, December 1859)

stage of the Théâtre d'Orléans, but it was not until 1813 when John Davis, a local gambler, constructed the second Orleans that a structure existed to provide a permanent home for opera. The Orleans was remodelled in 1845 and expanded to hold 1,344 seats. In 1852 the *Orleanian* said of it:

> The theatre is a pretty one; [it] wears an ancient aspect, and in its style of galleries, dress circle etc. resembles much of the old world theatres. With great precision and judgment it has been constructed so as to afford a view of the stage from all parts of the house; then its compactness ... enables all to hear as well as see. The *loges* we think too small for convenience and comfort, especially when some five people are packed in them.

John Davis, and later his son, owned and managed the Orleans until 1853, when Charles Boudousquié assumed control. Dissatisfied with the shabby interior and cramped quarters of the Orleans, Boudousquié, with the support of local financiers, organized a company and constructed a new opera house. The Théâtre d'Opéra, built in the Greek revival style at an estimated cost of $118,000, opened on December 1, 1859, greeting 3,000 of New Orleans' *haute sociétié* with the rousing overture to Rossini's *William Tell*. The Théâtre d'Orléans was sold to a Parisian capitalist and operated with small success and a poor cast in 1859-1860 and 1860-1861. The antiquated and roach-infested house was simply unable to compete with the newer Théâtre d'Opéra; it was not reopened for opera after the Civil War.

The operas presented in New Orleans were the favorites of Europe. New Orleans audiences, like Parisians, especially enjoyed Meyerbeer — long four and five act grand operas with a heavy stress on tragic, romantic plots. Also popular were Verdi, Bellini, Donizetti, and Rossini as well as light nineteenth century French comic operas. Often two short comic operas were performed in an evening along with a "musical divertisement," a ballet, or even a bit of poetry reading, and culminating in a rousing chorus of "La Marseillaise." On rare occasions separate acts from individual operas were presented.

Operas were sung in French even when of Italian origin though Italian operas were sometimes presented in their native language by touring companies. Thus an erratic Italian company en route from New York to Mexico City staged nine operas at the St. Charles Theatre in March and April, 1852, four Italian operas

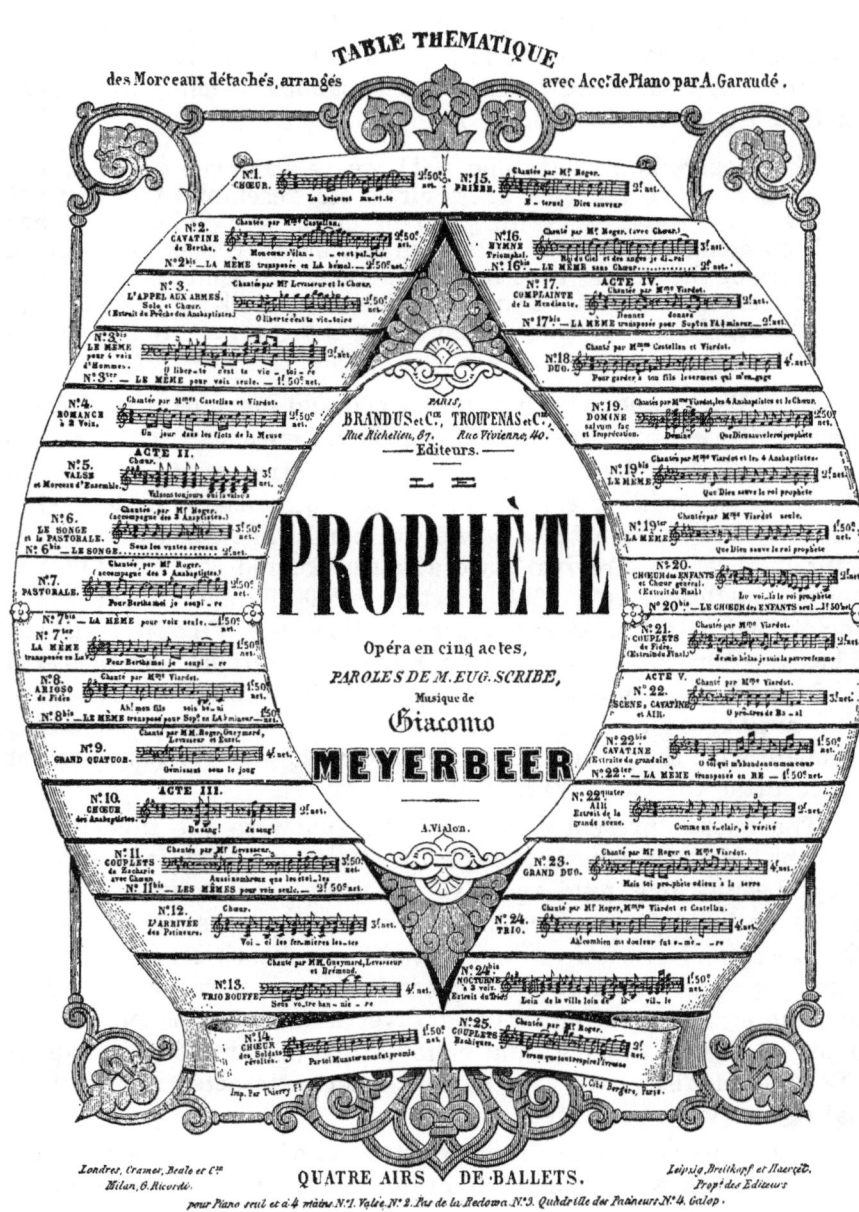

Program — "Le Prophète" by Meyerbeer

were produced in 1856 at the same theatre; a year later an Italian troupe "with small houses [and] fourth rate artists" had a brief run at the Gaiety Theatre.[15] On the eve of the Civil War the Parodi Italian Company put on several performances at Spaulding and Rogers Academy of Music; their appearance marked the first New Orleans appearance of Verdi's *La Traviata*.[16]

At the end of the opera season the cast broke up. A few members went to New York for a short opera and concert season; a smaller number remained in New Orleans or the nearby resort centers; most of the stars returned to France. The opera managers sailed to Paris to gather a company for the coming season. Using 1855-1856 as an example, the cast was composed of two first tenors, one baritone, one bass, and three "prima donnas" for grand opera. For comic opera, two tenors, two basses, and a "prima donna" were employed while five men and five women handled the Sunday theatrical and vaudeville roles. A chorus of thirty was recruited locally and in France; the thirty-five piece orchestra mostly consisted of musicians from abroad. The opera house employed also a stage manager, a scenic artist, a librarian, a treasurer, a prompter, a costumer, a mechanic, and three orchestra leaders.

The New Orleans opera companies were of first-rate quality, "excelled only by a very few in Europe."[17] Writing of the 1858-1859 cast the *Mirror* declared: "it is as complete and happy a selection of artists as the appreciative audiences who nightly crowd the Orleans have ever greeted with due need of genuine applause." The orchestra, reported a visiting Englishman, was the best in America and not inferior to most found in Europe. Perhaps the most eloquent proof of the company's excellence rests in the fact that Bellini's *Norma* was staged fifty-one times in this decade; *Norma* demands a soprano with extraordinary powers.

Davis and Boudousquié were able to command top talent by means of high salaries and profitable benefit performances given for the stars at the end of the season. In addition the chief prima donnas—Wideman, Colson, Lafranque, Fleury-Joly, Parodi, Paoli, Bourgois—had male admirers who frequently showered them with jewelry and money. While leading male singers might not have been the recipients of female largesse, at least not publically, they too basked in the overwhelming popularity which met opera stars. The applause at the Théâtre d'Orléans must have been heady indeed for singers not quite good enough or ready for the major European opera houses.

Apart from the music offered, opera was an important social institution. Attendance was "absolutely necessary" to the "social success and happiness" of the upper class in the city.[18] On Thursday and Saturday nights, the "fashionable nights," the Théâtre d'Orléans was the "select resort of the bon ton."[19] Socially prominent families subscribed to season private boxes, loge and balcony seats, lattice boxes, or parquette chairs for these two evenings. "Some were blase," remembered Eliza Ripley, "and looked dreadfully bored, a few were young and frisky, but everyone of them possessed a pompous and self important mien." The women, "demi-parisiens à demi-créoles," were dressed with *Directoire* simplicity.[20] "They were," reported an enchanted visitor, "attired in Parisian fashion, not over dressed . . . their luxuriant hair tastefully arranged, fastened with ornamental pins and adorned with a coloured riband or a simple flower."[21] The men, according to another visitor, were "moustashed and bearded dandies with Parisian cut coats, and a most undeniable odour of tobacco."[22] The daughters of wealthy Creole and Americans were the objects of amorous stares by bachelors who wandered about the opera house in the intermission or stood in the lobbies. Undoubtedly many of these young blades allowed their glances to move upward to the galleries where sat the wealthier free Negro families and the women of the demi-monde.

In its origins opera-going was Creole, but by the 1840's upper-class Americans were common and by the 1850's attendance had become popular among a sizeable element of the American middle class. In 1851 the *Picayune* remarked: "We are pleased to see so many of our Anglo-Saxon population attending the Orleans. . . ." "Lately," stated the *Delta* in 1853, "fondness for the opera has become disseminated throughout our population, and all portions of our citizens, indiscriminately, have taken in hand the support and encouragement of this refined order of amusement." Three years later the *Picayune* reported that the French opera "is in a very great degree, if not in the larger, supported by the people who reside or sojourn out of and above the French section of the city." American interest in the opera was expressed by financial support in organizing the Théâtre d'Opéra in 1858; about a fourth of the stockholders were Anglo-Saxon merchants. Other indications of American involvement in the opera may be seen in the fact that librettos sold at the door were in French and English with the enclosed advertisements being almost entirely in English and in the appearance of a bi-lingual opera news magazine published in the mid-fifties. Certainly the English press took an active interest and pride in the affairs of the opera company, and rose to the barricades whenever the ability or the character of the local company was questioned by the "Gascons of Gotham." "We have the only *real* opera house in the United States," an irate editor informed his New York compatriots.[23] Opera had become a city-wide institution.

Concerts were a regular feature of the winter season. And of all the concert series during the 1850's none attracted as much attention as the one given by Jenny Lind. Under the sponsorship of master showman, P. T. Barnum, the "Swedish Nightingale" arrived in the Crescent City on February 16, 1851, to present thirteen concerts. The city was in a fervor; in what was supposed to be a musically sophisticated center Miss Lind was greeted by shouting crowds (she had to go to her apartment in disguise), parades, firemen's concerts, and curtain call after curtain call. Whether she sang folk songs or opera, audiences were in a frenzy. Nor were music critics far behind. After her first concert the *Picayune* panegyrized: "Jenny Lind has been seen and heard, and all the most partial report had heralded of her unmatched sweetness as the Queen of Song, was more than justified in the unparalleled success of her debut." The paper declared that "Not to have heard Jenny Lind, is to have heard nothing." Her concerts were "an era in the history of our city." Even the music critics of the French newspapers overcame their initial coolness and awarded her their accolades.

Hardly less emotional was the treatment of the pianist Louis Moreau Gottschalk, a one-time resident of the city, who arrived in New Orleans on his American tour in 1853. His entrance into New Orleans, records an early biographer, "was triumphal;" city fathers, free masons, musicians, militia units, and private citizens accompanied him on a parade to the city hall where he was given a gold medal.[24] Called America's first matinee idol, Gottschalk's dramatic langour made him a favorite of women; "he is just too wonderful," wrote a New Orleans belle, captivated by his "large dreamy blue eyes & beautiful smile & the most perfect teeth I ever saw." She "nearly died with delight" over his music.

> ... I can not tell you how divinely he plays—such execution, such power & at times such extreme delicacy of touch, at times so melancholy & then brilliant beyond anything. ... I don't believe I can enjoy hearing the piano played by anyone else again.[25]

Jose Mandeville was not the only female to be aroused by Gottschalk's charm; while practicing in a Canal Street music store he was mobbed by a phalanx of squealing women. It was no wonder that the concerts of the "New Orleans Virtuoso" however saccharine his style and selections, were tremendous successes.

A far better pianist was Sigismund Thalberg, the first significant European pianist to come to America, who gave a series of concerts in 1858. In deference to the musical taste of the city, he did not restrict his repertory to the classical. The flighty Stella Bringier cried over his rendition of "Home Sweet Home," and his version of the "Last Rose of Summer, played with the left hand alone," left her in a state of ecstasy. "It is something sublime. Something that your imagination could never have conceived and that never can be forgotten."[26] Thalberg's reaction to the Stella Bringiers in the audience is not known; he was probably too preoccupied counting (with both hands) the sizable box office receipts.

The extensive interest in music, the presence of talented musicians and singers from the opera company, and an abundance of French and German music teachers, fostered local musical aggregations. Thus in 1853 the first symphony orchestra — actually a small string orchestra — the Philharmonic Society of the Friends of Art, was founded by four or five French, Italian, and German musicians. The yellow fever epidemic of that year carried off all but one of their members and the society ceased functioning. Its place in the musical world was taken by the Classical Music Society, which was organized in 1855 and reconstituted with a longer subscription list and a larger orchestra in 1858. The Society gave a series of six concerts yearly at the Odd Fellows Hall under the baton of George Collignan, a conductor of the opera orchestra. An example of its programs may be gleaned from its bill for January 31, 1860; Gluck's Overture to *Iphigenia,* Mozart's *Jupiter Symphony*, Von Weber's "Oberon," Mendelssohn's "Fingal's Cave," a song from *Die Freischutz* by a soprano from the opera company, the opening movement from Beethoven's *First Symphony,* and the Overture from Rossini's *Masaniello*. In spite of the expensive subscription price — thirty-five dollars for six concerts — the crowds were large and appreciative. In 1856 the Celia Music Society was established and presented four concerts. Organized in the manner of the New York Philharmonic with a regular subscription list and a mixed professional and amateur orchestra, it was unable to compete in the long run with the Classical Music Society and disbanded after a few seasons. Pops concerts, begun in the summer of 1856, were held at the Odd Fellow's Hall every Wednesday and Friday evening under the baton of a local music teacher. During the summer of 1855 and 1858 concerts of a similar nature were given at the lakeshore in Milneburg.

Among the composers claimed by New Orleans the greatest without doubt was Gottschalk. Of Creole and Jewish stock, he lived in the city until the age of fourteen, when his parents sent him to France where he studied under Charles Halle and Hector Berlioz. He became a renowned pianist and composer — the first American to "crash" European musical circles — and returned to the United States in the early fifties and remained until the close of the Civil War. He spent the rest of his life in South America. Gottschalk did not compose a single bar of music in New Orleans, but his native city furnished the background for his most original numbers. He was the first composer to adapt Negro music to a classical form. His piano pieces like "La Bamboula," "Le Bananier," "La Savanne," "Ojas Criolles," and "The Banjo" were based on Creole Negro dances and songs. He all but destroyed their primitive passion and beauty with a stylized form and sentimental manner, but the originality of the adaption was nonetheless significant. It was these pieces that won Gottschalk his European fame and for which he is chiefly noted today. The bulk of his work is hopelessly trivial; or, to use a contemporary appraisal, it reveals a "tender, dreamy languor, a delicious egotism," leaving "an impression of dreamy yet positive delight upon the mind."[27]

A number of local musicians composed serious music which was known and played in New Orleans but did not evoke enthusiasm in national or international musical circles. Theodore La Hache, organist, music dealer, bookseller, and music teacher, wrote art songs and minor classical numbers for chamber music groups. At the request of the Catholic Archbishop, La Hache occasionally was commissioned to compose a mass for a feast day. These masses varied from arrangements for organists (La Hache was the organist at the St. Louis Cathedral) and single singers (motets) to

Title Page of "The Banjo" by Gottschalk

pontifical high masses. Gregorio Curto, like La Hache a man of many talents, dabbled in serious composition. He wrote several operas in the 1830's and over two hundred motets, solos, trios, quartetos, quintettes, etc. Curto's most monumental work was his *Grand Mass of the Immaculate Conception,* which was performed at St. Eustache's Church in Paris with a full orchestra; it was the first mass written to honor this feast day. Eugene Prévost, the leading opera house conductor, composed a set of operas and classical numbers between 1835 and 1850. One of his operas, *La Chaste Suzanne,* was performed once in the 1850's. Prévost also composed a few masses and a *Te Deum.* Given the operatic background of Curto and Prévost, and La Hache's melodic sense, their church compositions probably owed more to Guiseppi Verdi than to Gregory the Great. In addition to the above figures Eugene Chassignac and Hubert Rolling, the latter with a local reputation as "une compositeur très distingé and "une pianiste de première force," wrote some light classical pieces and art songs.

A few prominent free Negro musicians and composers of classical music were born in New Orleans; however the Crescent City was no place for sensitive free Negroes and they lived abroad most of their lives. Edmund Dedé studied violin in New Orleans, but in 1848 he migrated to Mexico and then to Europe where he eventually became conductor of the Bordeaux Symphony Orchestra. Richard Lambert, born in New Orleans around 1828, left to study in Paris; there he and his son became popular French concert stars and composers. The only outstanding free Negro musician to remain in New Orleans and Eugene Macarty.

New Orleans popular music writers contributed to the sum national total of light and fleeting tunes and songs. Stage managers needing a novelty number or a piece to honor a local event often had a member of the cast prepared it or, like Dan Rice, wrote it themselves. "Dixie" was one such song. Written by a minstrel actor, Dan Emmett, and played first in New York City in 1859, the song was ignored until John E. Owens, manager of the Varieties Theatre, used it as a marching song for a troupe of forty female Zouaves. The song, catching the spirit of Southern nationalism, was immediately popular. "Dixie's Land," reported the *Delta* in April, 1860, "has been the musical furore for the past week of brass bands, whistling darkies, burnt cork melodists, and Tuscarora braves."

Among the local citizens who turned their hand to composing popular songs were Hubert Rolling, Jules Nores, Harry McCarthy ("The Bonnie Blue Flag"), G. Schmidt, George Collignan, G. A. Montmain, Eugene Chassignac, H. E. Lehman, Basile J. Bares (free Negro), and the ever-prolific Theodore La Hache. There were even a few women composers. In 1849 a local musical review declared that Mme. E. Lavillebeuvre's "Reverie" was "la première composition musicale écrit par une dame Créole." With more ardor than accuracy Mme. Lavillebeuvre was compared favorably with Franz Schubert.[28] Another Creole woman, Mme. Thomas Morphy, also composed songs and music in the 1850's. These local composers wrote songs for organizations to be used at anniversaries, dances, or other special occasions. Frequently they wrote songs dedicated to some local beauty to be given to her by a beau. These little songs—canzonetta or cantilene—were arranged for the piano and were romantic and sentimental. Songs like "Aime Moi Toujours," "Rappele Toi," "Reverie to I . . . x E . . . x," and "La Clematite," must have caused many a heart flutter. While sons as "L'Adieu d'une Mere," "La Vierge du Chemin, No. 5," and "Pour Ma Mere," were evidently designed to reach the young lady's heart through her tear glands.

Separate from the main trend of white man's music was the development of a nearly indigenous Negro music and dance with a beauty and originality of its own. A shrewd contemporary observer contended that the Southern Negro had developed America's only folk music, but except for Louis Moreau Gottschalk's insipid versions of a few Negro pieces, their music was considered beyond the pale for respectable people. Travellers, often more objective than local citizens, heard Negroes singing "their wild fantastic, yet harmonious"[29] songs at work on the wharves or on steamboats, but only one, the observant Frederick Law Olmsted, bothered to put down on paper the words he heard. In the following work songs of a group of Negro steamboatmen, a sample of which is given below, the lead line was improvised by a single Negro with the group forming the "chorus;" basically this is the call and response technique which came from West Africa.

    Ye see dem boat way dey ahead
        Oahoiohieu
    De San Charles in arter em, dey mus go behine
        Oahoiohieu

Odd Fellows Home, 1858

City Hall, 1858

United States Mint, 1858

Touro Building on Canal Street with Chrst Church in the distance, 1858.

Steele Chapel (Methodist) was one of the rare examples of Greek architecture in New Orleans churches. Designed by Thomas K. Wharton. This illustration made from Wharton's diary of 1855.

So stir up dah, my livelies, stir her up
 Oahoiohieu
Dey's burnin not'n but fat and rosun
 Oahoiohieu
Oh we is gwine up de Red River, oh
 Oahiohieu

Ime gwine away to-morrow
 Oh John come down in de holler
 Oh work and talk and holler
 Oh John, come down in de holler
Ime gwine away to marry
 Oh John, etc.
Get my doves in order
 Oh John, etc.
I'se gwine away to-morrow
 Oh John, etc.
. . . .
Work all day Sunday
 Oh John, etc.
Massa get de money
 Oh John, etc.

After conclusion of the song, and after the Negroes had left the bows, and were coming aft along the guards, we passed two or three colored nurses, walking with children on the river bank; as we did so the singers jumped on some cotton bales, bowed very low to them, took off their hats, and swung and waved them, and renewed their song.

God bless you all dah! ladies!
 Oh John, etc.
Farewell, de Lord be wid you, honey
 Oh John, etc.
Don't cry yerself to def
 Oh John, etc.
I'm gwine to New Orleans
 Oh John, etc.
I'll come back, dough, bineby
 Oh John, etc.
So far-you-well, my honey
 Oh John, etc.

Creole Negro songs were more elaborate than the work songs and were generally related to dances. From colonial times Negroes had gathered in Congo Square on Sunday to engage in dancing and singing. When Benjamin Latrobe visited New Orleans in 1818 he noticed that Negroes utilized hand drums (tomtoms), a primitive form of banjo, tambourines, and a bone clapper ("bones"). The instruments and dances, both fast and slow, were of African or at least Haitian origin, though the chants which accompanied them were sung in French. Words were often sounds used to capture the feeling of the instruments. Following are verses to accompany the Calinda, a popular dance.[30]

> Michié Préval le donnin gran bal.
> Li fait naig payé pou sauté inpé.
> Dansé calinda, boudoum, boudoum,
> Dansé calinda, boudoum, boudoum.
>
> Michié Préval li té capitaine bal,
> So cocher Louis to maitre ceremonie.
> Dansé calinda, etc.
> Dansé calinda, etc.
>
> Dans lequirie la yavé gran gala,
> No cré choual layé té bien étonné.
> Dansé calinda, etc.
> Dansé calinda, etc.
>
> Yavé des negresse belle passe maitresse,
> Yé voté be-belle dans l'ormoire mamzelle.
> Dansé calinda, etc.
> Dansé calinda, etc.

Other dances were the Bamboula, the Counjaille or Counjai, and the Juba. It is quite probable that these dances and the music for them had fallen into disrepute by 1850's for one traveller noted a violin being played and quadrilles danced by Negroes in Congo Square.

Reflecting an European rather than an African strain in Creole Negro music were the love songs. Sung in the mellifluous Negro-French dialect, they recounted love affairs — requited and unrequited. In feeling, though not in structure, these songs resembled the later blues. Prepared by well-known singers, they were passed down by word of mouth. In the 1850's the most famous of these singers was Joe Beaumont, a free Negro barber, whose "Toucoutou," recounting the story of an octoroon who attempted to cross the color line, was something of a classic in his time.

NOTES

[1] Moritz Wagner and Carl Scherzer, *Reisen in Nordamerika in den Jähren 1852 und 1853* (Leipzig, 1854), 353.
[2] "Musical Chit-Chat," *Dwight's Journal of Music*, IX (June 7, 1856), 87.
[3] *Weekly Mirror*, April 2, 1859.
[4] *Weekly Delta*, May 29, 1853.
[5] *Ibid.*, November 3, 1851.
[6] *Weekly Picayune*, July 23, August 6, September 10, December 10, 1855.
[7] *Weekly Mirror*, December 25, 1858.
[8] *Emile D. Baron* v. *Thomas Placide* (1852), 7, La., 229-231.
[9] *Weekly Mirror*, March 12, 1859.
[10] *Daily Orleanian*, January 4, 1852.
[11] *Weekly Mirror*, February 12, 1859, January 1, 1859.
[12] Sol Smith, *Theatrical Management in the West and South for Thirty Years* (New York, 1868), 233.
[13] Robert T. Clark, "The German Liberals in New Orleans, 1840-1860," *Louisiana Historical Quarterly*, XX (January, 1937), 150.
[14] *Louisiana State Republican*, November 25, 1854.
[15] *Porter's Spirit of the Times*, II (May 9, 1857), 148.
[16] There were isolated performances of now forgotten English operas such *Love Spell*, *Bohemian Girl*, *Rip Van Winkle*, and *Enchantress*. Short comic operas were common and at least once a year French and Italian operas in English were offered. The only German opera recorded was Von Weber's *Die Freischütz*.
[17] *Weekly Delta*, November 3, 1851.
[18] Eliza Ripley, *Social Life in Old New Orleans, Being Recollections of My Girlhood* (New York, 1912), 67.
[19] *Daily Picayune*, December 25, 1856; *Weekly Delta*, April 3, 1853.
[20] J. J. Ampére, *Promenade en Amerique*, II, 133.
[21] Charles Lyell, *A Second Visit to the United States of North America* (2nd ed., 2 vols.; London, 1850), II, 115.
[22] Edward R. Sullivan, *Rambles and Scrambles in North and South America* (London, 1852), 223.
[23] *Daily Crescent*, September 3, 1858.
[24] Luis Ricardo Fors, *Gottschalk* (New York, 1880), 64.
[25] Jose Mandeville to Rebecca Mandeville, April 9, 16, 1853. Henry D. Mandeville Papers, Louisiana State University Archives, Baton Rouge.
[26] Stella Bringier to Louis A. Bringier, February 18, 1858. Bringier Papers, 1850-1850, Louisiana State University Archives, Baton Rouge.
[27] *Weekly Delta*, March 27, 1853.
[28] *La Violette, Revue Musicale et Littéraire*, December, 1849.
[29] Frederick Pollard, ed., *Macready's Reminiscenses and Selections from His Diaries and Letters* (New York, 1875), 587.
[30] William Francis Allen, and others, comps., *Slave Songs of the United States* (New York, 1867), 111.

Statue of Henry Clay on Canal Street, unveiled April 12, 1860
(Frank Leslie's Illustrated Newspaper May 5, 1860)

Chapter XI

ART AND ARCHITECTURE

Under the pretext of art, the rich in particular, limit themselves to whitewashing the trees of their gardens; this luxury has the double advantage of pleasing the eyes and of being very cheap.[1]
In architectural matters, Louisiana is one of the richest, most varied and interesting places in the United States, if not in all of America. Diverse influences strongly contributed to the formation of an artistic expression, of a genius at times rational, gay, elegant, and reserved.[2]

ART.

Ante-bellum New Orleans, according to romantic tradition, was a "Mecca of American artists," and the city's aristocracy, especially the Creole aristocracy, were sensitive, enthusiastic, and discriminating partons of art.[3] This is highly questionable. In fact, as will be demonstrated below, there wasn't a single artist in the city with more than regional fame; of the hundreds of American painters who contributed to the National Academy of Design in New York and to the Pennsylvania Academy of Fine Arts in the ante-bellum period, none was from New Orleans; of the hundreds of artists listed in a history of United States art published in 1880, none lived in New Orleans in the 1850's. There were no art galleries and only one real patron of arts — and he was not a Creole.

The portrait painter was the most common artist in New Orleans. Wealthy persons desiring to be remembered by posterity by having portraits done in oils were numerous enough in the prosperous fifties to provide commissions and a fair living for several painters. These portrait artists generally drifted into the city from Europe or the East, set up a studio, painted a few years, and then restless, dissatisfied, or bankrupt they took up other occupations or left town. A few like B. F. Rinehart and R. Geshwindt were trained in Germany, a larger number — Lepelletier Duclary, Jacques Amans, Richard Clague, and Paul Poincy to name a few — were graduates of Paris art schools, while others like A. G. Powers and Theodore Moise were born and trained in America. The best portraitist in the city was Enoch Wood Perry who had been educated in Düsseldorf, Paris, Rome and Venice. After opening a studio in 1860 he painted John Slidell which remains as one of the better portraits of the decade.

For citizens unable to afford time or money for an oil portrait there were a growing number of studios where daguerreotypes and ambrotypes (photographs made on glass) were available. The portraitist's boast that he could paint an exact likeness was more than matched by the daguerreotypist who could capture a literal image on glass or metal — and for only one dollar! Even the color of the portrait painter might be rivalled by skillful painting over a daguerreotype or ambrotype with an oil base paint. Significant perhaps was an advertisement showing a painter abandoning his easel and fleeing in dismay at the sign of a sun representing an ambrotype.

Commercial art was not of course limited to portrait painters. Newspapers and job printers demanded the services of lithographers and engravers, and the ever-changing repertory at the opera and theatre offered employment for scenery painters. There was some call for skilled mural painters like Dominique Canova, Leon Pomarède, and Alexandre Boulet to decorate churches, public building, and few homes. Most of the painters specialized in decorative motifs in homes, public buildings, coffee houses, and steamboats. The coffee houses in particular provided abundant opportunities; "A naked Venus," declared one knowing reporter, "appears to be indispensible in such places." This same critic however did not consider these paintings provocative because the "paintings are generally so bad — such mere daubs of yellow ochre and Prusian blue, crossed with a dash of vermillion, that few, even of our 'fast young men,' can regard them for any length of time with pleasure."[4] Neither the names of these bar room painters nor the evidences of their work seem to be extant, but it is doubtful that any Charles Russell, Frederick Remington, or John Noble began their art apprenticeship in New Orleans saloons.

A few artists dabbled in landscapes and genre paintings, while B. F. Rinehart and Enoch Wood Perry attempted massive canvasses. Perry's "Signing of the Ordinance of Secession of Louisiana" executed in 1861 has some historical, but little artistic merit. Perry and his group were limited to the current Düsseldorf-Munich tradition — their paintings were generally brown, toneless, lifeless, and imitative ventures. Except by Richard Clague and Paul Poincy, both natives of New Orleans, and a few painters passing through the city, the spectacular subject matter-swamps, markets, steamboats, wharves, plantations — and the vivid color of the semi-tropical scene were ignored. Plein-air painting, then being practiced by the French Impressionists, would have given New Orleans artists a new perspective, but their training kept them inside their studios and at work on unbelievably sterile paintings.

Perhaps the lowly condition of the visual arts might have been improved by the existence of an art gallery. Two attempts to form a gallery were made in the 1840's and another in the early fifties, but as late as 1859 the Mirror could unhappily report that "so far no movement has been made to secure the advantages it [art gallery] would undoubtedly confer in forming and attuning the public taste to a correct appreciation of the beautiful." The only institution comparable to an art gallery was the Southern Art Union founded by Charles Galvani, an art dealer who kept on hand what the *Picayune* was pleased to call "a magnificent collection of paintings . . . worthy of the attention of the most accomplished judges." Whenever Galvani completed a special purchase he advertised it in the newspapers and invited all to view it and other of his paintings; he and other enterprising dealers, and sometimes even a lodge or church charged a small fee for the privilege of beholding works of art. Paintings were also shown by the local branches of the Cosmopolitan Art Association, the Cincinnati Art Union, and the Western Art Union, agencies designed to allow members to purchase paintings by subscription.

The poor man's art gallery was the popular panorama (sometimes called "cosmorama" if they were especially long or "tableau" if they presented a traditional story) shown in a hall or "museum" during the winter season. The panoramas were immense paintings — one was 1,325 yards long, another covered 100,000 square feet of canvas — executed by several artists and generally depicting some natural phenomena. They were viewed in a round room with the audience in the center; as the canvas was slowly unrolled (often accompanied by sound effects and mood music), a guide lectured on the subject. The quality of the painting was, to say the least, primitive, but curious New Orleanians looked at panoramas on Niagara Falls, Mammoth Cave, the Kane Artic expedition, Italy, the Crimean War, the Nile, the Western plains and Rocky Mountains, and a panorama painted by a former New Orleans resident, Leon Pomaréde's "Original Panorama of the Mississippi and Indian Life." A favorite in the city was the "Pilgrim's Progress Tableau," billed as "the great lesson of the Bible thrown on canvas," but which a local citizen felt was "merely coarse 'scene paintings'."⁵ In the same vein was "Williams' panoramic painting of Bible history" and a tableau entitled "The Captive Israelites" as well as the happy sequel on the "Departure of the Israelites."

Good sculptors in New Orleans, as in the rest of the ante-bellum America, were rare. Caleb G. Forshay, a professor and engineer, Achille Perelli, a painter, and J. N. de Pouilly, an architect, made serious but artistically unsuccessful attempts at sculpture. None achieved the fame of Eugene Warburg, a New Orleans free Negro, who went to Europe at an early age and remained there the rest of his life. Deserving passing mention were monument makers who created mourning angels and carved bas relief figures on tombs; occasionally one of these works took on a real charm and revealed an unknown talent.

Whatever the drawbacks of local sculpture, the fifties did see the erection of the two most famous public statues in New Orleans. Under the sponsorship of the city government and a private Jackson Memorial Association, Clark Mills was commissioned to make a copy of his equestrian statute of Andrew Jackson in Washington D.C., and on February 9, 1856, the duplicate was unveiled amidst an elaborate ceremony and the plaudits of an estimated 25,000 onlookers. Visitors however were less kind; one remarked that in the statute "everything is sacrificed to the position of the horse . . . [it] wants repose and has a clumsy look," while a Frenchman insisted that "this statute has no other merit other than being colossal . . . ."⁶ Shortly after the death of Henry Clay in 1852 a Clay Monumental Association was organized to arrange a memorial to him which took the form of a bronze statue of Clay done by Joel Hunt of Kentucky. In June, 1859, the statue of the Great Compromiser was dedicated and placed in a circle near the river end of Canal street. Many years later the statue was moved to Lafayette Square where it stands today.

The sad state of painting and sculpture might have been changed if, as in fourteenth century Florence or seventeenth century Netherlands, there had been wealthy patrons to encourage artists or at the very least to collect famous paintings. Such patrons hardly existed anywhere in the United States and in New Orleans the only real patron of the arts was James Robb, railroad builder and banker, and by all definitions a nouveaux riche. He was the only New Orleans member of the National Academy of Design and the Pennsylvania Academy of Fine Arts (he lent them

81 paintings and three statues for exhibit); he gave financial aid to Hiram Powers whose "Slave Girl" was the first nude sculptured by an American; and he was the largest contributor to the Clay monument. Robb had a private art collection that was both extensive and generally excellent, including over seventy-four major paintings, many from the Joseph Bonaparte collection. Among the artists represented were Rubens, Reynolds, Vanderlyn, Rosa, Vernet, Durand, Leutze and Snyders. Murals in his home were executed by Dominique Canova, nephew of the famous Italian sculptor Antonio Canova, who had earlier painted the impressive murals in the St. Louis Hotel. Robb's collection of statuary was less outstanding though it did include a number of extremely valuable pieces and he owned several folio volumes of original prints and engravings. So little interest was there in the city in this collection that in 1858 when Robb was forced to sell his art treasures, many paintings failed to final local buyers.

Probably the best summary on art attitudes in New Orleans is found in a delightful story recorded by Eliza Ripley.

> An Old Gentleman, called 'Old Jimmie Dick' when I remember him, a rich cotton broker . . . made a voyage to Europe, and brought back home some Apollos, and Cupids, and Mercuries, statues in the 'altogether,' for his parlor. Jimmie Dick was a bachelor, and . . . had a charming spinster niece keeping house for him, who was so shocked when she saw the figures mounted on pedestals (they were glaring white marble and a trifle under life size) that she immediately made slips of brown holland and enveloped them, leaving only the heads exposed.[7]

ARCHITECTURE

If the city was hard pressed to discover and maintain an artistic tradition, the same was not true in the field of architecture. No contemporary American city could equal the variety, the good taste, and the originality of New Orleans homes, places of business, and public buildings. Part of this architectural pre-eminence was atributable to a number of excellent architects. The Galliers, father and son, constructed many buildings in New Orleans from the 1830's to well after the Civil War, and were especially skilled in adapting Greek Revival architecture to fit urban requirements of space and location. James and Charles Dakin, like the elder Gallier born in Ireland, worked in a similar tradition. James Freret, J. N. de Pouilly, Henry Howard, and the free Negro, Joseph

Abeilard, also ably conributed to make this the golden age of New Orleans architecture.

Architecture in New Orleans is inevitably associated in the popular mind with the Vieux Carré or French Quarter, and evokes an image of a provincial French town set down in America. Actually most of the city burned down in 1788 and again in 1794 and the Ursuline convent is the only major building surviving from the French period, though the architectural tradition of the French *Côte d'Azur* remained in the curious story-and-a-half hipped cottages which housed Creole planters during the winter season. The Spanish influence in the Vieux Carré is more pronounced with the Cabildo and the Presbytere being classic examples of Spanish Renaissance style. In home architecture the Spanish touch (originally Moorish) was exercised in two or three-story buildings of brick covered with stucco and having an overhanging balcony to the street and an interior courtyard. However it should be noted that neither the French nor the Spanish made, except in a few public buildings, slavish copies of old world models; the functional problems induced by topography, climate, building materials, and long narrow lots fostered a number of significant local variations.

In the haze of romance concerning the French Quarter, American influences in that sector have been overlooked except by a few architectural historians. As American capitalists purchased more of the old city they naturally built and rebuilt to suit their own needs and traditions. Spanish homes were increased in size, with a third floor frequently added, the front enlarged to allow a carriage to enter the courtyard, and balconies were made heavier and wider. The older Spanish buildings were in this manner converted from places of business and residence to serve primarily as homes. Americans also introduced the Greek Revival style into the Vieux Carré, and it was widely adopted in business structures and private homes; its most prominent characteristic was the use of pillars supporting porch or portico or more commonly, superimposed about doorways. The American influence was especially evident on and a few blocks below Canal Street where old building were torn down and large windowed stores and plain brick warehouses were constructed which hardly differed from similar buildings in eastern cities.

Even wrought and cast iron balconies, so intimiately associated with New Orleans' colonial past, were largely of American introduction and manufacture. Wrought iron was used as grill work on balconies by the Spanish, though as late as the 1840's it was rare, but in the two decades before the Civil War cast iron was introduced as a replacement for wooden beams and mainposts in the construction of large edificies. It was a simple step from this point to the "new style" of cast iron pillars as balcony supports and lace work cast iron balcony railings. In 1853 a newspaper reported:

> The erection in front of stores and private residences of wide iron galleries two stories high, supported by substantial iron posts and extending over the entire sidewalk, *seems to be coming into general vogue*.[8]

The iron, brought to New Orleans from Pittsburgh and Baltimore, was processed to order in predominately American foundries by American workmen.

The American influence in the French Quarter was most aesthetically expressed in the Pontalba Building which in 1850 replaced "a poor delapidated [sic], skattered [sic] cluster of old cabarets and eating houses which used to throw a dingy gloom over either side of this beautiful [Jackson] Square."[9] The block-long apartment houses (supposedly the first in the United States) were designed by James Gallier Sr.; constructed of red brick the porticos, doorways, cornices, and dormers showed the mark of Greek Revival style. Superimposed on the building was the kind of iron awning-balcony then newly popular in New Orleans; the balcony was rimmed with an elaborate lace work wrought iron railing. The total affect was striking and handsome, but except for the balconies not much different from buildings that could be found in New York or Baltimore.

Commercial buildings in the uptown area were less complex in origin and appearance than those in the French Quarater. They were generally built to fit the contours of long narrow lots, two to five stories high, and fronted with "large, showy, and elegant" shop windows.[10] Most of these buildings were dull and plain, illustrating what Frederick Law Olmsted called "the characteristics of the unartistic and dollar pursuing Yankees," but some improvements were made in the fifties by the addition of cast iron balconies. The most interesting commercial buildings were those that employed iron "fronts," that is, the cast iron frame work (as in structural steel) on the street side of the building was partially exposed; the largest of these structures were the Touro Buildings, a set of ten stores four stories high on Canal street, and the grotesque, unfinished Moresque Building, "in the style of the Alhambra," on Poydras and Camp streets.

Mansions built after 1840 in the Garden District (uptown) and along the Bayou St. John (downtown) made lavish use of landscaping, placing the house within an environment of semitropical trees, shrubs, and flowers, and often surrounding the whole with an iron fence. Architecturally these newer homes represented several currents and mixtures. Southern Colonial, Georgian, West Indian, and Greek Revival homes could be found, though seldom in a pure state; rather most of the mansions revealed several architectural styles which, according to a noted authority, produced a "conscious original architectural design."[11] Local improvisations are best observed in the use of columns. Instead of running continuous pillars up the front of a two story building, it became popular to employ two single-story sets of wooden pillars separated by a balcony with the pillars and their capitals, Ionic and Corinthian usually, different for each level. The affect was further enhanced by adding side balconies with elaborate cast iron grill work and supported by iron pillars. Probably the most interesting architectural merger was the raised single-story cottage resting on a high basement with stairs on each side running up to small colonnaded porch.

Interior arrangements of the city's mansions varied in accordance with the dictates of the exteriors. Where Spanish and American colonial influence prevailed large windows and shutters were employed and wide central galleries separated the rooms. In the Vieux Carré rooms opened on to an interior patio directly or by means of an enclosed gallery; elsewhere there was a plain two-story back wing to accommodate the kitchen and servant quarters. Greek Revival homes often had a diminutive circular vestibule which opened into a hall room whence a delicate semi-circular stair rose to the upper floors. Rooms were high, regardless of the style, and end chimneys with tall mantles were common. By the 1850's gas lit chandeliers were utilized for light and heat.

If the homes of the wealthy showed a general beauty and simplicity in structure, their interior decorations and furnishings left much to be desired. Walls were occasionally frescoed, but more often they were covered with ornate floral wall paper, which in turn clashed with the gloomy sepia-toned landscape paintings of the age. The color conflict was however not too obvious because heavy purple or rose drapes eliminated light and breeze. Rugs, used in the winter months, were customarily of Belgian or French manufacture and were of good quality and acceptable taste. Furniture in the fifties had passed from the pleasing simplicity of the colonial period to the eclectic taste of the "Second Baroque" and "Gothic" Victorianism. Chairs, chaise longues, and couches, covered in silk brocaded patterns and embellished with elaborate carvings, were often ostentatious, grotesque, and ugly. It was truly the "age of upholstery."[12] Cluttering the rooms and hallways were bric-a-brac side boards and shelves and large vases mounted on fancy carved bronze pedestals. Cabinets of rosewood and mahogany with marble tops were in better taste — sometimes! Bedrooms, whether done in the eclectic fashion or in the current "Style Neo Grec," were scant improvements over the parlors and dining rooms. Beds were likely to be lacy four posters with some frilly charm, but unfortunately the gross iron bedstead came to be accepted in the 1850's; a variation of highly doubtful taste was the iron four poster bed. No less ornate and clumsy were the stoves and the immense cast iron baths. Patios or front yards were littered with stone or cast iron figures and fountains which, if they did not meet the canons of decent sculpture, at least provided the birds with water. The whole impression revealed, to quote Frank Lloyd Wright's view of Chicago interiors in the Victorian age, the "fifty-seven varieties of banal sentimentality."

Among the middle class a "cottage" type of home was popular. There is little information on these cottages, but judging from sale notices in newspapers and samples still standing, they were often two-story frame homes with a small upper balcony and containing from four to six spacious rooms. Such houses cost between two and six thousand dollars and rented from four to five hundred dollars a year. The poor, as noted in an earlier chapter, were crowded into large brick or wooden tenements constructed with a minimum of architectural embellishments, or they lived in makeshift shanties valued at a few hundred dollars. Many of the shanties, especially those in or near the swamp, had their origin in the flatboats which were dismantled after a trip down the river. The planking, if not the entire keel, was placed in the mud and a narrow house built up from it; unfortunately the structures frequently sank, allowing water and mud to seep through the floors. It may not be unreasonable to assume that the present "shotgun" houses in New Orleans (long, narrow homes placed on posts, fifteen to twenty feet wide, without interior hallways) is an institutionalized form of the older barge houses.

The churches of New Orleans were not, taken as a group, on par architecturally with the better homes. The Greek Revival style which graced so many homes and public buildings was often replaced by the less attractive and more derivative Norman and Gothic strains in the churches. There was, however, no lack of variety.

Built in 1798 by funds provided by the Spanish official, Don Almonaster de Rojas, the St. Louis Cathedral was the largest Catholic church in the city. As originally constructed it was a clumsy-looking building covered in grey stucco with a tower on either side of the front and the appearance was not much improved by the addition of a bell tower in 1819 designed by Benjamin Latrobe. In 1850 after Latrobe's tower fell into the church, the wardens employed Louis Pilié to re-design the side towers and replace the bell tower with a larger central spire; at the same time the present sanctuary and vestries were added and the inside of the church was covered with wall murals and frescoes done, supposedly, by the French artist Alexandre Boulet. As a result of these changes the Cathedral lost its awkward appearance and became the imposing structure that has never failed to impress four generations of residents and visitors.

Only a few other Catholic churches were worthy of notice. St. Patrick's Church, designed by Gallier and Dakin and begun in 1837 though not completed until the fifties, was considered very attractive by New Orleans residents, but was actually a rather dull-looking pseudo-Norman edifice. It was decorated by Leon Pomaréde, with murals and frescoes copied after Italian masters, though they look a bit more like set backgrounds for one of the contemporary biblical operas like *Moise* or *La Juive*. St. John the Baptist Church, an architectural oddity on Dryades Street, employed a suggestion of a flying buttress, something of a Greek mausoleum in the steeple, along with an onion-shaped spire more typical of the Ukraine than the American Gulf Coast. The Church of the Immaculate Conception also had about it a romantic air of distant lands. It looked like a mosque. Designed by Father Cambioso, a local Jesuit, it was the first public building to use a Moorish motif and the first to employ extensive tile work. It was, stated a local booster, "an ornament to the city and a creditable monument to the skill and perseverance of the society which has erected it."[13] The Ursuline Convent on Chartres Street was the oldest (1748) religious house in the Mississippi Valley. It was a simple building and probably because of this St. Mary's Italian, which in 1845 was cut into a corner of the old convent, was done in the classic high-vaulted simplicity often characteristic of early eighteenth century French architecture. It was quite possibly the most beautiful church in the city.

The First Presbyterian Church on Lafayette Square was the most striking Protestant house of worship in New Orleans. A Gothic style with a long delicate spire towering over the neighboring buildings gave it a more monumental effect than might have been expected from its modest dimensions. Decorations included extensive murals, faced oak carvings on the pews, and Gothic stained windows. The Canal Street Presbyterian Church, completed just before the outbreak of the war, was an attractive church of simple design with a tower done in the Christopher Wren manner. Norman influences were reflected in the Coliseum Place Baptist Church; like St. Patrick's and St. Theresa's which it resembled, it had a main floor and a side gallery, but because of Baptist theological tenets it was unadorned on the inside. Christ Church (Episcopal) was an elaborate mixture of Norman and Gothic which made it appear, in the eyes of one critic, "to be staggering under a weight of spires."[13] A sort of architectural marzipan seems also to have characterized the new (1855) Unitarian Church on St. Charles Avenue; it was, stated a *Picayune* reporter, "pretty to look at, but the gazer is irresistably inclined to associate its fanciful outlines and numerous turrets with the fragile temples which adorn confectionary windows." The Steel Chapel (Methodist) was one of the rare examples of Greek Revival architecture in New Orleans churches. Designed by Thomas K. Wharton, it had a narrow spire, superimposed pillars about the front of the church, and was built of brick covered over with a "warm coloured stucco."[14]

Government buildings varied from plain and functional jails, fire houses, recorders' courts, markets, hospitals, detention homes, and most schools to more significant structures. The Greek Revival style was personified in the City Hall of the Second Municipality (later of the entire city) designed by the elder Gallier. The beautifully balanced and proportioned two-story United States Mint was done in the same style. Together they were the most attractive public buildings in the city. The Cabildo, which housed the district courts and parish offices, had been constructed by the Spanish in the eighteenth century. It, along with its "twin," the Presbytere, showed strong Castilian and Spanish Renaissance influences rather than the expected ornate Spanish Colonial style. Unfortunately, the over-all effect of the buildings were ruined by the addition in the nineteenth century of a third floor with an "absurd" mansard roof.[15] The United States Custom House, the largest building in New Orleans, was designed by A. T. Wood, a contractor and part-time architect. The cornerstone was laid down on Washington's birthday in 1849, and construction began slowly under the supervision of Major P. G. T. Beauregard; by 1854 part of the building was in use, but final completion did not take place until the mid-1880's. Built of marble, brick, and iron, supported by hundreds of pilings driven into the soft batture soil, the Custom House was a third larger than the national capitol. On the inside there was a cavernous marble hall with fourteen massive columns supporting an arched dome fifty-four feet above the floor. The effect of the whole resembled, what Talbot Hamlin has called, a "rather uneducated person's idea of the Egyptian."

The best known of the city's large buildings was the St. Charles Hotel. The first St. Charles was built in 1837 and was a mammoth three-story wooden building with columns that ran the full height of the building and a large cupola which served as a landmark for seamen and an observatory post. It was, according to a visiting Englishman, "a most magnificent structure." In 1851 the hotel burned to the ground and the new St. Charles which rose from its ashes boasted no cupola and except for fourteen large fluted pilars was otherwise less grandiose than its predecessor. The street floor of the hotel was occupied by shops and a large tavern located in the center of the building; on either side of the tavern were flights of stairs that led to the main entrance and lobby. In the center of the lobby or rotunda eight Corinthian columns supported a large dome from which was suspended a gigantic "noble chandelier." The columns also helped support on three sides of the lobby a gallery which led to the second floor rooms. Most observers of the new St. Charles were pleased by its appearance; Charles Mackay was reminded of the palace of the King of Belgium in Brussels, while Frederica Bremer, otherwise hostile toward the Crescent City, declared that the hotel was a "magnificent building resembling the Pantheon at Rome." Far less enthusiastic was Frederick Law Olmsted who considered the St. Charles "stupendous, tasteless, ill-contrived and inconvenient."

The St. Louis Hotel was a block-long structure, two stories high, and topped by a large copper-plated dome which covered the rotunda for which the hotel was famous. Viewed from inside the building the rotunda presented "one of the finest pieces of architecture in the United States."

> It is a lofty, vaulted hall, eighty feet in diameter, with an aisle running all round, supported by a row of fine pillars fifty feet in height; the dome rises nearly as many feet more, and has a large skylight in the centre; the sides thereof are ornamented by well-executed works in *chiaroscuro*, representing various successful actions gained during the struggle for independence, and several of the leading men who figured during that eventful period.[16]

On the floor of the rotunda was a circle sixty-six feet in diameter paved with vari-colored marble in a geometric design. Unfortunately when a new hotel was recently built on the site the outward appearance partly resembled the old St. Louis Hotel, but no effort was made to reproduce the eye-catching rotunda.

U. S. Custom House on Canal Street as it appeared in 1860. Not completed until years later

After the Custom House and the second St. Charles Hotel, the Odd Fellows Hall on Lafayette Square was the largest constructed in the 1850's. It was a five-story domed structure "in the Corinthian order." The heart of the Hall was a second-floor ballroom, "the most magnificent room in New Orleans," and the most popular place in the city for large meetings. Flanked by a balcony and a special orchestral gallery capable of holding one hundred musicians, the ballroom was decorated with frescoes and hung with "curtains of the most gorgeous description."[17] Other large halls were located in the Mechanics Institute, a massive, clumsy-looking building with a poorly-designed Greek Revival front, and Banks Arcade on Magazine street. The latter was constructed in the 1830's from designs of Charles Zimpel; it was a three-story block-

The Mechanics Institute

long brick building, much resembling the later Pontalba Buildings but without the balconies. Dividing the building was a glassed-over arcade which ran from Gravier to Natchez streets; the building contained a hotel, offices, the armory of the Washington Artillery (Armory Hall), saloons, a restaurant, and the Toutine, a spacious, lushly decorated coffee house which—at least by one account—could hold 5,000 persons. Combining size, with food and drinks, it was, quite naturally, a favorite center for political rallies.

From a twentieth-century perspective the verdict upon New Orleans ante-bellum architecture must be a favorable one. The major influences at work — Spanish, American, Colonial, Georgian, and Greek Revival—made for good taste, and the local styles, blended from several architectural influences, possessed a grace unusual in eclectic designs. The "carpenter Gothic" movement — "la decadence romantique" — which even before the Civil War had begun to lay its palsied rococco hands on northern urban centers hardly touched the Crescent City. As two experts have stated, ante-bellum architecture in New Orleans was the "most eloquent testimony to the age. . . ."[18]

NOTES

[1]Eliseé Reclus, "Fragment d'un Voyage a la Nouvelle-Orleans, 1855," *Tour du Monde, Nouveau Journal des Voyages*, I (1860), 191.
[2]Marcelle Péret, "L'Architecture en Louisiana aux XIXe Siècle," *Comptes Rendus de l' Athenée Louisianais* (November, 1952), 5.
[3]Isaac M. Cline, "Art and Artists in New Orleans Since Colonial Times," Louisiana State Museum, Board of Curators, *Biennial Report*, 1920-1921, p. 33.
[4]*Weekly Delta*, March 10, 1851.
[5]Wharton, diary, March 24, 1855.
[6]Kingsford, *Impressions of the West and South*, 56; Reclus, "Fragment d'un Voyage a la Nouvelle-Orléans," *Tour de Monde*, I, 191. In a more generous and professional opinion Loredo Taft pronounced the statue "an attempt of surpassing audacity." "Nobody knows or cares whether the rider looks like Jackson or not; the extraordinary pose of the horse absorbs all attention, all admiration." Taft, *History of American Sculpture* (New York, 1903), 126-127. This was the first equestrian statute cast in the United States.
[7]Eliza Ripley, *Social Life in Old New Orleans*, (New York, 1912), 40.
[8]*Commercial Bulletin*, October 17, 1853. Italics mine.
[9]Wharton, diary, May 23, 1854.
[10]Mackay, *The Western World*, II, 296.
[11]Talbot Faulkner Hamlin, *Greek Revival Architecture in America: Being an Account of Important Trends in American Architecture and American Life Prior to the War Between the States* (London, 1944), 219. There were a few Victorian Norman homes, James Robb's "Italian Villa," and at least one Swiss chalet that were constructed before the Civil War.

[12] *Weekly Picayune*, October 22, 185.
[13] *Ibid.*, September 22, 1856. Another Episcopal church, Holy Trinity, was executed in the same fashion.
[14] Wharton, diary, August 12, 1855.
[15] Cable, *The Creoles of Louisiana*, 236.
[16] Murray, *Lands of the Slave and the Free*, 141.
[17] *Weekly Delta*, May 30, June 20, 1852.
[18] Christopher Tunnard and Henry Hope Reed, *American Skyline: the Growth and Form of Our Cities and Towns* (Mentor Books edition; New York, 1956), 89.

Charles Gayarre

Chapter XII

LITERATURE

> In a city like New Orleans, where the great mass of the people are absorbed in business . . . it is not astonishing, though it is much to be regretted, that the cultivation of letters should have been so much neglected.[1]

There was a general feeling in New Orleans in the fifties that the city, as a literary center, was hardly more than a "half way house between Civilization and California," producing more real achievements than the frontier, but fewer than eastern and northern urban centers.[2] If there were few works of creative genius in New Orleans, it was in part the result of an environment that placed small premium on the poet, novelist, essayist, playwright, or historian. But whatever the causes may have been, the lack of literary spirit was reflected in the sad state of the city's bookstores and literary journals.

In 1847 the poet-lawyer, Richard Henry Wilde, declared that there was "not even a tolerable bookstore" in New Orleans.[3] Thirteen years later there were fourteen bookstores in the city, but none of them appeared to be of first rank. William T. Sherman, President of the Louisiana Seminary of Learning, complained that he found it impossible to obtain a necessary supply of books from New Orleans book dealers. The firm of Ticknor and Fields, a major publishing house in the 1850's, sold only a fourth as many books in New Orleans as in Cincinnati, a city of comparable size; and this was true despite the fact that New Orleans was a shipping point for books to a large planation area. One of the major book sellers in New Orleans, B. M. Norman, was unable to make a decent living from his occupation.

There were several newspapers that were partly literary in scope and interest. The *Weekly Mirror*, which claimed (incorrectly) to be "the only literary paper in the South," was sponsored by the Southern Literary Society, whose members contributed poems, essays, short stories, and occasional novelettes to its pages. Denis Corcoran of the *Delta* edited the *Sunday Magnet*, but since there are no copies extant neither the character nor the duration of the journal can be ascertained. At least two French literary newspapers made their appearance in the decade. In 1851-1852 Charles Testut, a French immigrant, published *La Semaine de la*

Nouvelle Orléans, a Sunday journal, the chief purpose of which appeared to be the publication in serialized form of Testut's romantic stories, "Les Mystères de la Nouvelle-Orléans." Theatrical criticism, poetry, and polite essays were also included. *La Renaissance Louisianaise,* a weekly printed on gaudy yellow paper, was founded in 1861 as the "Organne des populations des Franco-Américaines du Sud." It had a staff of some of the outstanding French writers in the city and like the *Mirror* mixed national and topical local news with literary productions. By some miracle the *Renaissance Louisianaise* survived the Civil War and lasted until 1871. Nor should *Der Alligator* and the *Pekin-Democrat* be ignored. Edited and published in 1851 and 1852 by an irrepressible German journalist, Ludwig Von Reitzenstein, the principal contributor was Von Reitzenstein himself, as the local German population refused to support experiments in the belles artes.

A well defined form, the French revue included literary works as well as music, theatrical, and literary criticism. During the 1840's there were several revues, but in the fifties they were rare objects. *La Violette Revue Musicale et Littéraire,* sponsored but not read by the "Dames de la Louisiane" began in 1849; by early 1850 the editors were forced to announce "La Violette va mourir . . . ." The birth to death cycle of *La Semaine Littéraire,* a weekly magazine devoted to literature and general art criticism, was completed in one year, 1850. In 1851 Louis Audibert as editor-publisher brought out *L'Album Louisianais, Revue Littéraire et Artistique.* It failed quickly.

Nor were literary magazines in English any more successful than those in French. *The Southern Ladies Book: A Monthly Journal of Polite Literature,* edited by L. Virginia French of Memphis and Dr. William T. Leonard of New Orleans, made a fervent editorial appeal for the support of Southern literature and lasted from November, 1852 to May, 1853. But at least it did better than *The New Orleans Noesis or Journal of Intellectual Amusement: Popular Literature, Science and Arts* whose ambitious title could not save it the ignominy of lasting precisely one issue. More successful was *The Parlor Magazine* which was published twice. Edited by Mrs. V. E. Wilhelme McCord, a local authoress, it was "Devoted to Literature, Science and General Intelligence" and its main purpose was to "advance the literature and general interest of the South." Indeed its articles, Mrs. Mc-

Cord promised, would breathe "the very essence of the Southern land . . . ."

> The *Parlor Magazine* is a book for Southern homes; it will contain no word that the pure and gentle may blush to read; it will seek constantly to encourage the patriotism and the devotion of Southern institutions, to unite all the sister States of the South in the bonds of amity, and to cultivate the beautiful in literature and art.

The magazine contained an abundance of poems, a few short stories, a serialized novel, local color sketches, polite essays, short book reviews, a fashion column, and some theatrical gossip.

The only magazine associated with the Crescent City enjoying a national reputation was *De Bow's Review*. But as a newspaper man sarcastically suggested, it was not entirely a New Orleans publication; the editor was in Washington, the printer in Cincinnati, and only a sign in Exchange Alley was in New Orleans. This was a bit unfair since J.D.B. De Bow, editor and publisher of the magazine from its inception in 1842 until its demise in 1867, considered New Orleans his home and the *Review* had numerous articles and editorials that dealt with New Orleans and Louisiana. *De Bow's* was chiefly devoted to articles on southern agriculture, political economy, manufacturing, and commerce; in these respects it was truly a "complete encyclopedia of the Old South."[4] Its contributors included some of the outstanding thinkers of the South. Only two ante-bellum volumes had works of fiction and poetry and books reviewed were seldom on literary subjects. In his editorials however, De Bow made impassioned appeals for a southern literature, but the practical problems of the South occupied his greater attention; or to use De Bow's reasoning, "Ploughshares come before Philosophy."

French literature in New Orleans showed a wide variety of interests even if it failed in quality. The bulk of this literature was prepared by immigrant French intellectuals; the Creoles, like their native American counterparts, were not an eminently literary people. For example, of the fifty-six journalists and writers described by Charles Testut in 1850, twenty-six were born in France, five were born in or were from the West Indies, four were free Negroes, and only thirteen were native born; the origins of eight were unknown, though none belonged to any of the prominent Creole families.

French poetry, signed and unsigned, abounded in local newspapers, revues, albums and books, but failed to create a local school or tradition of French poetry; the obvious opportunity of using the fluid Negro French patois sems to have occurred only to Adrien Rouquette and even he only experimented with Negro dialect. Instead, French poetry in New Orleans was stilted and derivative. Of the many poets perhaps three are deserving of notice: Madame Emilie Evershed, Charles Testut, and Adrien Rouquette, the best poet of ante-bellum Louisiana.

Madame Evershed was born in France and came to New Orleans with her husband. After his death she had the good luck to marry a wealthy English immigrant who provided her with the money and tolerance essential to maintain a salon for local French writers. Her poetry found its way into newspapers and ephemeral literary journals and she published in Paris four volumes of poetry. Her *magnum opus*, a long epic poem, *Une Courrone Blanche: Roman Poetique*, was published in 1859. The poem recounts the morbid tale of an unfaithful husband who has a child by his mistress; the mistress dies and the selfless wife takes in the blind waif and raises it with her own daughter. This melodrama fairly dripped sentiment as witness the following lines from *Une Courrone Blanche*:

> Quand je ne pleure plus . . . je vois ces jours heureux
> Ou je pouvais baiser tes cher petits pieds roses
> Et tes petits mains, et tes levrès mi-closes;
> J'effeuille en souvenir tous ces biens precieux.

Charles Testut was born in France and came to New Orleans after a stay in the West Indies. He subsisted on writing for local papers and establishing short-lived literary journals of his own in New Orleans and Mobile. Testut published a collection of poetry, *Les Échos*, in 1849, and another, *Fleurs d' Èté*, in 1851. Carried away with his poetic success he contemplated publishing a monthly magazine of poetry to be called *L'Album Poétique de la Louisiane* and selling for a quarter. He accumulated enough material for six issues, but nothing came of his venture. Testut's poetry is filled with the usual romantic appeals to "le coeur" and "le sentiment" which tended to obscure his social commentary and vague socialism.

Adrien Rouquette came from an old Creole family. After education at Transylvania College in Kentucky and in Paris, he entered the Roman Catholic diocesan seminary of New Orleans and became a priest in 1845. He was attached to the St. Louis Cathedral until 1850 when, supposedly after giving an antislavery sermon, he was appointed to care for the religious life of a small and impoverished band of Choctaws in Lacombe, Louisiana. Despite his isolation, Rouquette maintained a constant interest in world affairs and in contemporary poetry. He corresponded with American Catholic intellectuals Orestes Brownson and Father Isaac Hecker and he exchanged ideas on poetry with Ralph Waldo Emerson. He was known in the proper literary circles in France where he was considered the "Lamartine of America."

The only volume of poetry published by Abbé Rouquette during the 1850's was his *Antoniade ou Le Solitude avec Dieu*, dedicated to Catherine Tehgahkwita, the famed "Lily of the Mohawks." Throughout this work the theme of nature, its beauty, its healing powers, and its inducement to contemplation is repeated. Without once losing his Catholicism, Rouquette brings forth the essential message of Rousseau's Sayoyard Vicar; and like his predecessor, the Abbé contrasts untrammeled nature with the horrors of the modern scene. In the prologue of the last division of the *Antoniade* he speaks of

> . . . à siècle éclaire, cet âge utilitaire
> Oü de l'humanité l'idole et la matiere;
> Oü le voi c'est le peuple et l'argent c'est le dieu,
> Faux dieu que l'on adore et pour suit en tout lieu;
> Dans un siècle de luxe, ivre comme le nôtre.

Certainly Rouquette revealed more depth and profundity than any of his Louisiana contemporaries and it is unfortunate that a later age is so little aware of his poetry.

The mid-nineteenth century was an intensely creative period in the history of the French novel and so it is not startling to discover in New Orleans, existing as it was in the backwash of French culture, several novelists. Charles de la Bretonne, a journalist who fled France after the 1848 revolution, published two novels in the fifties: *Le Soulier Rouge* and *Les Amours d'Hélène ou Deux Coeurs Brisés*. Bretonne had been strongly influenced by James Fenimore Cooper and the first of these novels was a sort of Leatherstocking Tale set in early Louisiana while *Les Amours d'Hélène* was a melodramatic novel set in contemporary France. *Rodolphe de Branchlièvre* by Charles Lemaitre, a twenty-seven year old native of New Orleans, made its appearance in 1851. Though set in contemporary New Orleans, it evoked no interest and Lemaitre having tasted the joys and sorrows of seeing his creation in print returned to the obscurity of his clerk's profession. Hardly more spectacular was the novelistic career of Armand Garreau who, at the instigation of Charles Testut, published a novel serially in the latter's *Veillese Louisianaises*. Garreau's *Louisiane* depicted the futile revolt against the Spanish general, Alejandro O'Reilly, in 1768-1769. Far more prolific was Charles Testut, a one-man literary scene. Believing that a novelist should supplement the work of historians, Testut took incidents from Charles Gayarré's histories of Louisiana to compose two novels, both of which were published in a weekly paper. *St. Denis* was based on an expedition to Mexico in 1748 by the Chevalier St. Denis; *Calisto* dealt with the adventures of a Russian emigrant in early eighteenth century Louisiana. These novels were no better or worse than most of the romantic sagas of the time. Probably the most interesting of Testut's novels was *Le Vieux Salomon, ou Une Famile d'Esclaves aux XIXe Siècle*. Written in 1858, but not published until after the Civil War, it owed much to the influence of Harriet Beecher Stowe's *Uncle Tom's Cabin*. The novel was frankly anti-slavery; to Testut New Orleans was "un véritable enfer pour les esclaves" and it was probably this fact as much as any that led him to move to New York in 1858 and not return until 1871.

Ante-bellum Louisiana could boast of one fairly prolific French language playwright, the "nerveux et impressionable" Creole, Louis-Placide Canonge.[5] He began writing plays in 1839 at the age of seventeen, but it was not until 1846 that his first major play appeared; it was an adaption, with slight variations, from Dumas' *The Count of Monte Cristo*. In 1849 the Théâtre d'Orléans produced two of his plays: *Juan, ou une Histoire sous Charles Quint* and a one-act comedy *Qui Perd Gagne*. In the following year Canonge wrote *France et Espagne* based on Garreau's novel *Louisiane*. *Un Grand d'Espagne* was published in 1851 though it had been staged as early as 1847. The play belonged to the bloody melodrama manner of writing so popular with nineteenth century audiences; it had the proper number of bandits, abductions, and murders set in a Spanish background. In 1852 the Théâtre d'Orléans presented Canonge's *Comte de Carmagnola*, based on a novel by Mole-Gentilhomme about life in Venice. It seems to have been a better-than-average play and after its printing in 1856 it was performed in Paris for a run of one hundred nights — a long showing for the time. Canonge's last ante-bellum play produced, but not published, was *L'Ambassadeur d'Autriche*.[6]

No discussion of French literature in New Orleans during the 1850's would be complete without mention of the most berated book of the decade, Madame de Grandfort's *L'Autre Monde*. Born Marie Barsala, she arrived in New Orleans in the early 1850's under the name of Mlle Barousse and claiming to be a French woman of letters. After creating a number of scandals (being a feminist was a scandal in the rigid Creole code for women), she married a French immigrant, de Grandfort, and returned to France in 1855 where she published *L'Autre Monde* under the pen name of Marie Fonteney. The book was influenced by Mrs. Trollope's work on American manners, except that it dealt solely with the French-speaking population of Louisiana and was written in a semi-fictional form. *L'Autre Monde* proved as shocking as it was popular; the author insisted that the Creole men and French immigrants were materialistic money-mongers, that Creole women were bores, and the Creoles' French was hardly above the Negro French patois; to climax her work she frankly praised the free Negroes and lashed out against slavery. She was viewed by the outraged Creole society as a combination of Lola Montez, Harriet Beecher Stowe, and a Bloomer girl. The book was quickly translated into English and enjoyed the notoriety of an official reply by a Creole dame. However Madame Frédéric Allain's *Souvenirs d'Amerique et de France par une Créole* was a weak and humorless answer, and on the subject of the dullness of Creole women re-enforced rather than refuted Madame de Grandfort.

Free Negroes, some of whom were educated in France where they had been influenced by French authors, had sponsored an active literary movement in the 1830's and 1840's. In the early forties a short-lived review, *L'Album Littéraire*, was founded as an outlet for free Negro poets and writers, and in 1845 under the editorship of Armand Lanusse an anthology of free Negro poetry, *Les Cenelles*, was published. Out of this free Negro group came Victor Sejour who after expatriation to France became a well known actor and playwright, boon friend of Hugo and the Dumases, and secretary to Napoleon III. Sejour was joined by several other free Negro writers who found New Orleans incompitable with their literary goals. By the 1850's the cascade of free Negro literature had been reduced to a rivulet; the few free Negro writers that remained published only incidental pieces for newspapers. The near-disappearance of a literate and articulate free Negro movement was a loss for the South and the Negro community.

Writing in English during the 1850's has often been overlooked by researchers, yet the quantity of works produced exceeded the local French literature. Several newspapers printed poetry and a number of New Orleanians availed themselves of this opportunity for publication. Many of the poetic contributions were unsigned, but signed and unsigned were of the same quality—bad!

A few English-language authors should be mentioned since they had a local reputation as poets. M. F. Bigney, a Canadian-born newspaperman, wrote numerous poems throughout the decade, but they were not collected in a volume until after the Civil War. Joseph Brennan, an Irish immigrant on the staff of the *Delta*, published poems weekly in that journal until his death in 1857. The best of several women poets in the city was Mrs. Mary Ashley Townsend who wrote for local papers under the name "Xariffa." (Alcée Fortier declared that "Xariffa is one of the greatest poets of America.")[7] Mrs. Marie Sophie Homes contributed essays and poems to newspapers under the sobriquet "Millie Mayfield." She has the dubious honor of having written the longest poem in the decade — perhaps in the city's history; her *Progression: or the South Defended* contained 201 pages of tedious and strained couplets. Another lady poet of note was Mrs. Anna Peyre Dinnies who wrote a regular column and contributed poems under the name "Moina" and "Rachel" for the *Southern Standard*, a Catholic newspaper edited by her husband. That her poetry did not challenge the Longfellows, the Whittiers, the Tennysons of the day may be seen in this stilted verse of a poem called "Lord, Keep My Memory Green."

> In the shifting scenes of life,
> Filled with sorrow, toil, and strife,
> May no shadow overcast,
> Those through which my soul has past!
> May no fabled Lethe pour
> Its dark waves my memory o'er;
> Hiding ought of pain or care
> God has traced in wisdom there!

Women dominated the field of the English novel and short story in New Orleans. Mrs. Mary McCord published a series of short stories for children in the *Mirror* and wrote an unfinished novelette in the *Parlor Magazine*. The *Mirror* serialized Elizabeth Mary Allison's mawkish historical opus, *Erena or The Christian Convert, a Tale of the Second Century*. Mrs. Mary Sophie Homes in 1857 published a sentimental period piece, *Carrie Harrington; or Scenes in New Orleans*. Perhaps emboldened by Mrs. Homes success, two years later Mary Ashley Townsend gave literary birth to *The Brothers' Clerks, a Tale of New Orleans*. In 1862 Mrs. Florence J. Willard, a contributor to the *Mirror*, wrote *The Heroism of the Confederacy; or Truth and Justice* which was set in New Orleans and on nearby plantations. The plot was romantic; it told of patriotic deeds and romances of the local Crinoline Confederacy. The dialogue, as in so many of these novels, was heavily interspered with inappropriately chosen bits of schoolgirl French.

A few New Orleans males turned their talents to the novel. Dr. J. S. Peacock published *The Creole Orphans* in 1855. William Henry Peck, who resided in the city from 1854 to 1859, published *Antoinette de Bordelais* (1857) and *The Brother's Vengeance* (1859); after he left New Orleans he wrote several novels which utilized local subjects. Charles Gayarré's sardonic *School for Politics* mixed sentimentality, moralization, and polemics against Pierre Soulé in about equal doses, but it was probably the best English novel of the decade.

The presence of several theatres prompted a number of New Orleanians to try their pens at playwritng. Theatre managers were often hard pressed for material and wrote short plays and skits themselves. Thus Dion Boucicault, already a well known playwright before arriving in New Orleans, in his year in the city wrote, acted in, and publically praised, *The Chameleon, Azael, Una*, and the saccharine *Life of an Actress*. His popular *The Octoroon*, which was written later, was suggested by his New Orleans experience. Managers also turned to members of the cast to prepare a play on short notice. The authorship of these plays, like those of the managers, was seldom announced, but it is known that actors Joseph M. Field, George Jamison (both did parodies on *Uncle Tom's Cabin*), Charles Bass, T. B. Logan, and Julia Dean wrote plays for the local stage.

The most prolific of the playwrights outside the theatre was E. C. Wharton. He wrote several dramas of which at least two,

THE OCTOROON;

OR

LIFE IN LOUISIANA.

A PLAY, IN FOUR ACTS.

By DION BOUCICAULT, Esq.,

AUTHOR OF

The Colleen Bawn; The Pope of Rome; The Young Actress; The Dublin Boy; Pauvrette; Life of an Actress; Jessie Brown; Azael; Blue Belle; Dot; &c., and part author of The Streets of London, otherwise, The Poor of New York.

Play by Dion Boucicault

The Young Couple and *Dick the Newsboy* appeared in the 1850's. Dr. William L. Leonard, a dabbler in the arts, wrote *Uncle Tom's Cabin in Louisiana* which had a run of twenty-three nights in March, 1854, and included the famous song "Wait for the Wagon." As for *The Lunatic and the Lover* which appeared in the *Parlor Magazine*, it is hard to determine if the author left the play unsigned as a result of modesty or shame.

The fifties are important in historiography because of the publication of the Gayarré studies on Louisiana history, which despite their faults, were the major historical works of ante bellum Louisiana. In 1851 Gayarré published *Louisiana, Its Colonial History and Romance;* he followed it a year later with *Louisiana, Its History as a French Colony.* Both of these books were based on his lectures before the Lyceum and Library Society and were inferior works. The author's real claim to eminence as a historian rested on his four-volume *History of Louisiana*. The first three were issued in 1854 and the fourth after the Civil War. Volumes I and II dealt with the French domination of Louisiana; the Spanish period was covered in the third, and the American in the last volume. Gayarré was convinced that history should illustrate the underlying romance in a nation's development and that the historian was to provide data for the playwright, poet, painter, and novelist. This fallacious attitude led Gayarré in his first two volumes into "rhetorical outbursts, pure fabrications, and lengthy digressions;" his style was 'florid, bombastic, and artificial."[8] Because of George Bancroft's influence and Gayarré's careful research in Spanish archives, the volume on the Spanish domination was a steadier historical work. It created a scandal by alleging the intrigues between General James Wilkinson and Spanish officers in Louisiana; Wilkinson was a popular figure in Louisiana history (the family resided in New Orleans) and the allegation that he had been a traitor raised a storm of protest and denial. Furthermore Gayarré's pro-Spanish attitude (his father had been a Spanish officer) was ill-received by a number of French Creole families.

As we look at literature produced in New Orleans the showing is meagre, especially if we contrast it with Boston, a city with only 16,000 more people, or even Cincinnati, a western city of nearly equal population. For example, in the fifties there were nineteen English-language magazines published in Cincinnati and seventeen in Chicago (100,000 population in 1860); New Orleans could boast of six or seven. Three causes appear to underlie the poor state of belles lettres in New Orleans: the intellectual colonialism characteristic of the entire South; an indifference to literature on the part of the mercantile community; and the feminine influence on literature predominant in this period.

New Orleans, like any other city in the South, was dependent on Europe or the North for the mass of its reading material. French journalists fostered an interest in the poems and novels of Dumas, Hugo, Chateaubriand, Murger, Sue, Lamartine, Sand, and Lamenais; their works were printed on the pages of newspapers and discussed in revues. English literary thought was filtered southward by periodicals and books printed in the North. There were no major publishing houses in the South to distribute and encourage a homegrown literature; the city's twelve printing houses were primarily job printers and none had a formal program of publication or outlets for distribution. Southern magazines could not compete with their northern counter parts in interest, quality, or numbers. Southern writers who wished to have a discriminating literary audience were forced to contribute to northern periodicals and publish books on northern presses. If they hoped to make a living as a writer, at best they could look forward to receiving no more than fifteen dollars an article from *De Bow's Review,* the South's leading magazine.

Ante-bellum New Orleans was primarily a commercial city. "Creative work in . . . literature," a discerning student has written, "was stifled in the vigorous business-like atmosphere."[9] According to George Washington Cable, the materialism of the Creole and American merchant fostered an "intellectual indolence" which prevented any literary flowering in New Orleans. Literature in the community had no prestige; it took the form of an "aside" — a task for dilettantes.

To the dearth of a reputable American literature nothing else contributed so much as did the growth of emotional female influences in fiction and poetry. The 1850's was an age of a "d - - d mob of scribbling women," as Nathaniel Hawthorne called them. The Susan Warners with their tear-stained pages vastly outsold the Herman Melvilles. Literature was often written by and for women and placed a premium upon emotional escapism, engendered an ignorance of vital problems, stressed artificiality in plot and subject matter, and substituted Victorian formalism for literary insights. "Realism in the feminine fifties," a literary historian has stated, "was rated with things vulgar and unrefined."[10] In the Northeast with its older intellectual traditions, a few male geniuses could hold back the cackling women, but on the southern side of the Magnolia Curtain ladies ruled the literary roost. Woman was the ideal of Southern literature; "a being whose chief aim is the cultivation of those sentiments and habits of thought that exalt the human understanding and heart at the same time."[11] Therefore it was understandable that "the gentler sex . . . have enriched the periodical literature of the South," and in so doing softened "by the graces of feminine delicacy the sterner emanation of earth's coarser vessels."[12] It is perhaps significant that in New Orleans a work (*New-Orleans Book*) intended to prove that the city had its quota of literary figures should be dedicated to the "Ladies of New-Orleans," and the only advertisement in a local

Christ Church erected in 1847 and demolished in 1883. The ground was then occupied by the Mercier Building for several years, later renamed Maison Blanche. This building was then demolished and replaced by the Maison Blanche building of today.

journal devoted to polite literature (*Parlor Magazine*) should be for "Madame Caplin's Prize Corsets."

NOTES

[1] Robert Gibbs Barnwell, "Preface," *New Orleans Book*, i.
[2] *Ibid.*, x.
[3] Aubrey Starke, "Richard Henry Wilde in New Orleans and the Establishment of the University of Louisiana," *Louisiana Historical Quarterly*, XVII (October, 1934), 619.
[4] Alcée Fortier, *Louisiana Studies; Literature, Customs, and Dialiects, History and Education* (New Orleans, 1894), 88.
[5] Edward Laroque Tinker, *Les Écrits de Langue Français en Louisiane au XIXe Siècle: Essais Biographiques et Bibliographiques* (Paris, 1932), 68.
[6] Creoles Charles-Oscar Dugue and Henry Vignaud each wrote two plays that were staged locally during the 1850's. Only one, Dugue's *Mila, ou la Mort de la Salle*, a three act verse drama, was published.
[7] Fortier, *Louisiana Studies*, 129.
[8] Herbert Howard Lang, "Nineteenth Century Historians of the Gulf States" (unpublished Ph.D. dissertation, Austin, University of Texas, 1954), 230.
[9] Harriet Houston Cale, "Cultural Life of New Orleans in the 1850's" (unpublished M.A. thesis, Baton Rouge, Louisiana State University, 1945), 127.
[10] Fred Lewis Pattee, *The Feminine Fifties* (New York, 1940), 30.
[11] "The South, What Is It?," *Southern Ladies Book*, I (November, 1852), 44.
[12] *Weekly Mirror*, February 26, 1859.

J. D. B. De Bow

Chapter XIII

THE FOURTH ESTATE

> I have mentioned something of the New Orleans press. the greater part of its elements are not merely the best altho [sic] dull [,] but the class will average better than most trades, callings, or professions.[1]

There were nearly two dozen newspapers, published in four languages, in New Orleans during the 1850's. The multiplicity of papers was due in part to diverse ethnic, factional, and political groups which demanded a degree of ideological unity in their press outlets. However several papers occasionally evinced the same political and economic creed, so that the reason for a proliferation of newspapers had yet other causes. An important factor was a purely technical one; existing presses were incapable of turning out enough papers to blanket the city for a morning or evening edition. Not until the *Picayune* purchased a Hoe press was it possible to print more than a few thousand newspapers in an hour. In light of newspaper competition it was probably financially impossible for any paper to purchase several presses. Then too the individualism of the editors and their writers gave even politically similar papers a special, personal touch which was savored by a small group of adherents.

To list all of the newspapers published in the city would tax the reader's patience and perhaps give undue significance to newspapers whose influence and importance was, to say the least, negligible. This is particularly true of French-language newspapers which, as one critic has pointed out, sprang up like "mushrooms and died like flies."[2] French revolutionaries who fled their homeland had a positive penchant for teaching school and then beginning a paper. Unfortunately the French-reading community seemed singularly indifferent to their journalistic endeavors. Following then, is a listing and discusison of the principal newspapers in New Orleans.[3]

The *Price Current Commercial Intelligencer and Merchant's Transcript,* the oldest of the city's commercial newspapers, was founded in 1822 and during the 1850's was owned by Francis Cook, George B. Young, and Samuel S. Littlefield; Young and Littlefield also served as editors. The *Price Current* was a four-page semi-weekly with a six-column spread until September, 1859, when an extra column was added and the length was increased to twenty-seven inches, the normal size of most of the city's newspapers. The *Price Current* contained material devoted to the merchant community; it listed ship arrivals and departures, imports and exports, stock quotations, weekly reviews of the market, Liverpool cotton prices, money markets, and on August 31, or during the first week in September, it compiled the year's commercial statistics on the city's river, railroad, canal, and ocean traffic and compared these statistics with each of the preceding ten years. The paper contained few editorials and almost no general national or foreign news. Perhaps because the editors were indifferent to politics the *Price Current* survived the Civil War while many of the city's papers failed.

The city's other commercial newspaper was the *Commercial Bulletin*, a four-page daily published and edited throughout the decade by Col. Isaac G. Seymour. Unlike the *Price Current*, the *Bulletin* sacrificed some of its market news to cover local and national news events and it was not politically neutral. It backed the Whig Party wholeheartedly; even after the rise of the American Party, it remained the voice of conservative, leaderless Old-Line Whigs and in 1860 it supported the Constitutional Union Party. The *Bulletin's* circulation remained around 3,500 throughout the 1850's.

The largest and most famous daily newspaper in New Orleans, with a circulation of 7,000 in 1850 and 12,000 in 1860, was the *Picayune*. It was founded in 1837 by George Wilkins Kendall and F. A. Lumsden as the first cheap paper in the city, a fact suggested by the title itself. Because of its racy treatment of police news and its rapid coverage of national and international affairs, the paper soon surpassed its older competitors and fostered, indirectly, a host of newer imitators. During the 1850's Lumsden and Kendall took no part in the daily activities of the *Picayune*; the latter spent part of the decade in Paris, after which he reveled "in the garden delights of sheep raising" in central Texas and occasionally contributed interesting accounts of events in the West.[4] The editor, and eventual owner, was M. A. Holbrook.

In 1850 the *Picayune* was a standard four-page paper, but with circulation expansion and with newer presses, the editors were able to bring out an eight-page edition in 1855, a morning and an evening edition in 1856, and a twelve-page newspaper on Sunday starting in 1860. From 1849 to 1859 the *Picayune* also printed a

California edition and the editors sought to reach the country trade with a weekly edition, which like the weekly versions of the *Bulletin, Delta, Crescent, Courier, True Delta,* and *Bee,* was a collection of articles and news stories taken from the dailies, but with few advertisements.

In policy the *Picayune* veered with the strongest political winds. It was an "independent" Whig journal until 1854, when it became an outspoken supporter of the American Party; it was a "Simon pure piously Protestant" journal according to the *True Delta.* As the American Party declined after 1856, the *Picayune* slowly reverted to a self-professed independent status. It drifted in this manner until the election of 1860 when it was vaguely pro-Union, without distinctly backing either Bell or Douglas. If the *Price Current* survived the Civil War because it was apolitical, the *Picayune* did so because it was politically opportunistic.

The *Crescent* was founded in 1847 by John W. Crockett (David's son), J. W. Frost, and Hudson A. Kidd. Three years later they sold the newspaper to the firm of Nixon and Adams and by the end of the decade it was owned and edited by James O. Nixon. The *Crescent* was a four-page paper published daily except Sunday, with a compensating eight-page edition on Monday. Politically the *Crescent* was more militant than the *Picayune.* It was a Whig paper until 1854, when it shifted its allegiance to the American Party until it broke with the Know Nothings in the spring election of 1860. During the national elections of that year and the Louisiana secession movement of 1861, it took an extreme Southern position; it was, according to Horace Greely's local reporter, "a little more insane than the rest" of the city's presses.[5]

The *Delta* was a four-page, seven-column paper edited and published by an Irish immigrant, Dennis Corcoran. During the fifties Corcoran experimented with different print and format so that by 1858 the *Delta's* typography was the best in the city. This improvement may have been partially responsible for the increase in the newspaper's circulation from 3,380 in 1850 to 4,500 in 1860; the *Weekly Delta* grew faster and was the largest weekly in New Orleans on the eve of the Civil War. Like the *Picayune* the *Delta* staff prepared a very popular California edition which was sold to voyagers leaving on ships for the gold fields. They in turn charged in California whatever the news-starved market would bear.

As the only uptown Democratic paper, the *Delta* came into editorial collision with the *Picayune* and *Crescent*. However these conflicts were usually over state and national issues; the *Delta* was frequently neutral or backed independent candidates in local political contests. While the paper was hardly a red republican organ, as the Abbé Napoléon Perché viewed it, it was probably the most liberal journal in New Orleans. During the Soulé-Slidell fight for control of the Louisiana Democratic Party, the *Delta* supported Soulé, but in 1860 it did a flip-flop and backed Slidell's presidential choice of John C. Breckinridge and became a rabidly secessionist paper. Probably because of this it failed, like the *Crescent*, to survive the Civil War.

The *True Delta* was owned and edited by John Maginnis from its inception in 1849 until after the Union occupation when it was sold to Michael Hahn. It was a four-page paper with a weekly and semi-weekly edition, and for a short time a California edition. Between 1850 and 1860 the *True Delta* doubled its circulation and became the second largest daily in the city. It claimed that its operation was "entirely independent of party" but its editorial policy was generally inclined toward the Democratic side, a necessity perhaps in view of its appeal for Irish readers. The *True Delta* remained pro-Union as late as February, 1861, but after Sumter it openly espoused the Confederate cause.

For a few years in the middle of the decade the American Party's direct voice was the *Daily Creole*, a four-page paper published by J. M. Weymouth & Co. For part of 1856 it was the official city paper, but despite this aid, the *Creole* died sometime in 1856 or 1857.

No direct relation to the *Daily Creole* was the *Semi-Weekly Creole* published by Latham & Co. The choice of the word "Creole" in both papers was strange in light of their strongly Protestant cast; however the editors stressed the kinship between all native Americans, whether Creoles or Anglo-Americans. The *Semi-Weekly Creole* professed a pronouncedly puritanical character. The editor claimed that his newspaper "carries nothing into the family circle, in advertisements or original or selected matter, which can corrupt the young heart or bring a blush on the cheek of innocence." Apparently he did not think innocence would be affected by blistering tirades against the Catholic Church and Irish and German immigrants, the *Creole's* stock in trade. Like the *Daily Creole,* the paper probably closed shop in 1856.

The Know Nothing movement also fostered a weekly, the *American Exponent*. It was published by Joseph Etter who spread his principles on the front page; just beneath George Washington's visage were the words: THE PERPETUATION OF AMERICAN FREEDOM IS OUR OBJECT; AMERICAN RIGHTS OUR MOTTO; AND THE AMERICAN PARTY OUR COGNOMEN. The *Exponent* began in February, 1855, and, since a year later the editors were complaining of a lack of funds, the paper probably did not see many more editions beyond February, 1856. Except that it was less newsy and less anti-Catholic, the *Exponent* did not differ greatly from the *Semi-Weekly Creole*.

Without doubt the best-written weekly in New Orleans was the *Mirror* published by Joseph H. Wilson & Co. and edited by M. F. Bigney and F. E. Macnamus. Bigney had worked as a literary editor for several papers and had a fair reputation as a poet. The *Mirror* contained local and national news, but it took no part in city politics nor did it appeal to any particular ethnic group. Its forte was essentially in the arts and its theatrical and opera criticism were superior to those found in any other English-language newspaper. The *Mirror* began operation in August, 1858, and it died sometime the following year despite an endeavor to garner readers outside metropolitan New Orleans.

Three newspapers were published in the Lafayette-Fourth District area. The *Louisiana Spectator* was a four-page journal published by J. M. Weymouth and edited by John P. McMillan. The editor revealed an antipathy toward the local Germans, but perhaps due to flagging sales, he sacrificed his prejudices for *gelt* and published part of the paper in the "Deutsche language." The change did not help; the paper went *kaput* around 1852. In politics the *Spectator* was Whig, though it opposed the party on the annexation of Lafayette. The *Louisiana State Republican* was a semi-weekly which in 1850 was the most successful paper in Lafayette with a circulation of 3,000. The paper was published and edited by Horace L. Marshall who transferred it on May 23, 1855, to Thomas S. Moore, printing foreman of the *Delta*. Moore brightened up the paper by publishing police news and accident reports, but in spite of his efforts the paper appears to have failed a short time later. The *Louisiana State Republican* subsisted on a set of negative beliefs; McMillan opposed the Know Nothings and he disliked Roman Catholics; on the other hand he offered no sympathy to either Old-Line Whigs or to Democrats. The paper's one positive characteristic was a sort of Fourth District jingoism. The third Lafayette paper was a bi-weekly, the *Louisiana Statesman*, a Democratic paper owned and edited by James G. Fanning. With only 900 readers in 1850, the editor transferred his paper to the greener pastures of Carrollton where it managed to survive for a few more years.

There were no major daily newspapers published solely in French, but there were three bi-lingual dailies. Starting in 1847, J. C. Pendergast published the four-page *Daily Orleanian-L'Orléanais*. Pendergast, who served as editor of the English half of the paper, had a remarkably deft style, but the physical appearance of the newspaper was no index to the quality of the writing; the *Daily Orleanian* was the poorest printed daily in the city. Though mildly Whig in politics, Pendergast spoke out for the Irish immigrant (he was one himself) and when many of the Whigs joined the American camp, he supported, with some misgivings, the local Democrats. The French section was edited in the early years of the decade by Paul Boutet. Pendergast allowed Boutet a free hand and on such matters as the Catholic Church and acceptance of unification, the *Orléanais* differed in policy from the *Orleanian*. Boutet was succeeded by Edouard de Lauc-Maryat and later by Paul Villiars, a French-born journalist, who brought the French side of the paper closer editorially to its English counterpart and who attempted to attract the immigrant French to the Democratic Party.

Despite the excellence of its editors, the *Orleanian* appealing almost entirely to the poverty-ridden Third District, found even more financial difficulties than the *Spectator* and the *Republican* in the Fourth District. The *Orleanian* was the official printer for the Third Municipality, but it was unable to compete for a city printing contract after unification. In 1858 the *Daily Orleanian-L'Orleanais* was laid to rest in the already-crowded tomb reserved for defunct New Orleans newspapers.

The *Louisiana Courier-Courrier de la Louisiane*, founded in 1807, was the oldest newspaper in New Orleans. A small four-page afternoon paper, in February, 1852, it was enlarged from six to seven columns and isssued in the evening. In 1856 the paper was reduced in length and width and the number of pages increased to eight. It was published by Thomas Théard from 1849 to 1852, then by Emile La Sere until 1856 when it was purchased by Claiborne & Co. In 1859, after the *Courier* ceased publication for two and a half months, it was purchased by John Slidell and Emile La Sere, who operated it until shortly after the outbreak of the Civil War, at which time the paper was discontinued. During the fifties there were several editors, including Théard, La Sere, Felix Limet, and Emile Hiriart. The latter was hired by his one-time opponent La Sere because, as one author has suggested, he had the two qualifications of a successful editor — he was an excellent writer and a first rate marksman.[6]

In politics the *Courier* was Democratic; in religion it was anti-clerical. However the anti-clericalism was somewhat muted during the rise of the American Party as the *Courier* found itself in an uncomfortable journalistic alliance with the Catholic papers. When the paper was purchased by Slidell and La Sere it became the official voice of the conservative (Slidell) faction in the Louisiana Democratic Party.

The best known French-English daily was the *New Orleans Bee-L'Abeille de la Nouvelle Orléans*. Begun on September 1, 1827, it passed through several hands until 1844 when it was purchased by G. F. Weisse who retained sole ownership until 1861 when he sold half interest to Felix Limet. In size, the four-page *Bee-Abielle* was the longest and widest paper in New Orleans; it had ten columns and employed a print small even for an age of nearly miscroscopic newspaper type. Throughout the decade the paper was aided financially by printing contracts from the Second Municipality, the City of New Orleans, and the state government. Unlike the *Orleanian* and the *Courier*, the *Bee's* editors, Dr. Samuel Harby (1844-1862) and Cyprien Dufour (1848-1860) maintained an editorial continuity and harmony.

The *Bee-Abeille* was a stoutly Whig paper which backed the American Party through its rise and decline, but in 1858 it broke with the party over the municipal elections. It assumed a semi-independent position until 1861 when it backed the secession movement. Though suspended for three years during the Civil War, the paper was reorganized and lasted until 1923.

One other local paper deserves special mention, for while it was hardly the most widely distributed paper in the city, it was in many ways the most readable. The *Propagateur Catholique* was started in 1842 to support the Bishop's side in the trustee conflict. The editor and owner, Abbé Napoléon Perché, had without doubt the most stimulating style of any journalist in the city; his invective, his satire, and his irony were masterpieces in torrid journalism and in conversation he was a master in cutting repartee. Perhaps this is why a contemporary declared that Perché was "esteemed rather than loved."[7]

Though normally sympathetic to the Creole element, he did not hesitate to attack Creole leaders or French editors (he once called Cyprien Dufour an Albigensian) who he felt were indifferent to their religion. Perché showed no definite political affilation, but in the early part of the decade he railed against the Democratic *Courrier de la Louisiane*, *Staatszeitung*, and *Delta*. He was slow in attacking the Know Nothing movement, but he was effective when he entered the lists against their editors. In turn he was called an ultra-montane Catholic; actually he was quite orthodox and the paper's motto "La Religion et Le Pays" was rigidly adhered to. After the middle of the decade, probably with the Archbishop's prodding, the *Propagateur* took an increased interest in the local Irish and German Catholics; it stressed inter-ethnic harmony among members of the faith. Perché retired in 1857 because of bad health, later recovering sufficiently to become Archbishop of New Orleans from 1870 to 1883. The *Propagateur Catholique* survived the Civil War and continued to be printed until 1885.

Except for the weekly editions, much of the space in the city's newspapers went to advertising. The captains, agents, and owners of river and ocean craft paid for, during the cotton season, nearly a full page of the major dailies. So important were these advertisements that shipping companies were able to bring pressure on local papers to standardize advertising rates. Reflecting a sellers economy many storekeepers advertised by simply listing products they had received in their latest shipments. Slightly more elaborate were amusement playbills, which listed performers and performances. Slave auctioneers declared in print how many slaves were available, where they were from, and when they could be seen. The most "modern" advertisements in terms of size and appeal were for patent medicines, retail clothing, and certain competitive national products like sewing machines and cotton gins.

In their coverage of local, national, and international news, the city's presses did not differ greatly. By 1850 most of the newspapers had followed the example of the *Picayune* and contained semi-humorous descriptions of recorder courts trials. The best of these, certainly the most personalized, were found in the *Daily Orleanian* which titillated its readers with accounts of recorder

"Awful John" Suzeneau and the girls of "Sanctity Row." Usually police court news was included with accident accounts, strange happenings, cemetery interments, and so on, in a column entitled "Local Intelligence.' Reporters (or editors themselves) covered special events. Since there was little opportunity to "scoop" opposition papers, these events were often described in lengthy and moralistic essays rather than in concise statements of who-where-when-what. Strangely enough the *Crescent*, which seldom carried long accounts of local happenings, printed two of the outstanding descriptions of events in the decade: the yellow fever burials on August 11, 1853, and the "seige" of the Vigilantes in 1858. As a space filler and a form of advertising most papers periodically employed a reporter to do a feature article on some local store, factory, institution, movement, transportation innovation, or on subjects such as railroads, insurance laws, free banking, etc. Frequently these feature articles were contributed by individuals not connected with the newspaper and often lapsed into a form of special pleading: Race track news was covered by most of the dailies during the winter season and the regattas during the summer. Except for a sudden interest in sports by the *Crescent* in the summer of 1858, possibly to turn attention away from the yellow fever epidemic, other forms of sports were largely ignored in the local press. An exception was a weekly chess column in the *Delta* starting in 1859. Religious material was found in a few dailies usually in the form of printed sermons. The *Semi-Weekly Creole* was the only secular newspaper with a column devoted to religious news and topics. Certainly on local subjects the overall picture was one of a highly personalized journalism; it was leisurely, at times provocative and intelligent; at other times it was, as a reporter complained, only a question of "grinding out inanities," column after long-winded column.[8]

For national news the local press relied on several sources of information. There was, of course, the old stand-by of clippings filched from other newspapers, though this was less common than in the decades previous to the 1850's. The *Picayune* during the Mexican War had pioneered a method of newsboats and horse relays to bring the war news quickly to the press; in the fifties they expanded their system to include parts of the United States. News was also transmitted to the city's papers by telegraph from their special correspondents in New York and Washington. In order to provide an equitable share of the telegraphed news several New Orleans newspapers joined the Associated Press cooperative after its founding in 1851. The *Picayune* however refused to join and contested the use of telegraph lines by the Association. The local papers also relied on informal correspondents to provide news from various parts of the nation. The *Picayune*, for example, printed the letters of George Wilkins Kendall in Texas and the accounts of "First Corporal" in Mobile. The network of the Roman Catholic Church provided sets of interesting letters from the western frontier to the *Propagateur Catholique*.

Coverage of international news was likely to vary according to the newspaper's ethnic appeal. French newspapers carried extensive accounts of events in France while the *Southern Standard*, a Catholic weekly, kept its Irish readers informed of happenings in the "Ould Sod." Foreign news was chiefly provided by ships which deposited foreign newspapers or special dispatches for individual papers. The most important foreign news was the Liverpool market quotations; these were telegraphed from New York or from a telegraph station below New Orleans at Belize. Only the larger papers had regular correspondents who sent sealed dispatches. In the case of national news, New Orleans papers often printed eye-witness accounts of events sent by travellers.

Each French daily had its *feuilleton* which contained music, opera, and theatrical criticism. These sections were directed by literary editors who personally reviewed the latest concert and stage productions. The editors were accorded high prestige in the community and their opinions carried a great deal of importance— and vehement opposition. Among the better-known *feuilletonists* were Albert Fabre, Louis-Placide Canonge, Judge Paul Emile Théard, and Charles de la Bretonne.

English newspapers did not have a special section devoted to theatrical criticisms. However on occasion a stage personality or a particular play or opera was discussed in some detail. The *Picayune* had a weekly column called "Musical Chit-Chat" (copied from a New York newspaper) and near the end of the decade it printed a weekly "Musical and Dramatic" column to review the city's present and future entertainments. The *Weekly Mirror* was the only newspaper in English with extensive, and fairly good, theatrical and opera criticism. Its monthly survey of entertainment was undoubtedly the best in New Orleans outside of the special little reviews devoted to the opera and theatre.

Local papers were frequently graced with fiction and poetry—

the comic strips of mid-nineteenth century journalism. In the French journals readers could follow the serialized novels of Hugo, Dumas, Chateaubriand, Murger, Sue, and others. Novels on the installment plan were rarely included in the English-language newspapers or in the English sections of the bi-lingual press. The *Mirror, Southern Standard,* and *Weekly Delta* averaged three to five poems an issue; other papers printed poems only occasionally.

There was no adequate book reviewing in the local newspapers. Usually a paper would simply list new books available at book stores. Where any attempt at reviewing was made, only a brief digest and a few cursory remarks were offered. Except for a short period in the *Weekly Delta,* there were no regular columns devoted to literary subjects.

Local newspapers with relatively small circulation, often were a reflection of their editors. And in looking over the backgrounds of the editors in the city, one is struck by the number of Yankees who edited or worked on the city's presses. George Wilkins Kendall, co-founder of the *Picayune,* New Orleans largest newspaper, was a northerner and during the fifties, the editor, and eventual owner, M. A. Holbrook, was a native of Vermont and two of the three asosciate editors were northern-born. Holbrook's position as editor-in-chief was taken by New Yorker, Durant da Ponte, who had formerly worked for the *Crescent.* J. W. Frost of Maine was one of the founders of the *Crescent;* J. O. Nixon, its editor and late owner, was a Philadelphian. Of the three owners of the *Price Current* the birthplace of two is unknown; the third was born in Maine. Isaac G. Seymour, owner-editor of the *Commercial Bulletin* was born in Georgia shortly after his parents moved there from Connecticut and he later attended Yale College. M. F. Bigney who was employed on the *Delta, True Delta,* and *Picayune* before becoming co-editor of the *Mirror* was from Nova Scotia. The editor-publishers of two official American Party papers, the *Creole* and *Semi-Weekly Creole,* were New Englanders and the editor of the *American Exponent* was born in the nation's capital. Peter K. Wagner, long associated with the *Louisiana Courier,* was a Yankee as were the editors of the leading Protestant and English Catholic weeklies. Among the northerners who worked as reporters in the city were Walt Whitman, a writer for the *Crescent* in 1848, Frank T. Porter, whose brother William ran the best known sporting paper in the country, and Eugene Fuller, brother of the famous New England writer Margaret Fuller.

Whatever their origins the editors of the New Orleans newspapers were a testy lot with strong likes and dislikes, deep-felt hates and bitter memories; these attitudes were in turn reflected in their editorials. This was common in the nineteenth century, but it was accentuated in the Crescent City by conflicting ethnic and political struggles. The French editors were an especially pugnacious group. They were, reported one student of the type, "extremely individualistic, touchy and highly volatile . . . Everything written in a newspaper other than his [the editor's] own was taken personally by each of the French editors."[9] When the venom of the pen failed, editors turned to the field of honor; duels were not uncommon in the life of many newspapermen.

More significant than their differences were the common agreements among editors and publishers. One of the basic postulates accepted by all was the belief that commerce was king, a monarch *sans reproche*. A certain amount of reasonable pessimism was allowed by the local press, but it was always countered by the assertion that essentially New Orleans' economic position was impregnable. This meant that any news which might jeopardize the prosperity of the city was considered not fit to print. News of yellow fever epidemics were delayed until the frightful death toll could not be avoided and a strictly enforced quarantine was opposed by all editors. There were no voices which questioned the formation of free banks despite the danger of inflation. Railroads were endorsed as well as the shaky manner of financing them through municipal and state bonds. The capitalist John McDonogh was treated as a renowned philanthropist. Only the *Delta* refused to speak good of the dead usurer and raised its editorial voice against the management of one of the railroads.

On the nature, character, and necessity of slavery every editorial pen was agreed. The Southland and its peculiar institution was defended with equal vigor by all New Orleans editors, whether Creole, immigrant, southern, or Yankee. Slavery was accepted; it was considered by the editors — in their columns at least — a positive good. An editor might, it is true, be accused by another newspaper of being an abolitionist, but these charges were made less as literal truth than as attacks upon the degree of Southern sentiment held by the editor. "Abolitionism" was the red herring of the era.

NOTES

¹Samuel Walker of Elia Plantation, Diary of a Louisiana Planter (typewritten copy, Archives of the Howard-Tilton Memorial Library, Tulane University), March 3, 1856.
²Edward Laroque Tinker, *Creole City, Its Past and Its People* (New York, 1953), 164.
³A complete list of French newspapers may be found in Edward Laroque Tinker, "Bibliography of the French Newspapers and Periodicals of Louisiana," American Antiquarian Society, *Proceedings*, XLII (October, 1932), 247-370; for Spanish newspaper see Raymond R. Mac Curdy, *A History and Bibliography of Spanish-Language Newspapers and Magazines in Louisiana 1808-1949* (University of New Mexico Publications in Language and History, No. 8; Albuquerque, 1951), 17-22; German papers are listed in J. Hanno Deiler, *Geschicte der New Orleander Deutsche Presse: Nebst Anderson Denkwürdigkeiten der New Orleander Deutschen* (New Orleans, 1901); and for English papers not discussed in this chapter see United States Census Office, Tenth Census, 1880, vol. VIII, *History and Present Condition of the Newspapers and Periodical Press of the United States with a Catalogue of the Publicaions of the Census Year* (S.N.D. North, comp.; Washington, 1881).
⁴*New York Daily Tribune*, April 12, 1861.
⁵*Ibid.*, April 2, 1861.
⁶Edward Laroque Tinker, *Les Écrits de Langue Français en Louisiane*, 267.
⁷Charles Testut, "Protraits Litteraires de la Nouvelle Orléans," (translated by Olivia Blanchard, Division of Professional and Service Projects, Works Projects Administration of Louisiana, 1939, Archives of the Howard-Tilton Memorial Library, Tulane University; typewritten copy), 43-44.
⁸Francis Brinley, *Life of William T. Porter* (New York, 1860), 181.
⁹Marie Louise Lagarde, "Charles Testut: Critic, Journalist, and Literary Socialist," (unpublished M.A. thesis, New Orleans, Tulane University, 1948), 11-12.

Louis Moreau Gottschalk

Chapter XIV

THE LAST SEASON: 1860-1861

"The market prospects of the coming crops would appear to be favorable . . . ."[1]

"The Union is Dead."[2]

"The last ship on the berth for Liverpool cleared on Monday and has now gone to sea. There have been no arrivals by the passes. One or two vessels from trans-Atlantic ports have been stopped by the enemy and ordered off. We have had no receipts from the Ohio and Upper Mississippi . . . "[3]

New Orleanians surveying the business statistics of 1859-1860 in the September 1 edition of the *Price Current* must have felt self satisfied. It had been a record year with 2,214,296 bales of cotton passing through the city and with exports valued at $138,392,567 and imports at $22,020,849. Furthermore the "prospects for the coming year," announced the *True Delta,* "are auspicious." The hot summer had insured a bumper cotton crop and with European textile mills making seemingly insatiable demands for raw cotton the season of 1860-1861 appeared destined to be the most prosperous in the city's history.

After a summer enlivened only by a few amateur theatricals, lakeside picnics, thirteen murders, nine suicides, and thirty-eight drownings, the pace of business and social activities slowly increased. On the 7th of September, the levee was noisy with the sound of landing cotton bales and ten days later 15,000 bales were brought into the port; "things are looking up in every direction" reported a newspaper. Business slowed temporarily because of a "hurricane" (probably only a gale) on October 2, but by the 10th there were 102 ocean-going ships in the harbor. As early as mid-September, the *True Delta* observed that "Not a few of our absentees have returned, and we might look for hundreds soon by steamer and railway; and not long afterwards, will come the swarms of visitors in cloth and crinoline." A month later the season's first swindler was arrested, always a clear indication of the renewed flow of business and an influx of visitors. By Toussaint, hotel keepers, cotton factors, gamblers, merchants, draymen, stevedores, and others were well into another flush season.

Along with the business revival went the usual increase of entertainments. On September 7, the best a local paper could offer was a baseball game in Algiers, though four days later latent pyromaniacs and the curious were thrilled by a blaze which destroyed the Louisana Oil Company across from the Jackson Railroad depot, and there was the joy of paddling down many of the city's thoroughfares after a near deluge in early October. Finally on October 13, the St. Charles Theatre opened, its dingy and water-damaged interior forgotten in the delight of watching the "new and amusing features" of Campbell's Minstrels. Four days later the Rumsey and Newcomb Minstrel Troupe opened at the Academy of Music "in a series of amusing Ethiopian representations;" while next door at the Spalding & Rogers Museum the citizen could examine a two year-old hippopotamus, the first such "monster" ever brought to America. Or he could wander into Vannuchi's Museum which for the new season had prepared a series of wax figures depicting the Japanese ambassadors meeting President Buchanan; also in the museum were favorites from other years: Louis Napoleon confering with Garibaldi, a nativity scene, the Last Supper, "CRIMEAN HEROES AND EUROPEAN POWERS," and rather appropriately "OLD JOHN BROWN and His Associate Murderers." Drama came to New Orleans with the popular Ben De Bar opening at the St. Charles on November 8, in a "comic drama," "Wonderful Woman," followed by Tom Taylor's "Nine Points of the Law;" the Varieties, newly decorated by Boulet's murals, captivated its first audience with the usual "laughable farce," skits, and a play "Lady of Lyons," followed a few days later by Sheridan's classic, "School for Scandal." By late October three dancing studios were advertising in the local press and on the 27th the first of many fancy dress balls were held at the Odd Fellows Hall. Meanwhile the city was tantalized with the news that the Théâtre d'Opera had its dome and proscenium frescoed and that Boudousquié was gathering the usual superb cast. Finally after much excitement, on the evening of November 8, the season opened with Rossini's "Barber of Seville." "Fine singing, beautiful women, enthusiastic audience; what could be more wanting to make the hours pass rapidly," declared an entranced critic.[4]

Amidst the revived bustle of business and the renewed conviviality of bar, ballroom, opera, and theatre autumn brought also, what one scholar has called, "Louisiana's most exciting and colorful national political campaign" and one which would affect the future of the Crescent City as no election in its varied history.[5] Political activity began in April, 1860, when the Louisiana delegation, having gone to the Democratic convention dominated by the Slidell faction, bolted along with delegates from five other southern states. The Soulé wing of the party remained in Charleston and secured the nomination of Senator Stephen A. Douglas of Illinois. The bolters went to Baltimore where they nominated John C. Breckinridge of Kentucky. Louisiana voters had a choice then of two Democratic candidates for President. Since Douglas, Breckinridge, and the Republican candidate, Abraham Lincoln, were unsatisfactory to many Old-Line Whigs, a National Constitutional Union Party was formed and nominated John Bell of Tennessee and Edward Everett of Massachusetts. On May 30, a sizable and ardent group met at the Odd Fellows Hall where under the leadership of Randall Hunt and Christian Roselius they approved Bell's nomination and set in motion a local organization to campaign for a true-blue "union" candidate.

The campaign, like so much else, wilted in the summer heat of New Orleans, but with the coming of cooler weather and the November election, the city became politically alive. Hosts of party groups were formed — Little Giant Club, Bell Knights, Southern Guards (Breckinridge), Mounted Squatter Sovereigns (Douglas), Union Guards (Bell) — who regaled the city nightly with multi-bannered torchlight parades (a Canal street merchant advertised "a magnificent assortment of everything in the pyrotechnic line, suitable for political clubs") accompanied by brass bands and marching units. Occasionally parade routes would cross and there would be scuffling and later accusations in the party press. In Algiers a duel was fought between two overwrought men who quarreled over the relative size of the Bell and Breckinridge parades; as so often happened in these "affairs of honor" they shot their guns, missed completely, and at the suggestion of their seconds departed amicably. Political agitation was maintained by newspapers which in a plethora of adjectives attempted to convince readers that their candidate was a shining knight and the opponents were agents of Beelzebub; they agreed only in viewing Lincoln as "one of the most dangerous abolitionists in the United States."[6]

The Presidential election was held on November 6, and when the votes were counted in the city Bell had received 5,216 votes, Douglas 2,998, and Breckinridge 2,645; thus New Orleans supported unionist candidates, but Breckinridge picked up the country vote and carried the state. By the next day however it was obvious that the matter of tabulation had been academic, since Lincoln, a man whose name did not even appear on the ballot in Louisiana, won the national election. The immediate reaction to the election of a "Black Republican" was moderate. The *Bee* stated that "We are for the Union so long as it is possible to preserve it"; Colonel Isaac Seymour, editor of the *Commercial Bulletin,* cried "Oh for an hour of Henry Clay .... I have been asked, when I would consent to a dissolution of the Union. I answer never, never, NEVER, NEVER!" (In less than a year he was leading a Confederate regiment, and in two years was killed in action.) Perhaps many citizens agreed with Stephen A. Douglas who visited New Orleans two days after the election and in a speech to the crowd gathered around him in front of the St. Charles Hotel pointed out that Lincoln won the election, though the Democrats controlled both houses of Congress.

Slowly the pattern of cautious watching changed. By mid-November the blue cockade, a pelican button with two streamers, symbol of secessionist sentiment, became fairly common in the city; already the Minute Men of New Orleans, a quasi-military organization to protect southern rights, had been formed. Newspapers became more hostile toward the North with even the *Picayune,* which had once fought the fire eaters, shifting sides and soon it "out Heroded Herod" in demands for secession. (It later accepted Butler with equal ease.) Only the *True Delta* provided no talk of disunion even after formal secession; threats were made against the paper, but John McGinnis was a formidable individual who supposedly had a small arsenal in his office and the undying allegiance of the city's volatile Irish. Kerosene was thrown on the bonfire of secession by the Reverend Benjamin Morgan Palmer who in a two-hour Thanksgiving Day sermon — later reprinted and widely distributed — violently imprecated the abolitionists and in the manner of Pope Urban II declared that the South was fighting for "God and religion." By mid-December the *Bee* reported that New Orleans "is now the hot-bed of Secession," an impression which jibed with the observations of the British consul, William Mure. When news reached the city that South Carolina had seceded from the Union, the Pelican flag was displayed and guns were shot off in the streets.

Even before South Carolina's departure from the Union, Governor Thomas Overton Moore on December 10 called a special session of the legislature. The slave-holding Governor proclaimed the right of secession and the danger of living under a "Black Republican President"; and at his suggestion the legislature called for an election of delegates to a state secession convention. So for the second time in three months a state-wide campaign was held. In New Orleans 8,336 votes were cast and the secessionists won by a slim 380 votes over the "co-operationists" who opposed immediate secession; in the state the vote was 20,488 to 17,296 in favor of the secessionists, but almost twice as many secessionist delegates were elected as co-operationists.

When the state convention met on January 23, secession sentiment was overpowering, though opposition came from New Orleans delegates, Joseph A. Rozier and Charles Bienvenue. They were voted down and on the 26th Louisiana seceded and became, for two months, an independent nation with its own flag, army, and government. The convention sent Judah P. Benjamin and John Slidell as representatives to Montgomery and after the Confederate constitution was completed it was brought back to Louisiana for ratification. In the debate over the new constitution Christian Roselius, a delegate from Jefferson Parish, "raked the Secessionists, fore and aft" as he urged the constitution be submitted to the people for popular vote. To Roselius the Montgomery convention "had dug the grave of republican liberty . . . ."[7] His mordant speech went for naught and on March 21, by an overwhelming vote, Louisiana joined the Confederacy.

The events of the winter of 1860-61 had an unsettling effect on New Orleans business. Trade diminished gradually though the record cotton crop was removed to northern and European ports; imports declined and prices rose; and banks hedging against possible financial chaos refused loans and called in specie thus creating by spring a serious shortage of hard money. Northerners in the city were either carried along with the seccessionist fervor or they maintained silence; "commerce," Horace Greely's New Orleans reporter shrewdly remarked, "is not wont to array itself against a popular frenzy." There were undoubtedly Yankees like Paul Tulane who invested his liquid capital in northern corporations and sat out the war in New Orleans guarding his real estate. Though the city was filled with zealous "Minute Men" on the lookout for northern spies and sympathizers, and many an individual found himself in parish prison for indiscrete remarks, only one northern company was forcibly closed. As late as the firing on Fort Sumter northern ships were leaving the port and the United States mails were operating smoothly and efficiently.

Social life went on hardly vexed during the winter season. Perhaps visitors declined somewhat after January, but costume and fancy dress balls wer conducted with the usual zest and frequency. Mardi Gras, a warm beautiful day, was celebrated with its usual joymaking and pomp; the only sign of the changing times were slight economies in costumes and an effigy of Lincoln carried on a rail by two Negroes. Opera continued unabated with the high point of the season being the appearance in February and March of the young, talented Adelina Patti — "La fauvette méloddieuse."

Military preparations began with the expansion of the Louisiana militia and the seizure of federal forts, the Custom House, and the United States Mint in January and February. To meet the needs of the Confederacy and to defend the state, military units were hastily formed in the city. "Daily men and boys in uniform," reported an observer in March, 1861, "may be seen on all the thoroughfares; and every night, to a late hour, our ears are saluted by the spirit-stirring drum and the ear-piercing fife, the iron tramp of horses, the march of footmen, and the commands of 'Attention!' and 'Front Face!' as the companies are drilled on the principal streets."[8] Officers were easily obtained from the upper class of the city and with the stagnation of trade immigrants were encouraged to enlist; if all else failed shanghaiing, a venerable New Orleans practice, could be employed — much to the horror of the British counsel who had the Governor release sixty British subjects who inadvertantly found themselves in the Confederate army. Money to equip soldiers was provided by the state and by private bazaars and auctions; however merchants, who were keen on local guards to protect property, were notoriously cool toward spending money for "foreign" ventures. In general there was a carnival air about war preparations; it was all very colorful with the marching bands and the bright spangled uniforms, spiced nicely with the patriotic and romantic quality that home folk seem to be able to give to war. It was a warm, early spring, flowers blossomed everywhere and the markets were filled with fresh strawberries. War did not seem so forbidding — besides the Yankees might not fight.

The firing on Fort Sumter made a fighting war inevitable. New Orleans recruits were sent to Camp Moore in Tangipahoa

Parish (an early camp in the Metairie rack track proved unhealthy and too near city grog shops) and units already formed were transported to Pensacola and to Virginia. There was of course some fear of an Union invasion of Louisiana from the sea and General P.G.T. Beauregard, who visited New Orleans before going on to fame at Charleston, urged improvement of the forts protecting the city and construction of a boom between Forts Jackson and St. Phillip below the city. General David Twiggs, placed in charge of the city's defenses in May, was so old and infirm and the city so relatively indifferent that no concerted effort to defend New Orleans was made until the following fall. Business meanwhile had almost halted, shortages appeared, and the ugly spectre of mass unemployment forced the city to provide food at a free market.

On May 26, 1861 the U. S. steam sloop *Brooklyn*, under Commander Charles H. Poor, anchored off Pass a L'Outre and dispatched a long boat to Fort Jackson to inform Major John K. Duncan CSA that the port of New Orleans was now blockaded from the sea. Though it would be another year before the Bluecoats landed in the city, the trade on which the wealth, power, and commercial glory of ante-bellum New Orleans rested, its very *raison d'etre*, was terminated.

It was the end of an era.

NOTES

[1]*Price Current*, September 1, 1860.
[2]*Daily Picayune*, January 27, 1861.
[3]*Price Current*, June 15, 1861.
[4]*Daily True Delta*, November 14, 1860.
[5]John D. Winter, *The Civil War in Louisiana* (Baton Rouge, 1963), 6
[6]*Daily True Delta*, November 8, 1860.
[7]*New York Daily Tribune*, March 29, 1861.
[8]*Ibid.*, April 2, 1861.

A NOTE ON SOURCES

General Sources: John Smith Kendall's *History of New Orleans* (3 vols.; Chicago, 1922) remains the basic history of New Orleans. More readable is Edward Laroque Tinker, *Creole City: Its Past and Its People* (New York, 1953); the best single volume history of New Orleans is Harold Sinclair, *The Port of New Orleans* (Garden City, 1942). No study of the age is possible without use of newspapers. The *Picayune, Crescent, True Delta, Bee, Courier,* and *Delta* are well known to most researchers and all were examined in this study; less known, and often more valuable, are the *Orleanian, Louisiana State Republican, Commercial Bulletin, Price Current, Propagateur Catholique, Southern Standard,* and *Mirror*. There are many travel accounts for this period. Far and away the best is Frederick Olmsted, *A Journey in the Seaboard Slave States* (New York, 1856). A New Yorker, Olmsted understood American institutions better than the usual hostile and often priggish travellers like Cunynghame, both Mackays, Bremer, Rosenberg, Reclus, Ashworth, Creecy, Kingsford, Wagner and Scherzer, Murray, Pulszky, Shaw, Stirling, Sullivan, and Wortley. The most discerning travel books by foreign visitors are J. J. Ampére, *Promenade en Amerique* (2 vols.; Paris, 1855), Charles Lyell, *A Second Visit to the United States of North America* (2nd ed., 2 vols ; London, 1850), and William Howard Russell, *My Diary North and South* (Boston, 1863). Autobiographical material is scarce, though the quality of Theodore Clapp, *Autobiographical Sketches and Recollections During a Thirty-Five Years' Residence in New Orleans* (Boston, 1857). Eliza Ripley, *Social Life in Old New Orleans, Being Recollections of My Girlhood* (New York, 1912), and T. L. Nichols, *Forty Years of American Life* (2nd ed.; London, 1874) is excellent. There are many contemporary letters and diaries in the archive collections of the University of Texas, Louisiana State University, and Tulane University, and the manuscript City Hall Collection in the New Orleans Public Library is invaluable. The best single manuscript source for the fifties is the diary of Thomas K. Wharton, the original of which is in the New York Public Library. The reports of the Louisiana legislature and the annual reports of the mayors of New Orleans offer an abundance of information. Though overlooked by many historians the Louisiana Reports (decisions of the Louisiana Supreme Court) frequently offer excellent insights into local history. Many theses and dissertations are available and a few are mentioned below; however, one in particular deserves special notice: Harriet Houston Cale, "Cultural Life in New Orleans in the 1850's" (M.A. thesis, Louisiana State University, 1945).

Chapter I. Material in this chapter is largely based on Kendall's *History of New Orleans*. A detailed account of the formation and growth of New Orleans' suburbs may be found in Meloncy C. Soniat, "The Faubourgs Forming the Upper Section of the City of New Orleans," *Louisiana Historical Quarterly,* XX (January, 1937), 192-211 and William H. Seymour, *The Story of Algiers, 1718-1896* (Algiers, 1896).

Chapter II. In this chapter, and elsewhere in this book, I am deeply indebted to the superb study by Joseph G. Tregle, "Early New Orleans Society: A Reappraisal," *Journal of Southern History*, XVIII (February, 1952), 20-36. An earlier, and often critical, view of local society is found in George Washington Cable, *The Creoles of Louisiana* (New York, 1885); the romantic picture of New Orleans society is best stated in Grace King, *Creole Families of New Orleans* (New York, 1921). The Germans in New Orleans are depicted in several pamphlets by J. Hanno Deiler and in John F. Nau's recent study, *The German People of New Orleans, 1850-1900* (Leiden, 1958). The Irish are treated in Earl J. Niehaus, "The Irish in New Orleans, 1803-1862," (Ph.D. dissertation, Tulane University, 1961). Donald E. Everett, "Free Persons of Color in New Orleans, 1803-1865," (Ph.D. dissertation, Tulane University, 1952) and Charles B. Roussève, *The Negro in New Orleans* (New Orleans, 1937) provide the best recent accounts of the free Negro in antebellum New Orleans. Both works in turn often rest on the seminal work on the New Orleans Negro: R. L. Desdunes, *Nos Hommes et Notre Histoire . . .* (Montreal, 1911). For a brief picture of slavery see my "Slavery in New Orleans in the Decade before the Civil War," *Mid-America*, XLIV (October, 1962), 211-222.

Chapter III. There are relatively few good studies on New Orleans' ante-bellum economy. The principal sources of information are the annual market reports of the *Price Current* and the many articles on the local economy in *De Bow's Review*. Louis C. Hunter, *Steamboats on the Western Rivers: an Economic and Technological History* (Cambridge, 1939), Robert Greenhalgh Albion, *The Rise of New York Port, 1815-1860* (New York, 1939), Dale Odom, "Louisiana Railroads, 1830-1800: A Study of State and Local Aid," (Ph.D. dissertation, Tulane University, 1961), and Stephan A. Caldwell, *A Banking History of Louisiana* (Baton Rouge, 1935) offer much information on specific aspects of the New Orleans economy.

Chapter IV. Roger Shugg's brilliant *Origins of Class Struggle in Louisiana . . . 1840-1875* (Baton Rouge, 1939) and the more pedestrian book by James Kimmins Greer, *Louisiana Politics, 1845-1861* (Baton Rouge, 1931) place local politics in the context of the state scene. The American Party is treated in Leon C. Soule, *The Know Nothing Party in New Orleans: A Reappraisal* (Baton Rouge, 1962) and in my "The Louisiana American Party and the Catholic Church," *Mid-America*, XL (October, 1958), 218-228.

Chapter V. Thomas O'Connor's *History of the Fire Department of New Orleans . . . Down to 1895* (New Orleans, 1895) is, in view of O'Connor's limited education, a remarkably good study. On the militia there is the vast "Historical Military Data on Louisiana Militia" (245 vols.; New Orleans: Works Progress Administration, 1938-1942), in the library of the Louisiana Adjutant General, Jackson Barracks, New Orleans.

Chapter VI. The most complete contemporary information is found in the *New Orleans Medical News and Hospital Gazette*, the *New Orleans Medical and Surgical Journal*, and William L. Robinson, *The Diary of a Samaritan, By a Member of the Howard Association of New Orleans* (New York, 1860). The outstanding secondary works are John Duffy, *The Rudolph Matas History of Medicine in Louisiana* (2 vols.; Baton Rouge, 1958-1962) and Professor Duffy's "The Sword of Pestilence, New Orleans, 1853" which is soon to be published.

Chapter VII. Roger Baudier, *The Catholic Church in Louisiana* (New Orleans, 1939) is good though the files of the local Catholic newspapers are often more helpful. There are pious and not overly interesting histories of various local Protestant church bodies: Louis Voss on the Presbyterians, Henry Cope Duncan on the Episcopalians, Robert Alan Cross on the Methodists, John T. Christian on the Baptists, and John F. Nau on the Lutherans. Leo Shpall, W. E. Myers, and Maxamillian Heller have written histories of Judaism in New Orleans; none are products of extensive research.

Chapter VIII. An account of the public schools in ante-bellum New Orleans is found in my "New England Influences on the Formation of Public Schools in New Orleans," *Journal of Southern History*, XXX (May, 1964), 181-195. The monumental work on private schools is James William Mobley, "The Academy Movement in Louisiana," *Louisiana Historical Quarterly*, XXX (July, 1947), 738-978. Little has been written on collegiate education in ante-bellum New Orleans, though A. E. Fossier, "History of Medical Education in New Orleans from Its Birth to the Civil War," *Annals of Medical History*, VI (July, 1934), 320-352, (September, 1934), 427-447, is highly informative.

Chapter IX. The story of clubs in New Orleans may be found in Stuart O. Landry, *History of the Boston Club* (New Orleans, 1938) and the early years of Mardi Gras in Perry Young, *The Mistick Krewe: Chronicles of Comus and His Kin* (New Orleans, 1931). Of special value are master's theses by Arvilla Taylor, "Horse Racing in the Lower Mississippi Valley Prior to 1860" (University of Texas, 1953) and Ruth Irene Jones, "Ante-Bellum Watering Places of Louisiana, Mississippi, Alabama, and Arkansas," (University of Texas, 1954). For a picture of the wilder side of New Orleans life Herbert Asbury, *The French Quarter* (New York, 1936) is still helpful though limited for the decade before the Civil War. George H. Devol, *Forty Years a Gambler on the Mississippi* (2nd ed.; New York, 1926) is the best contemporary record of the sporting life in New Orleans.

Chapter X. No one working on the New Orleans theatre should overlook John Smith Kendall's massive *Golden Age of the New Orleans Theatre* (Baton Rouge, 1952). The autobiographies of Sol Smith, John Owens, Joseph Jefferson, William Charles Macready, and Mrs. Sam Cowell provide contemporary flavor. The German theatre is thoroughly treated in Arthur Henry Moehlenbrok, "The German Drama on the New Orleans Stage," *Louisiana Historical Quarterly*, XXVI (April, 1943), 361-627. The most definitive work on music in early New Orleans is Henry A. Kmen's forthcoming book, *A Social History of Music in New Orleans: The First Half-Century, 1791-1841* (Louisiana State University Press). Though often inaccurate, J. G. Baroncelli, *Le Théâtre-Francais à la Nlle Orleans* (New Orleans, 1906) remains the standard reference work on opera in the city. There are several biographies of Gottschalk; the latest is Vernon Loggins, *Where the World Ends: The Life of Louis Moreau Gottschalk* (Baton Rouge, 1958).

Chapter XI. The Works Project Administration collection on art and artists in New Orleans housed in Delgado Museum and Tulane University Library is the starting point for all local research on art subjects. The most noteworthy books dealing with New Orleans Architecture are Talbot Hamlin, *Greek Revival Architecture in America . . . Prior to the War Between the States* (London, 1954) and Italo William Ricciuti, *New Orleans and Its Environs: The Domestic Architecture* (New York, 1938).

Chapter XII. There is almost nothing of a secondary nature written on English language literature in New Orleans during the 1850's, though Harriet Houston Cale's thesis, "Cultual Life of New Orleans in the 1850's" is helpful. The best study of Gayarré is Edward M. Socola, "Charles E. A. Gayarré, a Biography" (Ph.D. dissertation, University of Pennsylvania, 1954). French literature is brilliantly analysed and catalogued in Edward Laroque Tinker, *Lee Écrits de Langue Français en Louisiane au XIXe Siècle . . .* (Paris, 1932) and Ruby Van Allen Caulfield, *The French Literature of Louisiana* (New York, 1929).

Chapter XIV. The most detailed study of New Orleans in the years 1860-1862 is Charles L. Dufour, *The Night the War Was Lost* (Garden City, 1960). Dufour's study, like those of Jefferson Davis Bragg and John Winter, centers on military history; more informative on the domestic scene is Gerald M. Capers' manuscript "Occupied City: New Orleans 1861-1865." By far the most interesting contemporary commentary was written by the New Orleans correspondent of the *New York Tribune*.

INDEX

A

Abeilard, Joseph, 202
Academy of Music, 175, 185, 240
Adams, R. P., 144
African Methodist Episcopal Church, 122
Agassiz, Louis, 144-145
Albion, Robert Greenhalgh, 42
Album Littéraire, 219
Album Louisianaise Revue Littéraire et Artistique, 214
Album Poétique de la Louisiane, 216
Alexandria, Louisiana, 43
Algiers, 7, 45, 48, 53, 67, 80, 147, 163-164, 239, 241
Allain, Madame Frédéric, 219
Alligator, Der, 214
Allison, Elizabeth Mary, 221
Almonaster y Rojas, Don Andres, 206
Amans, Jacques, 197
Ambassadeur d'Autriche, 219
American Colonization Society, 29-30
American Exponent, 230, 236
American and Foreign Christian Union, 124
American Home Missionary Society, 124
American Hook and Ladder Company No. 2, 75
American Missionary Association, 124
American Party, 18, 56-61, 64, 73, 83, 115-116, 126-127, 129, 227-228, 231-232
American Theatre, 55, 75, 174, 177, 179
American Tract Society, 124
Americans, 9, 11-16, 31n, 51-52, 56, 62n, 82, 85, 103, 110, 117-118, 143, 157-158, 185, 229
Amours d' Hélène, 217
Ampére, J. J., 12
Amphitheatre, 178
Antoinette de Bordelais, 221
Antonaide, ou Le Solitude avec Dieu, 217
Appollo Club, 163
Armstrong Foundry, 28
Armory Hall, 144-145, 154, 211
Associated Pilots of Louisiana, 21
Associated Press, 235
Atchalafaya Bay, 103
Audibert, Louis, 214
Autre Monde, 219
Azael, 221

B

Baldwin, Joshua, 131
Bamboula, 194
Bancroft, George, 228
Banks Arcade, 59, 79, 210
Banks and banking, 43-44
Bares, Basile J., 192
Barnard, Henry, 132, 148n
Barnum, P. T., 170, 187
Barton, Dr. Edward H., 102-104
Bass, Charles, 221
Baton Rouge, 53

Battle of New Orleans, 5-6, 83-84
Bayou LaFourche, 118
Bayou St. John, 2-3, 204
Bayous (raquette team), 163
Beard, Joseph A., 27
Beaumont, Joe, 194
Beauregard, P. G. T., 16, 60-61, 114, 208, 245
Belize, 235
Bell, John, 241
Bellegrove Institute, 138
Belleville, 7
Belleville Foundry, 45, 79
Benjamin Judah P., 14, 128, 243
Berlioz, Hector, 189
Bermudez, Edward, 144
Berwick Bay, 48
Bible House, 124
Bigney, M. F., 220, 230, 236
Bienvenue, Charles, 243
Blanc, Bishop Antoine, 113-116, 125, 137, 142
Blanchard, Albert, 12
Bloomingdale, 7
Bolles, Dr. D. D., 144
Bolton, Edward C., 145
Bonaparte, Joseph, 201
Booth, Edwin, 176
Booth, John Wilkes, 176
Booth, Junius, 176
Boré, Etienne, 5
Boston, 37, 43, 223
Boston Club, 158-159
Boucicault, Dion, 175, 221
Boudousquié, Charles, 182, 185, 240
Boulet, Alexandre, 198, 206
Boutet, Paul, 231
Boyer's School, 138
Boys' High School, 133
Brashear City, 48
Breckenridge, John C., 229, 241
Bremen, 37, 41
Bremer, Frederica, 208
Brennan, Joseph, 220
Bretonne Charles de la, 217, 235
Bringier, Stella, 188
Brooklyn (navy ship), 245
Brown, John, 127, 240
Brownlow, Parson, 144
Brownson, Orestes A., 125, 145, 217
Brothers' Clerks, The, 221
Brother's Vengeance, The, 221
Bullitt, A. C., 130n
Bucktown, 8, 46
Burtheville, 7

C

Cabildo, 112, 147, 202, 208
Cable, George Washington, 103, 137, 224
Caldwell, James H., 6
Calinda, 194
Calisto, 218
Cambioso, Father, 206
Camp Moore, 244
Camp Street Theatre, 180
Campbell, John A., 74
Campbell, Julia, 70
Campbell's Minstrels, 240
Canal Banking Company, 28
Canal Street Presbyterian Church, 207

Canonge, Louis-Placide, 218, 235
Canova, Dominque, 198, 201
Canton, Mississippi, 47-48
Carondelet, Don Francisco Louis Hector, Baron de, 4
Carrie Harrington, 221
Carrollton, 7, 46, 68, 80, 230
Cartwright, Dr. Samuel, 104-105
Casa Calvo, Marquis de, 4
Casanave, Pierre, 106
Cassidy, Charles, 164
Catholic Free School Society, 138
Catholic Institute, 144, 146
Catholic Society for the Diffusion of Religious and Literary Education, 142
Celia Music Society, 189
Cemeteries, 107-110
Cenelles, Les, 219
Chaillé, Dr. Stanford, 72-90
Chameleon, The, 221
Charity Hospital, 89-90, 96, 141-142
Chassignac, Eugene, 192
Chicago, 48, 223
Choppin, Dr. Samuel, 87
Christ Church, 117, 207
Christian Brothers, 113, 137-138
Church of the Immaculate Conception, 206
Church of the New Jerusalem, 130n
Cincinnati, 77, 213, 223
Cincinnati Art Union, 199
Circus Street Hospital, 90
Citizens Bank, 66
"Citizens" ticket, 59
City Hall, 207
Clague, Richard, 197-198
Claiborne, W. C. C. (first governor), 5, 12
Claiborne, W. C., C., (legislator), 53
Clapp, Rev. T. S., 120, 127
Classical Music Society, 188-189
Clay, Henry, 56, 120, 200
Clay Monumental Association, 200
Cohen, M. M., 144
Coliseum Place Baptist Church, 119, 207
College of the Immaculate Conception, 142
College of Orleans, 140
Collignan, George, 188, 192
Commercial Bulletin, 227, 236
Common School Journal, 132
Comte de Carmagnola, 218
Congo Square, 194
Congregation Dispersed of Judah, 128
Congregation The Right Way, 128
Constitutional Union Party, 227, 241
Continental Guards, 82, 84
Cook, Francis, 226
Cooper, James Fenimore, 217
Cooper, Joseph, 21
Copes, Dr. J. S., 145
Corcoran, Denis, 213, 228
Cosmopolitan Art Association, 199
Counjaille, 194
Courrone Blanche, Une, 216

INDEX

Courts, 73-74, 86n
Couvent School, 139
Cowbellions, 155
Crawcour, Dr. I. L., 144
Creole, 229, 236
Creole Orphans, The, 221
Creole Race Course, 161
Creoles, 5-6, 11-16, 31n, 51-52, 56, 62n, 69, 82, 85, 101, 103, 105, 117, 143, 148, 157-158, 185, 197, 219, 223, 229, 233
Crescent, 228, 234, 236
Crescent City Cricket Club, 162
Crescent City Yacht Club, 161
Crescent Dramatic Association, 180
Crime, 65-70
Crisp, W. H., 175
Crockett, John W., 228
Crossman, A. D., 52, 55, 61, 70
Cuba, 41
Curto, Gregorio, 191
Cushman, Charlotte, 176
Cypress Grove Cemetery, 77

D

Dakin, Charles, 201
Dakin, James, 201, 206
Dalcour, Pierre, 25
Da Ponte, Durante, 236
Davis, John, 165, 182, 185
Dean, Julia, 221
De Bar, Ben, 174, 240
Debrosses, Nelson, 25
De Bow, J. D. B., 146, 215
De Bow's Review, 215, 224
Dedé, Edmund, 25, 191
De Lemos, Manuel Gayoso, 4
Deléry, Dr. Charles, 105
Delta, 228-229, 234, 236
Democratic Party, 14-15, 53-55, 57-59, *3, 231-232, 241
De Pauger, Adrien, 3
Dewey, Rev. Orville, 144
Dick, James, 201
Dick the Newsboy, 222
Dimitry, Alexander, 114, 132, 136
Dinnies, Anna Peyre, 220
"Dixie", 191
Dolbear, Rufus, 143
Dolbear's Commercial College, 143
Douglas, Stephen A., 241-242
Dowler, Dr. M. Morton, 105
Drainage, 92-94
Druids, 160
Duclary, Lepelletier, 197
Dueling, 69
Dufour, Cyprien, 232-233
Dugue, Charles-Oscar, 225n
DuHart, Adolphe, 139
Dumas, Alexandre, 179
Duncan, John K., 60, 245

E

Echos, Les, 216
Egerton, Mary, 70
Elmore, William A., 59
Ely, Albert W., 145
Emerson, Ralph Waldo, 217
Emmett, Dan, 191
Empire Club, 163
English, 20
Erena or The Christian Convert, 221

Esplanade Ridge, 2
Etter, Joseph, 230
Eustis, George, 12, 74
Everette, Edward, 241
Evershed, Emilie, 216

F

Fabre, Albert, 31n, 235
Faget, Dr. Charles, 87, 105
Faubourg, Marigny, 6, 62n
Fanning, James G., 231
Fennessy, David, 169
Field, Joseph M., 221
Fillmore, Millard, 59
Fire department, 74-80
Fireman's Charitable Association, 77, 80
Fireman's Low Pressure Steamship Association, 21
First Christian Church, 130n
First Congregational Unitarian Church, 120, 127
First Presbyterian Church, 119, 207
Fisk, Abijiah, 146
Flatboats, 36
Fleurs d'Eté, 216
Flint, Dr. Austin, 142
Fontenay, Marie (Madame de Grandfort), 139, 219
Forshay, Caleb G., 200
Forstall, Elmund J., 146
Fort Jackson, 245
Fort St. Phillip, 245
Fortier, Alcée, 220
Foster, Thomas, 27
Foster, Thomas Gales, 144
Fowler, Orson Squires, 144
France et Espagne, 218
Franklin High School, 138
Franklin Street Infirmary, 90
Free Negroes, 22-25, 28-29, 139-140, 219-220
French, 15, 19
French, L. Virginia, 214
French Quarter, see Vieux Carré
Freret, James, 201
Frost, J. W., 228, 236
Fuller Eugene, 236
Fuller, Margaret, 236
Funerals, 106-107
Fury, Bridget, 70

G

Gaiety Club, 159
Gaiety Theatre, 175, 177, 179, 185
Gallier, James, 201, 203, 206
Galvani, Charles, 199
Galveston, 48, 113
Galvez, Bernardo de, 4
Gambling, 164-165
Garden District, 204
Garibaldi Legion, 82
Garland, William, 67
Garreau, Armand, 218
Gates of Mercy, 128
Gates of Prayer, 128
Gayarré, Charles, 22, 31n, 132, 144, 146, 168, 218, 221-223
Genoa, 37
Georgetown College, 143
German Society, 19
Germans, 7, 18-19, 23, 59, 75, 82, 85, 102, 121-122, 170, 179-180

Geshwindt, R., 197
Girls' High School, 133-134
Gliddon, George R., 144
Globe Ball Room, 96
Good Fellows, 160
Goodrich, William, 132-133
Gormley's aBsin, 93
Gottschalk, Louis Moreau, 187-189, 192
Goubault School, 138
Gould, B. A., 144
Grand d' Espagne, Un. 218
Greenville, 7
Gretna, 7
Gruber, John F., 75
Gutheim, Rabbi James Koppel, 128

H

Hahn, Michael, 229
Haiti, 25
Hale, Dr. Josiah, 145
Halfway House, 69
Halle, Charles, 189
Hamlin, Talbot, 208
Harby, Dr. Samuel, 232
Harvard College, 143
Hatcher, C. F., 27
Havre, 37
Hawthorne, Nathaniel, 224
Hecker, Father Isaac, 217
Hennen, Alfred, 146
Heroism of the Confederacy, The, 221
Heron family, 177
Hezeau, Louis François, 17
Hiawatha Club, 159
High School for Young Ladies, 138
Hiriart, Emile, 232
Histrionic Assocation, 180
History of Louisiana, 223
Holbrook, M. A., 227, 236
Homes, Marie Sophie, 220-221
Hôtel Dieu, 90
Howard Association, 98
Howard, Henry, 201
Hughes, Henry, 145
Hugo, Victor, 179
Humboldt, William, 145
Hunt, Joel, 200
Hunt, Randall, 56, 140, 241
Hurstville, 7
Hyams, Henry, 128-129

I

Immigrants, 16-20, 39, 56-59, 66, 89, 101, 121 137, 229
Improved Order of American Red Men, 160
Independent Party, 55
Independent Voters of New Orleans, 60
Industry, 44-46
Irish, 7, 18, 23, 58, 102, 163
Irish Channel, 18
Italians, 20

J

Jackson, Andrew, 5, 200
Jackson, Louisiana, 72
Jackson Memorial Association, 200
Jackson, Mississippi, 47
Jackson Square, 112, 203,

INDEX

Battle of, 60-61, 83
Jamison, George, 221
Jefferson Academy, 138
Jefferson City, 7, 137, 163
Jefferson and Lake Pontchartrain Railroad, 46
Jefferson Parish, 113
Jesuits (Society of Jesus), 3, 113, 125, 127, 142
Jockey Club, 160
Jones, Evan, 12
Juan, ou une Histoire sous Charles Quint, 218
Juba, 194
Judaism, 128-129
Judson, E. Z. C., ("Ned Buntline") 62n, 126

K

Kane, Elisha, 145
Kendall, George Wilkins, 227, 235-236
Kidd, Hudson A., 228
King, Grace, 9, 56
Knights of Jericho, 171
Know Nothing Party, see American Party

L

Lafayette, 7, 52-54, 230
Lafayette Square, 60, 77, 119, 200, 207, 210
LaHache, Theodore, 189, 191-192
Lake Borgne, 46
Lake Pontchartrain, 2-3, 37, 84, 161, 164
Lambert, Richard, 25, 191
Landis, Joseph, 143
Lanusse, Armand, 139, 219
LaSere, Emile, 231-232
Latham & Co., 229
Lathrop, Henry, 54
Lauc-Maryat, Edouard de, 231
Latrobe, Benjamin, 193, 206
Laveau, Marie, 124
Lavillebeauvre, Madame E., 192
Lavilles, 163
Leacock, Rev. William T., 145
Leeds Foundry, 28, 45
Lehman, H. E., 192
Lemaitre, Charles, 217
Leonard, Dr. William L., 222
Leonard William T., 214
Lewis, John L., 12, 55, 57-58
Lewis, "Count" Lorenzo, 164
Levy, Sam, 164
Liberia, 25, 30
Libraries, 146-147
Limet, Felix, 232
Lincoln, Abraham, 241-242, 244
Lind, Jenny, 170, 187
Lindsay, William B., 145
Littlefield, Samuel S., 226
Little Rock, 113
Liverpool, 37, 42, 44
Livingston, Edward, 12
Llulla, José, 69
Logan, T. B., 221
Louisiana Board of Health, 92, 103
Louisiana Club, 159
Louisiana Courier-Courrier de la Louisiane, 231-232, 236
Louisiana Greys, 181

Louisiana Historical Society, 146
Louisiana, Its Colonial History and Romance, 228
Louisiana, Its History as a French Colony, 222
Louisiana Legion, 81
Louisiana Manufacturing Company, 45
Louisiana Native American Association, 62n
Louisiana Oil Company, 240
Louisiana Seminary of Learning, 213
Louisiana Spectator, 230
Louisiana State Medical Society, 146
Louisiana State Republican, 230
Louisiana Statesman, 230
Louisiana Supreme Court, 123, 141
Lowell, Massachusetts, 44-45
Ludlow, Noah, 174
Lumsden, F. A., 227
Lunatic and the Lover, The, 222
Lutheran Church, 121-122, 126
Luzenberg Hospital, 90
Lyceum and Library Society, 144, 146-147, 222

M

Macarty, Eugene, 191
Mackay, Charles, 208
Macmamus F. E., 230
Madame Desrayaux's School, 138
Maginnis, John, 229
Maglone, James, 169
Maison de Santé, 90
Manchester, 37
Mandeville, Ellwyn, 171
Mandeville, Jose, 188
Mann, Horace, 131-132
Mansion, Lolo, 25
Mardi Gras, 110, 153, 155, 157-158, 244
Marigny, Bernard, 6, 11, 56, 62n
Markham, Thomas E., 32n
Marks, Isaac, 60, 129
Marsh children, 178
Marshall, Horace L., 230
Martin, François Xavier, 146
Mason, Lowell, 133
Masonic Grand Lodge, 144, 146
Masons, 115-116, 160
Mathew, Rev. Theobald, 170
Maury, M. F., 145
Mazareau, Etienne, 12
Maybin, Joseph A., 71
McCaleb, Theodore H., 74, 130
McCarthy, Harry, 192
McClellan, George, 145
McCord, Mary, 221
McCord, V E. Wilhelme, 214-215
McDonald's Restaurant, 152
McDonogh, town of, 7, 90
McDonogh, John, 30, 135, 139, 173n, 237
McFarlane, Dr. John, 104
McGinnis, John, 242
McGrath, Price, 164
McMillan, John P., 230

Mechanics and Agriculture Fair Association, 14
Mechanics Institute, 75, 145, 210
Mechanics Society, 144, 146
Medical College of Louisiana, 87
Menken, Adah Isaacs, 176-177
Mercantile Library Society, 144, 146
Mercier, Dr. Armand, 87, 90
Metairie Ridge, 2
Metairie Trotting Club, 161
Methodist Episcopal Church, South, 118, 121, 123
Mexican Gulf Railroad, 46
Militia, 63, 80-86
Mills, Clark, 200
Milneberg, 8, 46, 164, 189
Minstrel shows, 180
Minute Men of New Orleans, 242-243
Miro, Don Esteven, 4
Mirror, 201, 213, 230, 236-236
Mississippi Company, 3
Missouri Synod, 121
Mistick Krewe of Comus, 155, 157-158
Mitchell, D. F., 145
Mitchell, Ormsley M., 144
Mobile, 113, 162, 216, 235
Mobile and Ohio Railroad, 47
Moise, E. Warren, 74
Moise, Theodore, 129, 197
Monoma Boat Club, 161
Monroe, John T., 61
Montmain, G. A., 192
Montez, Lola, 176, 219
Moore, Thomas Overton, 242
Moore, Thomas S., 230
Moral Reform Society, 171
Moreau's Restaurant, 152
Moresque Building, 204
Morphy, Paul, 161
Morphy, Madame Thomas, 192
Mrs. D'Aquin's School, 138
Mure, William, 242
Murger, Henry, 179
Mysteries and Miseries of New Orleans, The, 126

N

Natchez, 113
National Academy of Design, 197, 200
National Guards, 81, 85
Negroes, 3, 21-31, 39, 69, 83, 98, 101, 104-105, 122-124, 163, 165-168, 192-194
New American Theatre, see American Theatre
New England, 131-133
New Iberia, 48
New Orleans Academy of Science, 88, 145
New Orleans Bee—L'Abeille de la Nouvelle Orléans, 232
New Orleans Bible Society, 124
New Orleans Board of Health, 97, 99, 102-103
New Orleans Book, 224
New Orleans Can't-Get-Away Dramatic Association, 180
New Orleans and Carrollton Railroad, 7, 46
New Orleans Chamber of Commerce, 14

INDEX

New Orleans Chess Club, 161
New Orleans Common Council, City of, 54, 96-98, 103
New Orleans Female Collegiate Institute, 138
New Orleans Female Seminary, 138
New Orleans Gas Light and Banking Company, 14
New Orleans, Jackson, and Great Northern Railroad, 14, 47
New Orleans Noesis, 24
New Orleans, Opelousas, and Great Western Railroad, 47
New Orleans and Pontchartrain Railroad, 46, 163
New Orleans School of Medicine, 90, 141-142
New Orleans Trotting and Pacing Club, 161
Neville, Julian, 27
New York City, 37, 77
Nixon, James O., 228, 236
Nores, Jules, 192
Normal School, 134-135
Norman, B. M., 213
Notre Dame Church, 112
Nott, Dr. Josiah C., 141

O

Octoroon, The, 221
Odd Fellows Hall, 84, 115-116, 145-146, 153-154, 160, 188-189, 210, 240-241
Olmsted, Frederick Law, 168, 203, 209
Opelousas, 48
Opera, 181-183, 185-187
Order of the Lone Star, 62n
O'Reilly, Alejandro, 4, 218
Orleanian-Orleanais, 231, 233
Orleans Academic Institute, 138
Orleans Battalion of Artillery, 81, 88
Orleans (baseball) Club, 163
Orleans (social) Club, 159
Orleans Fire Company No. 21, 74, 78-79
Orleans Parish Grand Jury, 93
Orleans Territory, 5
Orleans Theatre, 153-154, 175-176, 179-180, 182, 185-186, 218
Oskya, 47
Owens, John E., 191

P

Palmer, Benjamin Morgan, 119, 144, 242
Panoramas, 199-200
Parlor Magazine, 214, 224
Parodi Italian (Opera) Company, 185
Pass Christian, 161
Patent Medicines, 88-89
Patti, Adelina, 244
Paulding, Cornelius, 120
Peacock, Dr. J. S., 221
Peck, William Henry, 221
Peel's Original Campbell's Minstrels, 180
Pekin-Democrat, 214
Pelican Club, 159
Pelican Fire Company, 79

Pelican Theatre, 175, 179
Pendergast, J. C., 231
Pennsylvania Academy of Fire Arts, 197, 200
Perché, Abbé Napoléon, 99, 115-116, 125, 144, 229, 232-233
Perelli, Achille, 200
Perritt, Henry, 164
Perry, Enoch Wood, 197-198
Perseverence Fire Company, 79-80
Peters, Samuel J., 6, 11-12, 62n, 131, 146
Philadelphia, 43
Philharmonic Society of the Friends of Art, 188
Photography, 198
Physico-Medical Society, 146
Picayune, 227-228, 233-235
Pickwick Club, 155, 158-159
Pilié, Louis, 306
Pioneer Boat Club, 161
Pipkin, Isaac, 29
Pittsburgh, 21, 46
Place d'Armes, 83
Placide, Tom, 175-176
Planter's Press, 75
Poincy, Paul, 197-198
Police, 63-65
Polk, Bishop Leondias, 118, 143, 145
Pomarède, Leon, 198-199, 206
Pontalba Buildings, 203
Poore, Charles H., 245
Populus, Nathalie, 139-140
Porter, Frank T., 236
Porter Williams, 236
Potters Field, 106
Pouilly, J. N. de, 200-201
Powers, A. G., 197
Powers, Hiram, 201
Presbytere, 112, 202, 208
Presbyterian Church, 118-119, 121, 123
Preston, Isaac T., 74
Prévost, Eugene, 191
Price Current, 226-227, 236
Princess (Steamboat), 61
Prisons, 70-73
Proctor, Richard, 12
Proctorville, 46-47
Progression: or the South Defended, 220
Propagateur Catholique, 115, 126, 232-233, 235
Prostitution, 165-168
Protestant Episcopal Church, 117-118, 121, 123
Protestantism, 117-121, 124
Public Schools, 131-137

Q

Questy, Joanni, 139
Qui Perd Gagne, 218

R

Ravel family, 178
Redemptorists, 113
Reform Party, 58-59
Reitzenstein, Ludwig von, 214
Renaissance Louisianaise, 214
Republican Party, 241
Rice, Dan, 175, 191
Rice, Edward "Daddy", 180
Riddell, John L., 104
Riddell, W. P., 144

Rigolettes, 103
Rinehart, B. F., 197-198
Ripley, Eliza, 186, 201
Robb, James, 13-14, 54, 200 211n
Rodolphe de Branchlièvre, 217
Rogers, Charles J., 175
Rolling, Hubert, 191-192
Roman Catholic Church, 112-116, 124-126, 137-138, 229, 231, 233
Roselius, Christian, 140, 144, 241, 243
Rost, Pierre, 12
Rouquette, Adrien, 216-217
Rousseau, Joseph C., 25
Rozier, Joseph A., 243
Rumsey and Newcomb Minstrel Troupe, 240

S

St. Alphonsus Church, 112, 137
St. Augustine Church, 113
St. Charles Hotel, 27, 74, 151-153, 157-158, 208, 242
St. Charles Theatre, 154, 157, 174, 176-179, 182, 240
St. Denis, 218
St. John the Baptist Church, 206
St. Joseph's College, 143
St. Louis Cathedral, 112, 115, 189, 206, 217
St. Louis Institute, 138-139
St. Louis Hotel, 27, 151, 153, 157-158, 201, 209
St. Mary's Church, 112, 137
St. Mary's College, 143
St. Mary's Italian Church, 207
St. Mary's Market, 68
St. Patrick's Church, 78, 112, 137-138, 170, 206
St. Paul's Church, 117
St. Stephen's Church, 137
St. Theresa's Church, 207
Sanitation Commission, 103
Santo Domingans, 5
Sawyer, Franklin, 132
Schmidt, G., 192
School of Madame M. D. Giraud, 138
School for Scandal, 221
School Sisters of Notre Dame, 113, 137
Sculpture, 200-201
Seamen's Bethel, 121
Seamen's Mission, 121
Sejour, Victor, 25, 219
Semaine Littéraire, 214
Semaine de la Nouvelle Orléans, 214
Semi-Weekly Creole, 229, 234, 236
Semmes, Thomas J., 74, 114, 144
Seymour, Isaac G., 227, 236, 242
Shakespeare, William, 177
Shaw, John A., 131-132, 136, 148
Sherman, William T., 43, 213
Sherwood, James, 164
Ships and shipping, 36
Shugg, Roger, 15
Sisters of Charity, 89-90, 113, 138
Sisters of the Holy Cross, 137

INDEX

Sisters of Mount Carmel, 113
Slaughter House Point, 102
Slavery, 25, 27-28, 237
Slaves, 22, 25-31, 65, 69-70
Slidell, John, 11, 57, 59-60, 74, 197, 232, 243
Slidell, Thomas, 74
Smith, Sol, 174
Smith, Ashbel, 145
Société Catholique pour l'Instruction des Orphelins dans l'Indigence, 139
Solomon, Clara, 129
Sons of Temperance, 171
Soule Chapel, 122
Soule, George, 143
Soulé, Pierre, 12, 57, 59-60
Solue's Commercial College, 143
Soulier Rouge, Le, 217
Soulouque, Faustian, 25
Southern Aid Society, 124
Southern Art Union, 199
Southern Baptist Church, 119-121, 123
Southern Ladies Book, 214
Southern Literary Society, 213
Southern Medical Dispensary, 90
Southern Organ, 171
Southern Rifles, 82
Southern Standard, 220, 235-236
Southern Yacht Club, 161
Souvenirs d'Amerique et de France par une Creole, 219
Spalding, Bishop John, 144
Spaniards, 20
Spaulding, G. R., 175
Spaulding and Rogers Academy of Music, see Academy of Music
Spaulding and Rogers Ampitheatre, see Ampitheatre
Spaulding and Rogers Circus, 181
Sports, 160-164
Spriggs, Judith Ann, 129
Stanley, Henry Morton, 166
Steamboats, 35-36
Steel Chapel, 207
Stith, Gerard, 59, 61, 71, 157
Stone, Dr. Warren, 87, 90
Stowe, Harriet Beecher, 219
Sue, Eugene, 179
Summer, H. M., 60
Sunday Magnet, 213
Suzeneau, John, 73, 234

T

Taft, Loredo, 211n
Tangipahoa Parish, 244-245
Taylor, Tom, 177
Tehgahkwita, Catherine, 217

Temperance movement, 170-171
Temple Sinai, 128
Tertiary Carmelite Sisters, 137
Testut, Charles, 213-216, 218
Thackery, William Makepeace, 145
Thalberg, Sigismund, 188
Theárd, Paul Emile, 235
Théard, Thomas, 231-232
Théatre d'Opéra, 182, 186, 240
Théatre d'Orléans, see Orleans Theatre
Thierry, Camile, 25
Ticknor and Fields, 213
Touro Buildings, 204
Touro Infirmary, 90
Touro, Judah P., 90, 128
Toussaint (Feast of All Saints), 109
Towboats, 36
Townsend, Mary Ashley, 220-221
Trevigne, Paul, 139
Trieste, 37
Trinity Church, 118
True Delta, 229, 236
Tulane, Paul, 243
Turnverein, 159-160

U

Ulloa, Don Antonio de, 4
Una, 221
Uncle Tom's Cabin, 135, 218, 221
Uncle Tom's Cabin in Louisiana, 222
Union Race Course, 120
United States Army, 81
United States Custom House, 60-61, 208, 224
United States Marine Hospital, 90
United States Mint, 244
University of Louisiana, 140-142
University of the South, 143
Unzaga, Don Luis de, 4
Ursuline Convent, 112, 202, 207
Ursuline Sisters, 138, 142

V

Vanuchi's Museum, 181, 240
Variété Association, 175
Varieties Theatre, 174-175, 177-178, 191, 240
Variety Club, 163
Veillese Louisianeses, 218
Verandah Hotel, 75
Vicksburg, 181
Victor's Reasturant, 152
Vieux Carré, 3, 9, 51, 62n, 93,
202-204
Vieux Salomon, Le, 218
Vigilance Committee, 60-61
Vignaud, Henry, 225n
Vignie, N., 27
Villars, Paul, 231
Vincentians, 113
Violette Revue Musicale et Litteraire, La, 214
Volunteer Fire Department No. 1, 75
Voodoo, 123-124

W

Wagner, Peter K., 236
Walker, General Joseph, 146
Walther, C. F. W., 121
War of 1812, 5-6
Warberg, Eugene, 25, 200
Washington Artillery, 81, 83-85, 211
Water supply, 94-95
Waterman, Charles, 59-60
Wederburn, Dr. Alexander J., 87
Weekly Mirror, see *Mirror*
Weisse, G. F., 232
Wesley Chapel, 122
West Indians, 20
Western Art Union, 199
Weymouth, J. M., 229-230
Wharton, E. C., 221-222
Wharton, Thomas K., 16, 32n, 135, 207
Whig Party, 14-15, 51-56, 61, 148, 227, 230-232
Whitman, Walt, 236
Wilde, Richard Henry, 213
Wilkinson, General James, 5, 12, 223
Willard, Florence J., 221
Wilson, Joseph H. & Co., 230
Winans Chapel, 122
Winters, "Irish Kate", 70
Wise, Rabbi Isaac M., 128
Wood, A. T., 208
Workingmen's organizations, 21-22

Y

Yale College, 143
Yellow Fever, 92, 95-105
Young Bachelors, 153
Young Couple, The, 222
Young, George B., 226
Young Men's Christian Association, 124, 144, 146, 153

Z

Zimpel, Charles, 210
Zouaves, 82

www.ingramcontent.com/pod-product-compliance
Lightning Source LLC
Chambersburg PA
CBHW022107150426
43195CB00008B/304